Praise for *Divine*

"Adam C. Hall's book *Divine Genius* is a consciousness template to apply Quantum Physics in real life. He helps the reader rise above disempowering programs to manifest our intentions and thrive into the future. I highly recommend it as a guide to free ourselves by freeing our minds."

—**Bruce H. Lipton, PhD.**, epigenetic science pioneer, and bestselling author of *The Biology of Belief*

"*Divine Genius* chronicles Adam C. Hall's psychic journey that resulted in the creation of his Genius Process. Follow Adam's lead and prepare to be catapulted from fear to love, from darkness into the light."

—**Lynne McTaggart**, internationally bestselling author of *The Field, The Intention Experiment,* and *The Power of Eight*

"Adam C. Hall takes us on an inner and outer journey to rediscover the Grail and embrace it in each of our hearts. Nonstop enlightened action and wisdom in ancient sacred places. A guide to our collective destiny."

—**Alberto Villoldo, PhD.**, author of *Shaman, Healer, Sage* and *Grow a New Body*

"*Divine Genius* takes you on a spiritual adventure—a quest to reclaim the ORIGINAL WISDOM you were born with. Adam C. Hall is your trusted guide. He will show you the way."

—**Robert Holden**, author of *Shift Happens!*

"Walking a spiritual path has never been so important. Adam C. Hall beautifully lays out a path and helps us find a better way to live in the chaos of the modern world."

—**Dr. Pedram Shojai**, *New York Times* bestselling author of *The Urban Monk*

"*Divine Genius* is a searingly honest, courageous, and vital quest, laying bare the evolutionary rite of passage we are undertaking and seeking to understand and embody what it means to choose a new future for the betterment of all."

—**Dr. Jude Currivan**, cosmologist, author of *The Cosmic Hologram* and cofounder of WholeWorld-View

"In these murkiest of times, skillful tools for insight and guidance such as what Adam C. Hall provides are really essential. The soul feasts on Truth."

—**James O'Dea**

"*Divine Genius* contains the hard-won wisdom that comes from lived experience combined with the perennial wisdom of the shamanic traditions. The book has many important lessons and you will be well served to read it."

—**David Gershon**, CEO of Empowerment Institute and author of *Social Change 2.0*

"*Divine Genius: The Unlearning Curve* may be the most satisfying quest you've ever experienced. Adam C. Hall helps take the reader on a journey of awakening to discover what it means to be fully human. He offers Universal Wisdom Teachings to help us create spiritual, fulfilling lives in ways we never may have expected."

—**Debra Landwehr Engle**, bestselling author of *The Only Little Prayer You Need* and *Let Your Spirit Guides Speak*

"Adam C. Hall is an evolutionary entrepreneur and attuned guide. He is a Quantum Genius who has dedicated his life to help others realize their own spiritual, social, and planetary potential."

—**Barbara Marx Hubbard**, author of *Conscious Evolution*

DIVINE GENIUS

The Unlearning Curve

ADAM C. HALL

Waterside Productions

Printed in the United States of America

First Printing, 2021

ISBN-13: 978-1-945949-89-0 print edition
ISBN-13: 978-1-945390-72-2 ebook edition

Waterside Productions
2055 Oxford Ave
Cardiff, CA 92007
www.waterside.com

For my daughters, Heather, Ashley, and Hannah: your love, patience and courage has given my life meaning and purpose.

I am eternally grateful and blessed to share this life with each of you. I love you.

Forever grateful to:

Alberto Villoldo and Marcella Lobos for Sharing their Chilean sanctuary, Los Lobos, with me during the writing of this book. Your land and home held me as I made the journey from what no longer served my spiritual evolution.

Tom Woodard for hosting me during this journey to genius at Rancho San Basilio, Baja Sur, Mexico. It all began in the pristine beauty and purity of this land and stunning sea.

Debra Engle, my editor, collaborator, and soul companion. Your guidance, gifts, and genius touched my heart. I could not have done it without you.

Table of Contents

INTRODUCTION

In June, 2012, I embarked on a journey to Peru. I had no idea where it would lead. In fact, I didn't know for sure why I bought the plane ticket and left my home in Santa Barbara. All I knew was that, for years, spiritual teachings and the ego struggles of my everyday life had been propelling me inward and forward.

By the time I stepped on the plane headed to the Amazon, I had packed plenty of questions, the seeds of trust, and a knowing that something significant was about to unfold. I felt like Percival embarking on the quest for the Holy Grail. Little did I know how right I was.

The idea for the journey came from an ascended master I called Men—not out of a particular appreciation for the male gender. (In fact, as you'll see in the book, I think men have a lot to learn from women.) I called him by that name because it means "eagle" in ancient Mayan, a culture and society I've studied for its wisdom and advanced technologies.

Men introduced himself when I was meditating one day in April 2012. And for the next few months, we met daily. He told me I was embarking on an eighty-one-day journey, that I would make a trip to the sacred valley of Peru for the last ten of those eighty-one days, and that my quest was related to the fifty-second anniversary of my conception into this physical life.

Along the way, he also shared Thirteen Wisdom Teachings with me. While those teachings are as old as time and have been shared by many others, Men made them uniquely powerful. They were delivered in a manner that wasn't just intellectual thought and conjecture, but a direct transmission from one of the great masters of the ages. Sharing those teachings with you so you can experience the transmissions for yourself was one of the greatest pleasures of writing this book, and they are the basis for the subtitle, *The Unlearning Curve.*

As you'll see throughout this book, when we listen to Spirit and all that it has to teach us, the one thing required is a willingness to unlearn everything we thought we knew.

People always ask, "Why did you write the book?" In one sense, the book wrote me. It wasn't a question of me writing anything. My job was to be alive in real time in my own conscious evolution.

What I've found is that storytelling in and of itself is a release and an expansion of the Divine light and love that shines through each of us. It's uniquely personal and necessary for a storyteller's own growth. But we do this for the whole. Not to gain fame or fortune, but to inspire, to show the way. Words are like activation, awakening us into becoming. They're part of God's blueprint for who we are in human form as we shift our focus from "me" to "we." Godcentric, lightcentric, lovecentric.

This book is for anyone who seeks to take a deeper journey and intends to find the nature of their own reality and life experience. It's for those who have made a decision to no longer live a life of dis-ease, who choose to end their inner loneliness of their separation from God and nature. It's for those who have been seeking but not finding the nature of reality. It's for those who want to up-level their relationships—at home, at work, and within—and express their unique genius.

It's also for those who have been walking this path for a long time and want to explore the inner architecture of creation's genius. For those who want to experience the outer edges of their own consciousness and peer into the Truth and knowledge that the universe contains. It's for powerful creators, manifesters, and leaders who are interested in the Quantum Field of infinite possibilities.

Divine Genius is not a scientific journal that seeks to prove anything or the nature of reality in general. I live by the motto of not simply wanting to know the facts, but to know why an experience is factually true for me. When I'm with people, I have an experience with them because I adopt the beginner's mind, focused on why it's true for them.

The biggest challenge in writing the book was elucidating Men's wisdom and teachings in a way that didn't impinge on the depth of his Truth. To the best of my ability, I kept myself from judgment and projection. At the same time, you'll see my own process of understanding and applying the principles the master gave me.

What I learned was a deeper knowing of my commitment to fulfill my soul's work in this lifetime. As I wrote the book and revisited my journal from that time, I asked myself, "Did I really do that? What possessed me?" I saw how fully and deeply I surrendered myself, trusting spiritual guidance as I walked through the valley of my own death and into the unconscious nature of God's light.

It's humbling to bow to that deeper trust. While we have free will that can take us on detours, we eventually find our way Home again to God. In my journey, I had to give up my free will to receive Divine Will—a process that can seem like death but carries the promise of rebirth.

Ultimately, *Divine Genius* is the story of my quest in Peru for what came to be known as the Holy Grail—the answer to the question, "Can I get out of this lifetime alive?"

For better or worse, I was curious enough to go to whatever length it takes to move beyond the stories I've lived and the loneliness I'd felt. The questions I asked—and the answers I found—were not just for me alone. You will see yourself and your own path as *Divine Genius* brings my journey alive.

It shares a universal story of how we evolve as sentient beings on a physical, emotional, spiritual, and soul level. It's about a quest in which those four aspects of my life meet as one. It attempts to answer questions like these: What is the spiritual aspect of what I'm called to do in this lifetime? What is my mission? And how can I fulfill my soul's journey, which has been emerging through lifetimes?

Divine Genius is a deep interpersonal journey to my Truth of being one with—not separate from—God. For better or worse, I was curious enough to go to whatever lengths it takes to move beyond the stories I've lived and the loneliness that I'd felt in my estrangement from Mother Nature and the Divine.

My path has been uniquely my own. It called for complete surrender and what I'd known myself to be. It called upon fearlessness to do what one should never do in the darkness of the unknown. It called upon me to shed my skin like the serpent does, all at once. Hence this storyline takes us on a vision quest to various places around the globe, primarily to Peru, my holy land. And it explores the ancient wisdom of the EarthKeepers that resides here in the jungles and in the mountains.

The only way to come to these experiences was by embracing the unknown and shedding my limiting beliefs, traumas, and emotional and psychological pain. To actively engage in the unlearning curve.

To tell that story as completely as I could, I wrote *Divine Genius* using four interwoven threads:

1. My journey to Peru in June 2012
2. Back stories about my life experiences and my struggles in personal relationships and business
3. The Thirteen Wisdom Teachings from Men, the ascended master
4. You, the reader, who will experience the teachings within this book in your own personal and unique way

Along the way, you'll find references to different shamanic and spiritual teachings. Key among those is *A Course in Miracles*, which I've studied for many years. While many spiritual books move us forward, pushing us out of our ego mindset, this book has a different starting point, pulling us from the higher mind to unlearn the ego's fear-based thinking we have been programmed to believe.

This process of speaking to you from another place, from Home, is unique and powerful. This is your authentic Self. Constantly, my experiences invited me to make a choice in which voice I listened to either the ego or the genius Mind. *Divine Genius* invites you to do the same.

Within these pages, you'll find references to ego mind, genius Mind, Divine Genius Mind, God, Oneness, authentic Self, ego versus genius, Quantum Field, and others. Some are capitalized to indicate their Source, which is Love.

Because of the three threads of Peru, back story and wisdom teachings, this book is a weaving, a trinity. It gives you the opportunity to explore the layers on the page and in yourself. You can look at the stories on the surface, but underneath is fertile wisdom, knowledge, practical application, and reflection. It's written with three threads for a reason—for the active evolution into love beyond fear and loneliness.

There are many great spiritual books and wonderful teachings and modalities available to the everyday spiritual traveler. They all in their own ways support a path to return to the place where they all meet. The oneness of God. While I've taken and explored different pathways, this is a compendium of all that I've experienced in this lifetime and others, leading us to the place where we are One.

As you read, give yourself permission at any time to put the book down for reflection. Take a moment in nature, pick up the phone and call a loved one, follow your deep intuition as to what this story is suggesting you do.

Most of all, hold on. You're in for an adventure. Are you ready for the ride that changed my life forever? Are you ready to rediscover your authentic Self? If so, by reading this book, you will active your genius Mind. I'm here to share that with you to inspire you to accelerate your own spiritual journey and do what we all must do in this lifetime, not the next.

When it comes to unlearning, there is no time like the present. Simply say yes to the Divine Genius within, and you'll find there is no moment like now.

For a free companion ebook download, visit
www.adamchall.solutions/ebook

Prologue

The high mesa stretched out before me, a tangle of tumbleweeds and dusty sagebrush headed to the horizon. I surveyed the view, feeling as desolate as the empty space around me. Maybe a herd of wild mustangs would come thundering across the plain. Or a desert storm would blow in with crackles of heat lightning and wind.

But there was nothing. No color, no movement, no sense of being alive. I sat alone on the mesa, waiting. Simply waiting.

It was April 11, 2012, and I could see it all clearly in my mind's eye. Even though I was sitting by the fire in my home in Santa Barbara, I felt as though I'd been transported body and soul to that lonely landscape.

Then I heard it. A voice. It was coming from inside me and outside me at the same time.

"You will soon spend eighty-one days receiving essential knowledge about completion, harmony, and the seven planes of consciousness," the voice said.

I felt a chill throughout my body. Where was this coming from?

"The first forty days will ground you in a self-actualization process. The second forty days will lift you out of the lower self and into the higher Self."

I took a deep breath, trying to focus without fear on this disembodied voice. *But what about the eighty-first day?*

"The last day remains unknown," the voice said. "Although I can say this: it has to do with the Divine Design."

I wasn't sure what that meant. As if hearing my internal questions, the voice continued.

"During the eighty-one days, you will be given the treasures that have been found in the four Citadels and seven Temples of the ancient EarthKeepers. Should you choose to take this mission to infinity, you will be given the keys to the Divine Genius."

The Divine Genius? His voice was soft and monotone. *How did he understand what I was thinking when I didn't speak a word to him? He must be clairvoyant, or clairaudient—maybe even clairsentient or something beyond the human capacity.*

"I am all of the above," the voice said. "Every human has the capacity to access these tools."

"If it's alright with you," I said, "I'd prefer to speak with words."

"That would be fine under one condition," he said.

"What condition would that be?"

"That you feel what emerges from your intuition and practice speaking from that place."

"I think I can do that," I said.

"No thinking, Adam. Just do or don't. Act from the center of your being. By doing so, you too will learn to access the seven planes of consciousness."

I was taken aback by his insistence.

"I'll give it my best shot," I said.

"No thinking, no giving it your best shot. Just be in it. Just do it!" he said firmly.

"By the way," I said, feeling the heat of the desert sun on my face. "Who are you?"

"If you want guidance, Adam," the voice said, "don't ask silly questions."

Clearly I had no choice but to accept. The eighty-one days—or at least all but that last day—were already in motion.

"This knowledge will become essential to the redesign of the new humanity," the voice said. "Should humans choose not to craft a new future for the betterment of all, your species will become extinct."

I felt another chill as I realized the enormity of his words.

In the distance, a ray of light glanced off a boulder on the mesa. But in an instant, it was gone. And so was the voice.

I invite you to come on the journey. Not just as a reader but as an active cocreator of your destiny. I would recommend that before you read each chapter on the wisdom teachings, you read the Invocation to Men. With the assistance of Men, you can manifest the life you are meant to live. Please read it before you begin the book. The power and wisdom of this great archetype will help ensure the journey to discover your authentic Self will be full of joy and love.

Credit for the poem goes to Ariel Spilsbury & Michael Bryner.

Invocation to MEN

I am Men,
the eagle's vision and dream
gather about me, winged one, to take your place
upon the currents of our divine purpose.
Soar with the flow of consciousness in my massive wings.
Let us glide in the graceful expansive of planetary mind,
carving out the pathway of timeless beauty for all to follow.

Spread your precious wings,
sweet, blessed eagles of the new Sun of Flowers!
Flow with me upon the shimmering crest
of the new reality emerging,
and together we shall create
the joyfully awaited garden of the one world.
Feel my song stirring in every cell,
its refrain quickening you into resonance
with the golden octave now sounding
Through the consciousness of the Earth,
Gaia, singing likes a crystal
in the brilliant light of luminous love.

through you, Gaia, I also am transformed
I, too, am awakening
as the return of divine love and light.
We are One!

I am Men.
My gentle sound and touch ripple like waves of healing silk
upon the wounded body of the Earth
I am the crystal singer
At the heart of the labyrinth,
Whose crystalline core magically transforms this vibration
into the splendor of planetary mind.

Hear my impassioned call,
O radiant children of the Sun!
Lift with me the collect mind,
for we are the awakeners, the transformers!
Let the flowing beauty and power of my wings
inspire you are ascend to our committed purpose!
Find the gate of "I cease,"
The place where there is no "other"
Remember, alliance of the faithful of the stars,
Sun runners, your commitment
to hold the light high in this time.
Find the living consciousness of God within you,
Like a florid fountain, this place flows
With the elixirs of compassion
To create our ascended Earth!

Believe in yourself and your visions!
Sing the sparkling songs of hope
in a voice rich with the transforming power
Of your crystalline rainbow body!
Merge with the sublime vibrations

that lays the song of ecstasy ever so gently
upon the yearning spirit of Earth, Terra Gaia.

This, my beloved, is yours to do!
Build thy inner and outer temples, and adorn them
with the precious gifts you have carried
within you for so longs
On the winds of created by the moment of my might's wings,
Hear me,
Feel me,
Let us begin!

1
Arriving

June 21, 2012

"Let the beauty of what we do be the love of who we are."
—Rumi

Flying at more than twenty thousand feet over the Amazon rainforest, I witnessed the darkness of the night as it gave way to the morning light. Bright orange hues reflected off the rain clouds, filling the cabin of the plane with an otherworldly hue. What lay ahead, I didn't know. What lay behind didn't matter. Mother Nature's majestic sunrise inspired me to relax, reflecting on the long journey ahead and all I was leaving behind.

The grace of the sunrise invoked the depths of my feelings toward Lizanne. I must have done something right in the past to be gifted with a love like hers. We had made this journey together a few times over the years. But in her wisdom, she knew that this vision quest was only for me.

"You can't do it alone, and you can't do it with anyone else," she said. The axiom held true for our eight-year spiritual partnership. I felt her at my side, knowing that even from our home back in Santa Barbara, now thousands of miles and a different hemisphere away, she had my back.

"How are you feeling, love?" Lizanne asked me on the drive to LAX hours before.

"Solid, but nervous," I said, looking out at the California sky.

"Nervous about what?" she asked.

"That's what's strange," I said. "I don't know."

She assured me that everything would be okay, but I felt that something big was about to happen. "And I think the surprise is going to be on me," I said.

"Just know this, Adam," she said with her gentle smile. "I love you. And you will be in my thoughts and prayers."

"Lizzy, you always make me feel better," I said.

We sat in silence. I looked out to the blue Pacific as we drove the coast highway through Malibu to the airport. It was June 21, the longest day of the year in North America, and the shortest in South America. I felt I was turning my life upside down, from light to dark, old to new. I'd be home July 2. A short trip, but a potentially life-changing one nonetheless.

Before I knew it, we pulled up in front the American Airlines terminal. I unloaded my luggage, grabbed my Indiana Jones hat and backpack, and carefully set my guitar case on the ground. The case was the best thing I could find to transport the treasure inside. I looked Lizanne in the eye and welled up in tears.

"I love you, beautiful," I said.

"I love you, Chaska," she said, using the spiritual name she had given me several years ago on our first trip to Peru.

"I'll call you in the morning to let you know the eagle has landed," I said with a smile.

"Sounds good," she said, giving me a final hug. She waved as she got in her car, then drove off.

I checked in for my flight to Miami, taking a deep breath when it came time to let go of my bags. My clothes and toiletries didn't worry me, but the guitar case did. It was hard to hand over that precious cargo to the baggage handlers. But since I would have a two-hour layover in Miami, I trusted that it would transfer to the flight to Lima without incident.

I boarded the plane, sat down, closed my eyes, took a few breaths, and began to relax. As soon as I felt at ease, I heard Men's voice saying, "Catalyze your Being." What did he mean? Would this quest to Peru unlock the mystery of those words?

As we sat at the gate, our departure time came and went. I started to fidget in my seat as the minutes passed. Finally, we taxied toward the runway, only to face another delay.

"Hello folks, this is Captain Williams," the voice over the intercom said. "We're experiencing a malfunction with one of our electrical navigational devices, and we'll need to return to the gate and have it looked at."

There was only one problem: no gate to return to. Great. By the time the ground crew directed the plane into a gate, an hour had passed. Then it took twenty minutes to address the problem. And then another twenty minutes because the problem was bigger than they thought.

I was convinced I'd miss the flight to Peru, so I put in a call to American and explained the problem.

"We can book you on tomorrow night's economy flight from Miami, or I can put you on a nonstop flight tonight in business class, leaving from LAX."

"What time does the LAX flight depart to Lima?" I asked.

"At 8:00 p.m.," she said. "Just a couple of hours from now."

"I'll take it!" I said.

I grabbed my belongings and reached for my coat when the Captain came on.

"Folks, we've got the problem fixed, and we'll be leaving in just a few moments."

My mind was already made up. I'd get there faster on the direct flight—no more delays.

"I'm going to take another flight," I said to the attendant. "How can I get my baggage off the plane?"

"You can't," she said. "We're about to depart, and your luggage will have to be forwarded to your destination."

I nearly fainted. I had assumed that bags—and guitar cases—don't fly unless their owner flies with them.

"What would you like to do?" she asked. "We'll be closing the door in just a minute."

I hesitated. Then, saying a silent prayer that all would work out, I headed down the aisle and walked off the plane, hearing the thud as they closed the door and locked it behind me.

After the sleep deprivation and uncertainty of the previous hours, I was mesmerized by the sensations I felt as we approached our landing in Peru.

I was experiencing the change in time and hemisphere in a state of heightened awareness. Instead of attuning myself to the experience, I felt like something was attuning me. Knowing the mystery that is the Amazon rainforest, there was nothing to do but surrender. I was the arrow flying into destiny's dawn.

On many of my quests, Lizanne had been by my side, my partner in adventure and seeking. This, though, was a different mission. It was about a redemption of my soul, my deep inner Self and surrendering to Divine guidance.

The rainforest was a mystery, and so was the part of me that was preparing to emerge. I could feel it in my gut, and I knew my guides, my soul sage, and the Holy Spirit were directing me. My job was to remain open to their wisdom, and to trust.

Even though the seat next to me was empty, I could feel Lizzy's presence. "I'm here with you," I heard her say in her tender, beautiful voice. "I send you blessings for a safe journey and safe passage," she said. "I love you."

I could feel the shift in time and space as I left the linear world behind. I'd declined the processed food in a box that was offered as a meal since there was no life in it, and I could feel my body adjusting to the recirculated air on the plane.

I knew the Boeing 737 was the last piece of the modern world I would experience for a while, and I appreciated the shiny chrome of the seatbelt buckle, the neat uniforms of the attendants. From my previous trips to Peru and landing in the jungle near the Bolivian border, I was aware that everything would be dilapidated. No new buildings or roads. Few modern amenities. I breathed in, closed my eyes, and waited for the new world.

Soon I fell into a twilight state and began to have a lucid dream. I saw myself walking in Central Park in New York. Men was there, waiting for me.

"When you arrive, follow the butterfly," he said.

"Follow the butterfly? What do you mean?" I asked.

Before I heard Men's answer, the flight captain came on the intercom.

"Ladies and gentlemen, we're about to land in Puerto Maldonado," he said with a Peruvian accent. "Please prepare for landing."

I tried to get back into sacred space to continue the session with Men, but I couldn't. Apparently I had received the essential message—nothing else was required.

When I stepped off the plane, I felt the sun on my face. I walked down the steps onto the tarmac, taking in the fertile smell of the vegetation and a pungent odor of smoke in the air. The landing field was literally carved out of the jungle, and I felt myself being drawn back into the womb of the Amazon forest.

My friend Marcela was on the same plane and had sat a few rows behind me. In her early forties, Chilean by birth, she was married to Alberto Villoldo, one of the world's most respected Western shamans. I'd known both of them since 2005, when I first took part in trips with Alberto's company, The Four Winds.

Marcela and I share a birthday. We are both Aires, both fire signs. And she would be hosting a group at the same lodge where I was staying. Even though I was not part of her group this time, I was on a parallel journey.

"Did you sleep?" I asked her as we met up on the tarmac, walking toward the ramshackle terminal.

"*Un poco*," she said. A natural beauty with long black hair, she radiated light despite the long flight and little rest.

"And how about you?" she asked, shifting her backpack to her other shoulder. She wore jeans with a Patagonia vest, managing to look soft and feminine while being outfitted as a female Indiana Jones. "How was your flight?"

"Long," I said. "I'm glad we're here." It felt comforting to have this human connection.

After going through immigration, I waited with Marcela by the archaic conveyor belt that took the place of a luggage carousel, then helped her with her suitcase when it showed up. We continued to wait. One by one, everyone collected their luggage. But my bags didn't come.

I'd already felt out of my comfort zone at every leg of the trip, and now I was empty-handed. Walking into the womb with nothing but my backpack and a few basics. I bought a couple of things in the airport, adding a couple of plastic bags to my belongings. My guitar case could be anywhere in the world, and it was out of my control.

Marcela greeted the members of her group and included me, making me feel adopted even though I was on a solo quest. I helped her carry her bags to the curb, where an open-air school bus waited for us. Painted like a 1970s psychedelic van—and probably of that vintage—it was rickety—especially on the rugged streets of Maldonado.

As we drove through the city, I saw the motor scooters—familiar from previous trips to Peru—and busy city streets and smelled the exhaust. I could tell the petrol had more lead in it than we're used to. There were people everywhere. As the bus hit bumps in the road and potholes here and there, I hung onto the grab bars, bouncing up and down from my wooden seat.

A young girl of about eight caught my eye. She wore a pink outfit, which stood out from the throng of people. She was with her mother, but then let go of her mother's hand and ran off to check out something that caught her eye. I was struck by her innocence and purity, her simplicity within the hustle and bustle, where everyone was trying their best to survive in a difficult environment. I felt a bit like that child, hoping to focus on the gifts rather than the struggle.

It was a twenty-five-minute drive to the river where we'd meet our next mode of transportation. Marcela and I visited a bit, but I was still introspective, feeling into the next leg of the journey. My journey wasn't tourism. It was a spiritual adventure. "Get ready for the rabbit hole," I told myself. "That's where you're headed."

When the bus dropped us off in a cloud of exhaust, we walked down a ravine to a decrepit dock, carrying bags and loading them into a motorized canoe-shaped boat that smelled like gasoline. We were about to embark on the Madre de Dios—the Mother of God River—which flows into the Amazon.

As I'd experienced on previous trips to Peru, everything in time was radically altered as soon as I stepped off the plane. The smells, the temperature, the humidity intensified that feeling. It was like walking from one stage to the next in a complex play that twisted time and senses with every step.

The boat could carry twenty people with luggage. I sat near the front and kept an eye out for the life vests.

With the wind in my face and the sound of the motor behind me, I went inward, thinking about the jungle and the river slicing through it.

The lush landscape gave way to Amazonians' thatched hut homes. Most locals tended to the land and cattle. Far from the caricatures society has drawn of them and their heritage, they are not savages looking for their next human meal. They live in accordance with the laws of the natural world.

As we motored by, I waved at the children who danced on the banks of the *rio*. They always waved back, smiling their joy upon the boats as they motored up and down the river.

They seemed to know nothing of their parents' struggle and the persistent need to survive in the jungle of jaguars and snakes. Innocence, playfulness, and imagination ruled the day.

As I watched the shoreline go by, I began to reflect on the why. Why had I come to this remote outpost? I knew that, at least in part, it was about reclaiming my own innocence—an innocence I'd lost many years earlier when society's jungle dominated my life. Now at middle age, what would life offer? Innocence, survival, or something else? Intuitively, I sensed the answer would reveal itself during the next ten days.

I was in the home of the jaguar now, the king of the jungle. A powerful animal spirit, always tracking and stalking prey. It's an extraordinary gift to see a jaguar, and I hadn't done so on any previous trips. I wondered if I would have the honor of seeing a jaguar this time.

Already, though, Jaguar was teaching me. *What am I tracking?* I asked myself. *What am I stalking?*

And maybe more important: *What is stalking me?*

2
The Question

In 2005, I was emerging from my first year of being separated from my wife and family. I'd been going through the inner process that many refer to as the dark night of the soul. My life—my business, my community, my family—seemed to be unraveling, and each day brought a new problem that I could either resist or review.

I was in a process of searching for outer answers, not knowing I was being called to a deeper purpose and meaning in my life. Because I wasn't attracted to religion or other dogmatic theologies, I sought wisdom from Eastern and Western modalities, including indigenous traditions and shamanism.

I was searching for what I had not quite known. I was seeing something I hadn't quite seen. I was hearing something that was not yet heard. Inside, I felt an inkling, a spark within. But on the outside, my world was collapsing from top to bottom.

In the spring of 2005, seven years before my solo vision quest to Peru, Lizanne and I sat in a meeting room at a lodge in a fertile valley near Machu Picchu. The meeting room itself was ordinary, with plain walls, standard tables and chairs arranged in a circle.

A local shaman was there, sharing textiles, crystals, and condor feathers. Medicine women and men wore their Peruvian shamanic garb. Outside the lodge, the Urubamba River flowed from the Andes to the Amazon rainforest. And along with about seventy other travelers and seekers, we were about to hear from Alberto Villoldo, our teacher and guide.

Standing over six feet tall, Alberto is Cuban American, regal with a gentle aura and humble demeanor. He wore a shirt that repelled bugs, along with a vest and an easy smile. Each evening on this journey, called the Via Iluminada, he would share shamanic teachings and traditions.

It felt good to sit. I was still recovering from an experience a day earlier that had been a hike to eternity. Along with fifteen other travelers and Marcela as one of our guides, Lizanne and I had climbed the Pachatusan Mountain outside Cusco. Reaching the pinnacle at sixteen thousand feet was considered being on top of the world—an experience we didn't want to miss.

On a cool, sunny morning, we'd begun at an altitude of eight thousand feet in a small nearby village, where we'd visited a local shaman in his stone home with a thatched roof and dirt floor. Cows and roosters roamed freely, and the air was so thin and dry, I was already laboring for breath. The house, known as the Shaman's Lair, was owned by a powerful healer, Don Martin. It was said that he had dealt with black magic but now worked with the light. Still, when I visited his basement and saw the altar for his sorcery, I felt an uneasy heaviness and didn't linger long.

As a group, we began to climb another three thousand feet, past vast fields of quinoa and golden wheat. Unlike the sweetness of the jungle, the air smelled of smoke and dung. In the distance, we heard the sounds of children playing and the rush of water flowing down from the snowcapped peaks.

After continuing our steep ascent, we reached a donkey corral, where we could choose a mule to carry us the rest of the way. Lizanne and I declined—the only ones to do so—confident we could make our way on foot. I felt powerful, relying only on myself. But the feeling, it turned out, was short-lived.

We kept climbing above the tree line. I was wearing hiking boots and pants and my dark leather Indiana Jones-style hat, carrying a backpack, and I could soon feel the fatigue from the altitude and physical exertion.

Despite the inspiring views as we climbed higher, I felt increasingly weak. I was going through my gallon of water quickly but still felt dehydrated. And eventually I felt wobbly and fuzzy headed. At that point, it was Lizanne's love and energy that kept me going. Her encouragement and support meant everything, and we joked later that this was the time when we truly fell in love.

The group stopped for lunch at a stone monolith called the Philosopher's Stone, where I couldn't resist putting my ear against the smooth slab. "Listen to the voice within," I heard, "and you will hear of hidden treasures."

As we continued the climb, I needed the treasure of strength within, but it eluded me. Lizanne walked by my side, and her feminine energy lifted me. She was not big physically, but her inner power was immense, and I could feel her supporting me when I started to lag.

At about thirteen thousand feet, we looked out at the valley below and saw a lake in the shape of a heart. I stopped for a moment and felt my great appreciation for Lizanne well up in me. I took it as a sign, a valentine for the two of us, affirming the devotion to one another that was deepening by the minute. It brought tears to my eyes to feel such love from Lizanne, the landscape, and Spirit, all at once.

We hiked for another three hours, as switchbacks wound back and forth, carrying us ever upward. When we made it to the top—the last ones to summit, due to my weakened state—I knew it was because I'd been lifted by the heart of my love.

Lizanne and I embraced at the top of the mountain, feeling exhilarated despite our physical fatigue.

It was 4:30 in the afternoon, and the rest of the group had already started the descent. The temperature had dropped ten degrees, and the sun was getting lower in the sky. I was ready to relinquish my pride and ride a donkey down the mountain, but that was not an option. The descent was too steep for the donkeys to carry anyone on the way down.

With Lizanne's help and the guidance of Chino, a shaman who had a flashlight, we descended slowly, carefully taking each step. It was nine o'clock when we finally reached the bus at the bottom of the mountain, where everyone patiently waited for us.

My need for help, it turned out, was transformative for me, and for my relationship with Lizanne. She was touched by my vulnerability, and I fell in love with her strength.

The next day, we collapsed and spent hours sitting by the pool at the lodge in stillness. "The eagle has landed," I said to Lizanne. It was my way of saying we'd taken flight up the mountain and had come back to ground and nurture the experience—even though every bit of us ached, and we felt the fatigue of complete physical and emotional exhaustion.

My psyche had been cracked open. And that, of course, is what allowed the light to come in.

On the next leg of our journey, a trip down river into the Amazon jungle, Alberto gathered us together and talked about the wings that lift and carry us to a higher vision of what's possible. But that high perspective means nothing unless we bring it home and apply it in our daily lives.

"The eagle has landed," he said. My jaw dropped. They were the very words I'd said to Lizanne only hours before. She and I looked at one another as though we'd just been handed a surprise gift. With that, I knew the magic was active, and something unknowable was happening.

Sitting in the circle in the lodge that evening in 2005, waiting for Alberto's teachings, I didn't know that more light would be delivered in the form of a life-altering question. Something was bending reality as I knew it, and I was more than curious to find out what that something was.

As a shaman, Alberto abides by the traditional teachings of indigenous people who practice holistic healing and a spiritual understanding of what it means to be human. Shamanism is a spiritual technology that has the power to affect every aspect of life—past, present, and future.

That technology relies on three great symbols: the pyramids, the medicine wheel, and the staff. Through his nightly teachings on that trip in 2005, Alberto helped us understand the greater universal nature of who we are and how we're to fulfill our soul's purpose in life by serving as the conduit between heaven and earth.

As Alberto began to speak that evening, I wasn't anxious, but I did feel uneasy, as though I had stepped into the unknown. That's part of the magic of the shamanic journey—to simply step into the space and trust. The rest will take care of itself. Like other wisdom traditions, shamanism is as much about doing *nothing* as doing *something*.

I paid close attention as Alberto shared wisdom and answered questions. Then, as though he were speaking directly at me, he posed a question I'd never heard before:

"Can you get out of this lifetime alive?"

The question intrigued me immediately, hooking me as though I were a fish in the Urubamba River.

Can I get out of this lifetime alive? What did that mean? What would it look like? Was it even possible? Was there some advanced technology of the ancient Shamans/EarthKeepers that could help me accomplish this ultimate feat?

In this world, there are two things we know: we are born and we die. But could there be more to it than that? Are we, in actuality, eternal? Immortal? The question invited me to consider the possibilities of life beyond what I'd imagined before.

In the social time after Alberto's talk, I told him about the synchronicity of our "the eagle has landed" comments. His wide smile was like a wink that said, "Trust what you're feeling. Trust the connectivity. We are attuned beyond time and space. You are where you need to be."

For days after our experience with Alberto, Lizanne and I returned to the question: *Can you get out of this lifetime alive?* Neither of us knew what to do with it. Like all of life's most profound riddles, it doesn't offer the answer. It simply invites more questions. Yet oddly, somewhere deep inside me, I knew this was not just a question. It was a statement. *You* can *get out of this lifetime alive.*

How can we expand into a greater expression of who we are while we're in physical form? How can Spirit help us fulfill a greater human experience in our lives? Alberto's question fed my curiosity and inquiry, and along with it my own sense of being *in* the world yet not *of* it. There must be something else. There must be something more.

On April 11, 2012, I was guided to sit in meditation in a way I never had before.

As I sat in the sacred place of the home I now shared with Lizanne, taking one conscious breath after another, I observed my busy mind, thoughts flying like machine-gun fire.

They were about everything and nothing. In one moment, a feeling of remorse about my three beautiful daughters. In the next, a work-related worry. Then a thought about how much I love Lizanne.

It was an endless stream, and I decided to just surrender. As I did, the thoughts became fewer and fewer. And then there was stillness. Oddly, the stillness was always there, overlying busyness of the thinking mind and the brain that carries out the marching orders of the thinker.

In the stillness, I had a lucid dream, much like I'd had over the past few years. I began with a walk down Fifth Avenue in New York. Walking briskly down the street, crowded with what must have been thousands of people, I walked uptown and made my way into Central Park.

The fever pitch of city life began to subside a bit as I lessened my pace and began working my way up the meandering path toward the reservoir. I then veered right and headed down an obscure side street, where I was directed to an unmarked door, leading to a portal to the "other side."

This time, however, I was called to veer left and head down a narrow dead-end alley. The buildings on both sides, painted with graffiti, towered to the sky. Just as I was nearing the midpoint of the alley, I heard a voice.

"Stop," a man's voice said.

I froze, everything fell silent. To the right, I saw a massive graffiti image of a jaguar. The oversized eyes penetrated the very fabric of my being.

"Turn your head slowly and look the other way," the voice said.

I slowly rotated my head to the left, keeping my feet firmly in place.

"Turn and face the door," the voice commanded.

I continued following the voice's directions, trusting that I was safe and being instructed by a benevolent guide. Without resistance, I climbed a flight of eighty stairs, then stood next to a grand chair atop a towering rock. Fit for a king, the chair was oversized and golden, inlaid with diamonds, emeralds, rubies, and other precious stones.

Humbled, I looked around. The rock pinnacle rose a mile from the earth below, connecting with heaven above. It offered a 360-degree view of what appeared to be a kingdom.

The Kingdom of Avalon?

From the rock monolith, I took in the eagle eye view of the stunning landscape. In the far distance North, I could see a castle protruding from an outcropping. As I focused in on its grandeur, the voice broke into the reverie of the moment.

"Are you ready to take a seat and claim your castle?" it asked.

Taking a deep breath, I said, "Yes."

I moved toward the chair and took my place on the throne.

What seemed like just moments later, still in meditation, I found myself lying in the fetal position on sandy earth. Slowly, I got onto my hands and knees and stood up. It was pitch black on a moonless night. There were billions of stars shining. Glancing to the right, I noticed a small puddle on the ground. It was nearly frozen.

That's funny, I don't feel cold.

I began to look around and saw I now was on top of a high desert mesa. Off in the distance was a flickering fire, and I began to move toward it slowly. When I was twenty feet or so from the fire, I saw a hooded figure sitting by it, and I stopped.

The figure signaled me to come closer. As I stood at the fire, I saw that the hood hid any facial features. Beckoned to sit, I sat on a stone shaped like a chair, and we were silent for what seemed like several minutes.

Finally, the voice spoke.

"You have embarked on an epic quest of high adventure to receive the gift of completion and harmony from God," it said. "Along the way, you will receive many treasures. These treasures contain universal knowledge and Truth. What you do with them will be your choice. However, should you violate Divine Will, you will be expunged. Do you understand?" the voice asked.

"Yes, I understand," I said with a gentle bow of the head.

"Good. For the next eighty days I will be your guide. You will do as I say. Should you be unable to perform any part of this quest, you are to notify me immediately. I will be with you even outside of the lucid dream. Am I clear?"

"I am ready to begin, Master," I said.

"Let's skip the master label," he said.

As we sat in silence once again, my mind began to wander. *What did I get myself into? Who is this? Can I trust him? Can I really spend the next eighty days at this fire with this ancient man?*

"What is your name? I asked, thinking it was a simple question.

"It doesn't matter," he said. "Call me whatever you like."

I took a deep breath, wondering what the next eighty days would hold.

Over time, I came to call the voice Men, a name that was not a reflection of his gender. When we first met, I called him Horus for the ancient Egyptian deity who was said to have the head of a falcon.

Then, true to my study of Mayan shamanic traditions, I changed it to Men, a Mayan word meaning "the wise one." Men is the eagle who lives in the North, the higher mind. The eagle of the North connects with the condor of the South, which represents the heart. I also thought of him as Merlin, the magician who served as advisor to King Arthur.

No matter who and what he was, I began to find answers through his guidance and teachings.

"You can discard any and all of what I reveal," he said in the stillness of that first night in April, 2012. "Your free will remains, for now."

For now?

Looking at the state of my life at that time, it was clear that my *free* will had imprisoned me. I was still paying the price financially and emotionally from a brutal divorce, and I was estranged from my three daughters.

While I thankfully had found a deep love with Lizanne, the rest of my life was in limbo. My work as a real estate developer was gone, my role as an EarthKeeper unclear. I knew only that I did, indeed, want to get out of this lifetime alive. And I sensed that the voice I heard in the middle of the night might have something to teach me about that.

As I sat by the fire, Men said eight words that started the first of his Thirteen Wisdom Teachings.

"When you forgive, you begin to experience infinity."

Forgiveness. I took a deep breath. I had done a lot of forgiveness work, and while it had brought me some peace, I wasn't sure what else it could accomplish.

"Adam, this wisdom speaks directly to why you're here right now," Men said. "To move beyond the place where a problem was created, you must forgive."

I kept hearing the word "but"—a form of rebuttal— in my mind. My ego wasn't going to accept forgiveness without a fight.

"As you may know," I said, "I've spent much time in forgiveness. I've forgiven my ex-wife, mother, father, others, and myself. I can't imagine who else I need to forgive." I even forgave my assistant, who once stole my Lakers basketball ticket to the biggest game of the year.

"You have done good work," Men said, "and you have much more to do in order to bring a close to the past and find completion and harmony."

Then, as if in complete reversal, he said, "You have nothing to forgive."

"Wait a minute," I said. I'm confused."

"True forgiveness removes the obstacles that prevent your soul from fully emerging in the world," he said. "The challenge many people face results from a misunderstanding of forgiveness. Most forgive others for what they have done instead of forgiving them for what they have not done."

I shook my head slightly to try and understand. "What do you mean for what they have 'not done?'" I asked.

"Take a few breaths," he said. "Now say the word 'forgiveness' gently three times."

I did as he suggested, feeling into the word for-give-ness, until I heard it differently than I ever had before. *For giving.* Giving compassion and acceptance for all of us, for oneness.

"Forgiveness offers you the gift of life, Adam," Men said.

"It's hard to believe I've spent fifty-one years on this planet and haven't embraced that simple yet essential spiritual Truth."

"Not to worry," he said. "You're here now. You are being swept up by the winds of Grace. Your sail, your evolution, has been riding these winds. I invite you to hoist your sail and sail into destiny."

"What does this have to do with forgiveness?" I asked.

"Forgiveness is like the wind. Without it, your boat—your life—will drift on the vast sea of consciousness."

This put forgiveness in a completely different light. I realized that when we truly forgive others or ourselves, we are not forgiving an act perpetrated against us. We're simply forgiving an act of amnesia, forgetting we're all one.

In the end, there is nothing to forgive.

"Remember the words of the Buddha," Men said. "To understand everything, you must forgive everything."

"Ah," I said, reflecting on this first wisdom teaching. "If I forgive everybody and everything in my life, the great winds of evolution will blow."

"Yes," Men said. "And they will blow from your back, guiding you toward the future."

At that first meeting with Men, I had no idea that forgiveness was just the first of Thirteen Wisdom Teachings he would share with me over the next few months. And that, with his guidance, I would not only receive the answer to Alberto's question, but I would embark on my own quest for the Holy Grail, much like Percival in King Arthur's court.

In the end, I knew I would have to risk it all to have it all.

I knew that death was stalking me, and it would certainly win. But would that be the end?

Or could I be reborn?

Wisdom Teaching 1
True Forgiveness

"Forgiveness is a conscious act of non-judgment that restores the memory of God."
—Men

All thirteen of the wisdom teachings will help you on the path to genius. Each will guide you beyond the ego's thought system of separation and fear. We begin our journey together with the first teaching on Forgiveness, which happens to be the most challenging and essential of all the thirteen teachings. It's also the one I practice the most.

True Forgiveness, Men said, means understanding that your Divine Being—your essence, your Truth—can never be wronged. Our genius Mind remembers that we are one with God, one another, and ourselves. And it is only when we forget our genius and think with the ego mind instead that we can feel harmed by another.

"To understand everything is to forgive everything."
—Buddha

Five Insights for True Forgiveness

The genius path to true Forgiveness unburdens you from the past. Nothing is more critical on the return to your authentic Self. Without true Forgiveness, you will be unable to disempower the ego and activate your genius Mind.

Men put forth the following five critical insights to help you shed past events. Each will help you discover your authentic Self, the genius within.

1. **There is only one simple error.** True Forgiveness begins with forgiving yourself for making a simple error: believing that you are separate from others. From that one error comes the conflict and chaos in our lives. Also, from this one error, all problems are created. And by correcting this one error, you can find the solution to all questions.
2. **We all make the same error.** After you truly forgive yourself, you can forgive others for making the same error you did. When you truly forgive yourself and others, the experience that created the need for Forgiveness in the first place will no longer have the power to control your feelings and thoughts. By forgiving others, the events that happened will give meaning and wisdom to your life instead of painful memories.
3. **We are all connected**. True Forgiveness reminds us of this fact. The universe was created with a big bang, and everything was created from this one event. Science has traced the beginnings of the universe back to this one source. And everything—including every human being—is connected to this Source. This Source is the Divine Genius Mind of the universe and Forgiveness of others, and it allows us to remember our Oneness with this Source.
4. **There is nothing to forgive.** When we realize we are all the same, Forgiveness is no longer necessary. Blood, body, heart, mind, and spirit are all common and shared attributes of every human. We do not need to forgive others for anything when we are in a place of our shared humanity because we are connecting in this place of Oneness.
5. **We have nothing to defend or hide.** The ego mind must protect itself because it believes that you are separate, and that to remain that way, you must protect yourself from the

genius Mind. The genius Mind does not need to protect or hide anything.

To learn true Forgiveness, I needed to unlearn my beliefs around Forgiveness. I needed to think about Forgiveness in a new and radically different way. It has been the most challenging teaching to learn and practice, so be patient with yourself.

As Men returned to the wisdom teaching of Forgiveness again and again, I began to understand why my relationships with my wife, daughters, and colleagues had collapsed. Without Forgiveness—of ourselves, God, and one another—we can't experience or share real love. Could it be that true Forgiveness is the highest form of earthly love?

"Forgiveness is a conscious act of non-judgment that restores the memory of God," Men said.

I had long thought about the meaning of Forgiveness. I forgave others and myself, yet it never really freed me from what had happened in the first place. I kept holding onto the judgment and guilt, and they were the very things I needed to shed.

Men was teaching me from the other side of judgment and guilt. In other words, he was teaching the meaning of true Forgiveness from a place of non-judgment and innocence. This place I call the genius Mind. As compared to the ego mind, the genius Mind offers each of us a new perspective on how we want to forgive.

When I started to forgive from this place, I felt a surge in my power to choose and not have unfortunate situations control my thoughts, feelings, and life. I began to unlearn the ego's thought system of Forgiveness and began learn the Truth about Forgiveness and the reality of who I am. We are all on this continuous journey, and Forgiveness is a process, not an ending.

Think about it. You learn that you are a victim of someone else's angry deed. You struggle to let go and forgive that person. You surrender and ask that these feelings of shame and guilt be gone. The emotional and physical pain persists. You cannot escape this person or the traumatic event. The dictionary says Forgiveness "is a conscious, deliberate decision to release feelings of resentment or vengeance toward a person or group who has harmed you." That form of Forgiveness simply perpetuates a belief that you're being treated poorly.

For instance, my relationship with my ex-wife was based on my attachment to her playing specific roles as mother, housekeeper, and wife. I forgot that we were both created by God from the same genius Mind—the One that fills our individual genius Mind with peace, love, and prosperity. And because I forgot, I saw her as separate from myself—a body that expects to make me happy in narrow and limited ways.

I blamed her for not giving me what I needed, and she did the same to me. We both believed we'd been harmed by the other. But in truth, we'd simply forgotten who and what we are as Divine Beings.

I had fallen asleep, living life unconsciously and thinking we were both our egos rather than our Divine selves. When, with Men's help, I finally started to wake up and become conscious of that fact, I saw that I had nothing to forgive her for.

The Genius Process on True Forgiveness

This five-step Genius Process on Forgiveness will help you let go of all things and people that have harmed you. It will help you move beyond the dysfunctional ego that never truly forgives. Men emphasized that reawakening your genius Mind will help you manifest a new Life as Beauty, Grace, Love, Compassion, Cooperation, Cocreation, Transparency, and Service. Peace and prosperity will become commonplace.

The Genius Process on Forgiveness asks one question, has one answer, identifies one problem, and offers one solution. If you understand the meaning and purpose and practice it every day, you will reawaken your genius Mind.

In the Genius Process on Forgiveness, Men reminds us that the insights you will be learning are useless unless you create an experience to go along with it. The Genius Process helps you create the experience and unlearn past ideas about Forgiveness.

1. **Ask the question: "What do I need to know about the ego?"** Forgive yourself for judging others for what they have done. You simply made an error by judging. This is the true meaning of "Thou shalt not judge."
2. **Listen to the answer: "Whom should I listen to?"** Forgive yourself for feeling that you could be separate from God, your Source.
3. **Acknowledge the problem the ego caused in your life by asking, "What do I see that has yet to be seen?"** Remember that you and others are all One, part of the same Divine Universal Genius Mind, and forgive yourself for believing anyone could be apart from you. They, too, simply made an error in forgetting this Truth.
4. **Ask, "How do I do things in life without doing them from the ego?"** Choose your genius Mind. Know that there is nothing to forgive because everything is One in the genius Mind. Whatever seemed to harm you occurred simply because you and others forgot who and what you are.
5. **Activate your genius by asking, "How shall I be?"** When I choose the genius Mind, I become a forgiving person who has nothing to defend or hide.

In each of the coming chapters on the Thirteen Wisdom Teachings, you will be given five insights and a five-step process that will help you begin to manifest an extraordinary life of peace and prosperity.

You, too, can take these steps and practice vigilant Forgiveness. By using Men's teaching on true Forgiveness, you'll be reminded that peace begins within. The journey to peace, prosperity, and love never ends. It can be challenging, and there were times when I wanted to give up, but true Forgiveness reminded me that, in the end, there is only peace and love.

You can choose not to commit the error of believing in separation. No person or thing can take away your power of choice. You can truly forgive others and yourself for merely forgetting that we are One. And you can choose to respect others for their uniqueness and differences. This understanding changed my entire life.

Life, at times, has made me feel hopeless. True Forgiveness reminds me that there is hope, and we have a choice.

"You who want peace can find it only by complete forgiveness."
—A Course in Miracles

As *A Course in Miracles* says, I simply erred in my thinking. No separation or sin. No need for guilt. Only innocence.

"Forgiveness has nothing to do with an actual event," Men said. "It is necessary only because you've judged yourself and others as separate and guilty. Forgive yourself and others for forgetting who and what you are, and you will be restored to the peace of your genius Mind."

What if I had known this during my marriage, I wondered. What if I had seen my ex-wife as part of the Divine Genius where everything is One? What if I had loved my daughters with all my heart rather than "protecting" myself, the little wounded Adam? What if I had run my business with a desire for the highest good rather than the highest profits?

What if I had lived with an understanding of Oneness, knowing there was nothing to forgive?

When I asked these questions, filled with possibilities rather than remorse, I started to dream a new life into being. I was determined to find the answers so that, someday, I would no longer need to ask myself *what if* questions.

Little did I know how much I would need this understanding during my eighty-one-day quest.

3

Halcón

June 23, 2012

The boat pulled up to the banks of the river, where one hundred steps led up to the Eco-Amazonia Lodge. We all carried luggage and set it on the high bank, where I took in a view of my surroundings.

Situated on approximately ten acres of river frontage, the lodge was cut out of the thick jungle. It reminded me of an arboretum near my house in Pasadena where I went as a boy to run and play. Abundant with flowers and large, colorful parrots, the area around the lodge was practically vibrating with life, a natural playground in its own way.

The lodge had an open courtyard in the center with a covered pool. The dining hall was on the left, and on the right were individual huts. It was well maintained, definitely built for tourism. I anticipated a shower, some food, and a nap.

"It's a beautiful day to be in the womb of Mother Earth," I said to Marcela as we met at the entrance to the lodge.

"Indeed, brother," she said. "I feel blessed to be sharing this journey with you."

"I'm hungry," I said. "Do you want to get something to eat after we settle in?"

"I'll have something very light," she said. "I'm planning to do medicine tonight. Are you?" Her tone was soft, reflecting the importance of preparing for the evening ceremony.

"Yes," I said. "My stomach may have gotten the best of me."

Marcela was perhaps the most powerful shaman on the planet. She was gifted in the ways of indigenous cultures of the area. Through my own studies of shamanism, I knew she was known as a WisdomKeeper, a title conferred on a person who has gathered much life experience and knowledge, then translated it into wisdom. The term also honors someone who has been initiated by a community to carry forward the wisdom of their culture or tribe.

She also was known as an EarthKeeper. These individuals also are WisdomKeepers, but they've been given the power to preserve the soul of humanity and that of Mother Earth, working in harmony with the elements of nature, from the stones to the planets to the animals.

Marcela was one of few Wisdom and EarthKeepers walking the planet, and none is more dedicated to serving the sacredness within each human.

Fernando, our valet, appeared from the lodge and seemed distraught. He spoke to Marcela in Spanish, and she translated for me as he headed back to the lodge.

"Apparently they were mistaken when they said there was a room for you," she said. "They're totally booked for the next four nights. Fernando's going to check with the owner to see what options are available." I could hear the concern in her voice—and I felt the frustration in my own mind.

Great, I thought. *I don't have my luggage, and now we're in the jungle and I don't have a roof over my head.*

I immediately went into masculine control. "But I sent them a deposit," I said. "This is not acceptable." I felt exposed and vulnerable, and being aggressive was my default mode.

I had called and made arrangements through the main office, and they'd confirmed that I would have a room. Apparently they thought I was accounted for in the group that Marcela would be hosting.

I saw Fernando walking back toward us. My heart began to race with anticipation, and I tried to let go of my need to control. Worst case, I could sleep in a hammock in the pool house.

Marcela and Fernando exchanged a short dialogue in Spanish.

"He says tonight you can stay in one of the huts nearby," Marcela said. "Tomorrow the owner will clear out a hut that's used for storage. It's not near the main huts, but it should be fine for a few nights. Does that work for you?"

"Yes," I said, giving a nod of gratitude to Fernando. "Thank you both."

"*Llevaré el equipaje a la habitación cuando está lista,*" Fernando said.

"What did he say?" I asked Marcela.

"He said he'll take your bags to your room when it's ready."

"No need," I said, handing him the sum total of my possessions in the moment— my two plastic bags from the airport.

In the dining hall, I managed to eat a couple of bites of fruit, but I lost my appetite thinking about what might unfold at tonight's ceremony, starting at nine o'clock in the Ayahuasca Lodge.

Known as "The Doctor of Death," or "Ayi," ayahuasca is a tea brewed from two powerful plants. When combined, they possess psychoactive properties for visions and healing. The nickname comes from what Alberto Villoldo called a "death of the old order. Embrace the medicine with love and forgiveness to move beyond into the new order."

The medicine had always proved profound for me. I'd come to understand that every human has a coding within his or her DNA sequencing genes that are similar to everything in the universe. When you access that code and unlock that DNA, you become a cocreator and coparticipant with Mother Nature, gaining access to the inner workings of the natural world. This process, activated by ayahuasca and other non-mind-altering practices, can best be described as conscious evolution in real time, when the past, present, and future all merge in the present moment.

When you take the medicine under the right protocols, using the highest and best practices, the medicine helps you align with your higher purpose. Typically before an ayahuasca ceremony, I would prepare questions for the Doctor. Then, after taking the medicine, I sometimes received an instantaneous answer. Other times, the Doctor took me back in time to retrieve old memories or gave me a glimpse of the future.

No matter what, I'd found that the medicine never delivered small news. I would often come back from these trips knowing I was being called by something greater than myself. In fact, sometimes it took years for answers to fully download.

Certainly ayahuasca is not for everyone. While it provides a portal to remote domains of the mind, those hidden places can also be accessed through meditation or lucid dreaming. But I had found that the Doctor expanded my consciousness more readily than any other. Far from a "Disneyland" experience, it's an intersection with the spiritual world that transcends physical reality.

At times I'd say I'd had enough of the medicine. Experiencing ayahuasca is always rigorous, with a deep psychological processing that's not easy. It also causes physical discomfort and ego confusion. Whenever I participated in an ayahuasca ceremony, I always felt conscious and lucid, yet I surrendered to Spirit's voice and that which is completely unknown.

As I sat in the dining hall and pondered tonight's ceremony, I knew it was important to have clarity of intent. What outcome did I want to emerge? But unlike the other times I'd used ayahuasca, no clear intentions came to mind. I felt unprepared, wondering if I could simply show up and listen.

I knew that by spinning the ego and disrupting your sense of identity, the Doctor creates havoc. Within a few hours, I would be like a gyroscope, spun completely around by competing forces. And what would I hang onto? Where would I be?

The answers were simple: nothing and nowhere.

That afternoon, I noticed the arrival of the master of ceremonies, the *ayahuascero,* Maestro Panduro. His given name was Edmondson. He appeared out of thin air. It was as if one of the jungle trees shape shifted into Panduro. He was a stocky fifty-something-year-old man who grew up in the jungle. I had "done ceremony" with him in the past. He was an extraordinarily powerful healer. His medicine and the songs he sang during the ceremony were magic.

As I approached, the maestro turned and looked me straight in the eye.

"*Hola, mi hermano,*" he said, smiling as if I were a long lost friend. I appreciated his recollection of our last encounter at the lodge in 2008.

"*Hola, Maestro, como está usted?*" I asked, giving him a big hug.

"*Muy bien, y tú?*" he responded politely.

Maestro Panduro was legendary in these parts. And as a guide into other dimensions to hundreds of seekers over the years, he had become famous for his service as a master ayahuascero. His medicine, "Jungle Juice," was guaranteed to change your life forever.

"Señor Hall, your room is ready," Fernando said in broken English.

"*Nos vemos mas tarde,*" I said to the maestro.

He nodded his head and smiled, and I followed Fernando. We walked past guest huts with small wooden signs that said Jaguar, Toucan, Monkey, Serpent, Boa, and Tortoise.

Then we kept walking, and I wondered where Fernando was leading me. Finally, away from the main camp and near the edge of the jungle, he stopped by a rickety hut, opened the door, and stepped aside to indicate we'd arrived.

Even before I entered, I could smell cleaning supplies and a musty odor. As Marcela mentioned, it had been used for storage, and it hadn't been cleaned out completely. Despite its rough appearance, though, it had an auspicious name.

Halcón.

It's the Spanish word for falcon, a bird indigenous to South America.

As a spirit animal, Halcón is known for vision and protection. I wondered if I would need those two attributes with me for the ceremony that night.

In three short hours, the ceremony was to begin. The light of day was diminishing. As I sat in my Halcón hut, I could feel the jungle as it transitioned from day to night in the beginning of the Southern Hemisphere's winter. The ecosystem went into changeover mode. Perhaps this was happening to me, too. Many of the plants and animals called it a day and tucked in for the night, while others were awakening from their daytime dreams.

Among those creatures were insects and spiders that could kill you with a single bite. This was the wildest of the wild, high adventure, and I was well aware of the risk.

Having been to this particular lodge, to this jungle, to this appointment with the Doctor two times before, I could feel the magnitude of what I was about to do. The first time I'd experienced the medicine, I'd done it out of curiosity. Now I understood the deep significance, and my ego was busy trying to talk me out of it.

From my studies of *A Course in Miracles*, a channeled text known as spiritual psychotherapy, I understood that my small ego mind was dedicated to keeping me stuck, small, and always seeking happiness, but not truly wanting to find it. Any experience that could lead to self-knowledge, wisdom, or joy threatened the ego's commitment to struggle and misery, and my ego tried to redirect me from it every time. In this case, it didn't mince words.

What am I doing here? Are you kidding? You're going to do this again?

Make no mistake, the fear was as present as the sounds of the night creatures outside my hut.

Frustrated by my lack of focus in the dining hall, I stretched out on the hard bed in my hut with its tired sheets and lumpy pillows, watching the ceiling fan go round and round and trying to think of questions I would ask the Doctor. This time, all sorts of things popped into my head.

What do I still need to clean up from the residue of karma in this lifetime? How can I cultivate a closer relationship with my children? How can I serve the planet? And, on a more practical note, *Where the heck is my guitar case with my treasure? I was planning to have it on hand for the ceremony.*

No question was more or less important than the other. During the past nine years on the road to completion and harmony, I had explored many questions. As a matter of fact, I made it a point to question "intelligence"—mine and others'. I was still trying to figure out my self-identity. I knew how strongly the world tried to label me and imprint an identity upon me—and how many years I had accepted that identity and all the chaos it caused.

But who was I really? To understand my purpose, what did I need to unlearn from the world?

Unlearning, I'd discovered, is an art form that requires acceptance and Forgiveness. By conforming to familial, societal, and cultural imprints that dictated who and what I was to do, I'd been living an unconscious lie. As I moved further into my own conscious evolution, it was time to take my seat at the table as my authentic Self.

The ceremony would begin shortly. I got up to head over to the sacred Ayahuasca Lodge where the ritual would be held. As I opened the door to the Halcón, I heard a voice.

"Adam, don't do or ask for anything. Just receive."

I turned to look behind my back. "Who is that?" I asked, but heard no response. Just the sounds of the jungle as they rose with the moon.

"Well, it's good advice," I said to the empty hut, "whoever or whatever you are."

Then I stepped out into the dense jungle air.

4

A Stand for Love

It was a beautiful day in Santa Barbara. Under a light cover of clouds, I stood under the granite pillars where our Evolutionary Leaders Circle would soon gather. Rows of white folding chairs were set up in a semicircle facing a tall Stonehenge-style arch, with other similar stone arches off to the sides of the chairs.

In front of the main altar was a small stage with two comfortable chairs, a reed side table, and a vase of orange Asiatic lilies. Deep red and pink bougainvillea cascaded over the tops of the arches, and a grove of trees formed a backdrop for this beautiful natural setting.

My friend Barbara Marx Hubbard had invited me to join the global Evolutionary Leaders Circle a few years earlier. Part of a global organization founded by her, Deepak Chopra, and Marianne Williamson, along with the Source of Synergy Foundation and the Association for Global New Thought, this group shared a vision for expanded states of mind and evolution of consciousness.

I decided to start a local chapter and invited some local millennials to cohost a multigenerational gathering on my land, Casa EarthKeeper. We hoped to expand in Santa Barbara and welcome more people of all ages into the circle.

Soon, several dozen seekers would gather near the stone arches to share fellowship and ideas for raising the vibration of our community. In all, more than fifty people showed up, spanning seven decades in age. It was an extraordinary display of wisdom, wealth, heart, and soul. On this particular day, I was the designated convener, which served as a coming out of sorts. For the first time publicly, I was claiming my own light as a leader, as a steward of our community.

And more than anyone might have known, I was taking a stand for love.

On the same day in Utah, an altar of another kind was set up in a church near my ex-wife's home. My daughter Morgan, the youngest of my three girls, would walk down the aisle and say her vows of marriage.

As her father, I'd envisioned this day for years, just as she had. I would wait for her at the back of the church, where she would take my arm, and I would proudly walk with her past friends and family and deliver her to her groom.

But the reality didn't meet the fantasy. My ex-wife Gigi and I had split up when Morgan was eight years old, and years of Gigi's ongoing resentment had erected a wall between me and my daughters.

This wasn't the first time her fury had poisoned a wedding. Two years earlier, Lizanne and I arrived at the ceremony for my oldest daughter Maya, not sure what to expect. We had been formally invited to the wedding out of obligation. I was determined not to miss this special day in my daughter's life.

The wedding took place in the garden at Gigi's home. I hadn't been there for several years. Not since a cold winter night when her entire family turned on me and unleashed their fury.

The vitriol I experienced that evening was a striking contrast to the nuptial setting in Gigi's backyard. Flowers lined the aisle, and white chairs with sashes were set up for all the guests. Lizanne and I headed toward the back and waited for the ceremony to begin, but within minutes, my former mother-in-law headed toward us. She looked me up and down and said, "Only a fool would wear white to a wedding." Then she turned and walked away. Gigi, meanwhile, was giving Lizanne and I the evil eye.

Before long, Gigi's brother came up to us, face to face. Both his body language and his tone were menacing as he said to me, "I'd leave if I were you."

Despite the threat, we chose to stay. And when the music started, I saw Maya in her wedding dress for the first time. My beautiful daughter was escorted down the aisle by her grandfather, not by me.

I looked around at the beauty and exquisite attention to detail, all in the name of love. The vows came with deep emotion. But when the ceremony was over, Lizanne and I were openly attacked.

My other two daughters wouldn't come near us. My new son-in-law's father came over, leaned in close and said, "You were brave to come," then ambled away.

At the reception, Gigi's best friend made a speech about what an amazing mother Gigi is, how she had "done it all on her own, with no money, support, or anything."

The atmosphere grew darker and more hostile by the minute. I wanted peace for all of us—for Gigi, Maya, her new husband, my other daughters, and for Lizanne and me. But as hard as I tried to keep the peace that day, I felt my ego fighting to be heard, to be in control, to lash out and hurt others the way they were trying to hurt me and Lizanne. The same way they were hurting themselves.

Lizanne took my hand and looked into my eyes. "Are you ready to go?" she asked quietly.

"Yes," I said. "I think I am."

On the day of the Evolutionary Leaders Circle gathering, with the heady fragrance of the flowers and the ancient energy of the stone, our sacred space in Santa Barbara felt like an open cathedral. Women wore sundresses and hats, men came in jeans and polo shirts.

Feeling reverence for the spirit of communion, I stood on the stage and called in the directions to open the space shamanically.

"We are gathered here today not only to meet new friends," I said, "but to celebrate a time of communion, of shining light together into the center of the circle. We come together to see how we can support one another with the wisdom of the ages and our collective resources. Today is about helping you to shine your light, knowing you no longer need to play small."

I acknowledged the breadth of ages present, and the fact that "our eldest is only as good as our youngest."

A slight breeze stirred the leaves on the trees, and I heard a young girl giggle. A spontaneous expression of delight.

"We want to hear from each of you," I said to the crowd. "The people of Santa Barbara. We are innovators, collaborators, cocreators, and people of the heart. Compassionate, loving people, surrounded by geniuses, and planetary stewards."

With that, each person introduced themselves, speaking into the community and symbolically taking the torch and spreading their light.

"We are here for the good of the whole," I concluded. "For our children's children. We are living in the light, coming together. It is incumbent on us to shine and guide others home."

After Maya's wedding, I vowed never again to be a party to such verbal and physiologically hostile circumstances, nor subject anyone I loved to such an event. So when it came time for Morgan's wedding, I agonized over whether to go.

Gigi set the tone when she told Morgan, "If you ask your father to walk you down the aisle, I'm not coming to your wedding." Immediately I was put in a divisive position, feeling the same energy brewing that we'd experienced at Maya's wedding.

I had to make a choice. I could go to Morgan's ceremony and experience darkness. Or I could stay in Santa Barbara and lead a communion, a gathering for spiritual peace.

I knew that if I went to the wedding, I'd be on the periphery, simply making an appearance. Certainly my ego felt dishonored and wanted to retaliate. But my presence would have cultivated hate and animosity by Gigi and her brother. How could I dishonor the sanctity of love's presence on my daughter's special day?

The morning of Morgan's wedding, I sat in the family room, just off the kitchen, and called in love for her and her groom.

It was as though I sat above the wedding venue, looking out over it with the eyes of an eagle. I had visited the venue's website and knew what it looked like. I saw the flowers that had been my contribution to the wedding, even though I'd kept my distance during the planning.

Even two weeks earlier, I was still undecided about going and struggled deeply over it. Lizanne supported my staying in Santa Barbara, knowing the ugliness we'd experienced before. I felt every iteration of the ego mind: complete loss, shame, guilt, and self-loathing. My daughter was about to embark on a rite of passage. And I was clearly experiencing my own.

Morgan had always been our miracle child. Tough, brilliant, and deeply wounded, she had undergone years of programming from Gigi that I was a monster, the enemy, that I didn't love my girls. And now here I was, deciding to miss her wedding. It brought back every moment of regret and shame from all the years I'd missed with my daughters.

And yet, there was love.

I was choosing love.

In *not* going to her wedding, I was choosing to save her from a potential scene of darkness and ugliness, of confrontation and blame.

I wasn't sure she would understand. I could only hope that someday she would. She had to know I was doing this on purpose. And the purpose, from that day forward, was love.

It's hard to describe the feeling of the Evolutionary Leaders Circle that day. I breathed in the powerful presence of love and was able to share it openly, without drama, in the total absence of fear. It was as though I broke through a sheet of ice, publicly proclaiming my own commitment to love, and creating a space in which others could do the same.

As I visited with all who had joined us for the communion, I thought about Morgan. Had she said her vows by now? Had she and her husband signed the marriage license? Were they all raising a glass of champagne? A part of me ached to be with her, to look in her eyes and tell her how much I loved her, how proud I was to be her father. Maybe one day she and her husband would renew their vows, I thought to myself. And I'll be there. I will pinky swear with her to be there.

Even though no one but Lizanne knew it, when I stood on the stage in Santa Barbara, I was standing directly in the intersection of love and fear—of my old, unconscious self and the real Self of my Divine Genius. Inwardly, I was weeping and rejoicing simultaneously. My greatest heartache, right next to my greatest celebration.

As a long-time student of *A Course in Miracles,* I asked myself, "What purpose did this serve? What was my decision *for*?"

"Forgiveness," I thought to myself. A stand for love. And, in the end, the only path to peace.

Wisdom Teaching 2
True Purpose

"To know your true Purpose, look within. Emotions, when expressed from the heart, will help you remember your authentic Self and discover what you are here to do on earth."
—Men

Everything has a purpose, and that purpose is the same for everything: to point us back to our authentic Self, the genius Mind within. Built on forgiveness, true Purpose doesn't depend on what you do, but on the soul's alignment with your heart and genius Mind. When your actions are true to your Purpose, you become aware of the authentic emotions of the heart and soul.

It wasn't until I spent time with Men that I understood a new definition and perspective on Purpose—one that comes from the inside out rather than the outside in. I always thought that Purpose was about what I am to do in the world. Trying to figure out where I belonged and what I was to do was not only stressful but also confusing and tiring. Often I felt lost. Men's teaching made it simple for me to understand my true Purpose.

Interestingly, Men linked Purpose to our emotions. Our purpose impacts not just what we do but the emotions that govern our lives. Life, he said, is as much about feeling your way through it as thinking your way through it.

I had long forgotten the feeling part.

Five Insights to True Purpose

Men's teaching on true Purpose helped me reawaken my genius Mind. Like Forgiveness, it has made a profound difference in my relationships, with my work, in my health and mind. Why? Peace and prosperity prevail. As you get in touch with your genuine emotions, you will become more balanced and present to deal with life's inevitable disruptions.

These five critical insights put forth by Men will help you understand that emotions project themselves from either the separate ego mind or the genius Mind. As you choose the genius path to true Purpose, you will discover your authentic Self.

1. **Surrender to your emotions.** Surrender does not mean suffering defeat or losing control. It's just the opposite when understood in the context of true Purpose. Emotions, when expressed from the ego mind, either get repressed or project themselves into your outer life from the unconscious. They feel conflicted and promote chaos in your relationships. These are projections of the shadow or ego self. Authentic emotions that stem from the genius Mind come from the heart. They express themselves in your relationships as kindness and compassion. These are aspects of your light and authentic Self.
2. **Become aware of childish emotions.** The ego always reacts first and loudest, expressing childish emotions. The ego acts out and fights with other people to prove itself right. On the other hand, childlike emotions are innocent and can be sweet. They are genuine and share from a place of tenderness. The separate ego reacts and rejects authentic emotions, whereas the genius Mind that is living its authentic Purpose allows and accepts emotions. The path to true Purpose always guides you to the place within that is aligned with your heart and soul.
3. **Listen with your heart.** The voice of the heart will guide you to the innocent, childlike emotions within. On the genius

path to true Purpose, you can listen *to* your heart, and you can listen *with* your heart. Both are important. It's best to begin by connecting with your heart's voice. Take a moment and close your eyes. Feel your breath and ask yourself, "What does my heart desire?" When you hear its voice, you can begin to listen with your heart. When you listen with the heart, you can listen to what others are asking from their heart. When you do this, you are authentic and genuine to yourself and others.

4. **Take authentic action.** Insights are only as good as your willingness to take action. The path of genius requires two things:
    a. Your willingness to show up to learn and unlearn.
    b. Taking authentic action from your heart and soul. To take authentic action, ask yourself in everything you do, "What is the Purpose of this person, place or thing?" Remember that true Purpose points you back to the Home of your authentic Self and genius Mind. If you take action(s) from the separate ego mind, conflict and chaos will result. When you choose authentic action from the genius Mind, you will express your genuine nature and share peace and prosperity with everyone.
5. **The path to genius is a journey without distance.** The authentic Self doesn't ever go away. When you choose the ego mind instead of the genius Mind, you forget about what has been and always will be: your authentic Self.

Learning to feel the world around us from the authentic Self of genius is not always easy. Unlearning habitual thinking and unhealthy patterns of emotions requires a vigilant practice of true Forgiveness. It necessitates constant reminders to live your true Purpose and take the path of genius back to heart and soul, where we are one with each other. When we do, we practice the wisdom and intelligence of the emotional body and intelligent heart.

Remember that feelings originate from the pain body that's governed by the ego mind. Emotions emanate from our inner psychological self. When your emotions express themselves as feelings from the ego mind, you're reacting from the place of separation and woundedness from past events. These emotions are childish and inauthentic. When emotions emanate from the genius Mind, they are expressions from the heart. These emotions are childlike and authentic.

True Purpose begins with Forgiveness. When I was living the life of a hard-charging businessman trying to conquer the world, I was all too often unkind to people. I'll never forget the time I scolded my assistant Stephanie for making a simple typing error. "You're incompetent," I shouted at her. My childlike emotions brought her to tears.

I needed to forgive myself for the thousands of moments in which I acted from the inauthentic ego mind. If I continued acting the same way, the genius path Home would have been like driving down the road in a dense fog going a hundred miles an hour. My destination would have been death.

"Everyone has the same path to travel to discover that Purpose," Men said, "and it begins with Forgiveness. With True Forgiveness, you will be able to flower into your Purpose and live in abundance."

"I've been a seeker of purpose," I told him. "I decided my purpose was twofold: to be of service to others and to shine light and love into the world. That's it."

"Those are admirable acts in the outer world," Men said. "However, they are outward projections of Purpose. We need to ensure that your outward expressions are not originating from your ego's small mind, but your inner genius Mind.

"How can we determine that?" I asked.

His answer seemed confusing—until it didn't.

While we think we want to know our Purpose, we're asking, "Where do I belong? How can I fit into the world? What can I do that will help me feel like I matter?"

The cause of those questions, Men said, is our ego mind. Feeling separate from God, it believes its worth is always in doubt. Because of that, it searches the world for a role or job to fill that empty void. And it operates within a limited view of reality. The effect? We keep searching but never find what we're seeking.

It goes right back to the ego's desire to get rid of peace, as explained in *A Course in Miracles.* By projecting a belief in separation onto the world, our egos build walls, keeping our sense of Purpose always beyond reach no matter how much we strive to find it.

However, when we ask, "What is my purpose?" from our genius Mind, we get a different answer. Our genius Mind remembers that we're one with Spirit, the Divine Genius Mind, and can never be separated from it. So its solution is not about doing something important; it's about being the love and light that we already are, the geniuses that we already are.

In the end, our only purpose is to find our way back to God by remembering that we never left. Your authentic Self has always been there. It was simply hiding in the shadows of the separate ego mind. Everything and everyone can help us find the path back to genius. Maybe it's a bird that makes you smile when you are down, or a flower that helps you feel the wonder of it all. People, places, and things are put in our lives to remind us of our true Purpose. All we need to do is remember our true Purpose.

To do that, says *A Course in Miracles,* we need to lift the veil of forgetfulness. Like the clouds that hide the light of the sun, this veil hides the light, love, and genius of our being from shining fully into our lives. To remember our way Home to God, we simply need to move beyond the ego mind.

"So whatever your purpose has been," Men said, "it must be revisited on occasion to ensure that it emanates from the heart and not the ego mind.

"Return to the emotions of the magical, innocent child," he said. "Find the joy and tenderness of that child within."

Genius Process on True Purpose

This five-step Genius Process on true Purpose will help you get beyond the ego mind. According to Men, true Purpose reminds us to take every life experience as a learning experience. We are here in the body and ego mind to reawaken the authentic Self, the genius Mind.

When you practice true purpose as taught by Men, you will always be moving closer and closer to your authentic Self. When you are genuine, life happens with ease and grace. The conflict and chaos created by the ego becomes a joke: "There you go again."

The Genius Process on True Purpose uses the same formula as the previous teaching. Ask the question, listen for the answer, acknowledge the problem, and be open to the solution. Yet it focuses explicitly on finding true Purpose. It gives us hope.

As you go through the Genius Process, be aware of the feelings that emerge from the ego mind. This will make the work of remembering your authentic Self and genius Mind more precise and straightforward.

1. **Ask the question, "What do I need to know about the ego?"** Sit with the emotion when it arises. Surrender to it. Let it feel into you. Write down the feelings.
2. **Listen for the answer, "Whom should I listen to?"** From there, you'll be led to the authentic action to take—or not—as part of your true Purpose. Practice sharing your emotions from the heart.
3. **Acknowledge the problem the ego caused in your life by asking, "What do I see that has yet to be seen?"** Remember that the ego always reacts first and loudest. It's likely that your initial emotional "hit" in any situation comes from the inauthentic ego self and will be childish—like a toddler throwing a tantrum.
4. **Be open to the solution by asking, "How do I do things in life without doing them from the ego?"** Whatever you're feeling, don't resist. Take a deep breath, and then listen

more deeply, getting past the ego mind to your quiet inner voice. That voice will guide you to the innocent, childlike emotions within.

5. **Activate your genius by asking, "How shall I be?"** When you choose the genius Mind, you remember that everyone and everything helps you to return to the place you never left: the Oneness of your authentic Self.

I thought of all the times I'd acted upon a feeling of want, need, or hurt, rather than acting from a heart-centered place of compassion and Forgiveness. Even at times when I thought I was living with Purpose, I could see that I was thinking and feeling from my ego mind rather than my authentic genius Self.

So now I had a new litmus test to use every day: Was I expressing myself from genius, or was I reacting from ego? Was I being forgiving of others and myself? Was I coming from a place where I was one with others? Did I remember my true Purpose, that I am one with others and that they are in my life to remind me of this Truth?

I was about to learn more about my Purpose than I'd ever understood before in the hands of the Doctor of Death—the one who reminds me to forgive, to be authentic, and stay on Purpose and to surrender all that no longer serves my soul's journey on the path to genius.

5

The Good Doctor

June 23, 2012

The Ayahuasca Lodge was located about four hundred yards from the main lodge and about six hundred yards from my Halcón hut. The lodge was twelve-sided with beamed ceilings and a series of trusses. The bottom half of the building was enclosed, but the top half was screened in, providing little between us and the night noises of the jungle. The entrance was on the west. In shamanic traditions, this is the direction of the setting sun, home of the jaguar, and the symbol of death.

It was 8:50 p.m., and I was one of four people scheduled to see The Doctor. Instead of sitting directly on the floor, I found a worn-out mattress that was ready for the trash. Like the others, I kept moving and shifting, trying to get comfortable before the journey began.

Maestro Panduro greeted us and declared that we were ready to begin. I didn't know if I'd ever be ready, but I was there, and the part of me that wasn't terrified was willing to see what would happen next.

Maestro pointed to a four-by-six-foot framed picture hanging on the south side of the hexagonal room. "The greatest ayahuascero ever," he said. The image was hand-drawn, depicting a dark-skinned man with strong features smoking a ceremonial pipe and wearing a necklace of feathers and beads. In his left hand, he held a bowl, presumably of Jungle Juice, and in the background were palm trees and a structure that looked remarkably like the lodge. In fact, handsome and elegant, the man in the drawing looked a lot like Panduro.

The Maestro smiled. "This was given to me by the owner of the lodge," he said. "I am the man in the painting."

Clearly, the master was in his house, and this was his kingdom.

Panduro came around the circle, stood in front of each of us, and met our eyes. I could tell he wanted to see if we were present. Satisfied, he said an Incan prayer in a soft voice. Then, from a plastic half-gallon jug, he filled an espresso-sized metal cup with Jungle Juice and handed it to me.

No matter how many times I visited the Doctor, I knew I would never get used to the taste of the medicine. My body tensed as I bowed in humility and brought the cup to my lips. In two gulps, it was part of me—its dark, primordial taste and its power over my mind, body, and spirit. Now all I could do was wait. And surrender to what may come. *Am I going to die?*

Panduro made his ritual last spin around the circle to "clear the energy field." He was smoking his famous jungle tobacco, made from dark leaves, with extremely high amounts of nicotine. It smelled as earthy as the ayahuasca tasted. This was Panduro's way of smudging the space. He stood directly in front of me and blew a huge puff of smoke toward the middle of my forehead. The force of this breath nearly knocked me over. If he wanted to clear any exterior energy lingering around us, there was no doubt he succeeded.

I settled in, sinking a bit into the comfort of my mattress. Then, suddenly, my body felt as though lightning had struck. The medicine was kicking in. I reached for one of the large plastic bowls placed around the circle and threw up violently, then vomited again. My human body was simply a vessel for the deep work of the medicine. But finally my body let go, and my journey began.

As I lay back on the mattress, I began to listen. The medicine recognized my energy field because it began to ask about issues we'd visited in the past, including the wounding in my childhood and past lives.

As I tuned into the questions of the Jungle Juice, I heard Panduro begin to sing. His ayahuasca songs are specifically for ceremony, calling on the medicine like a lover calling on its mate. The melodies brought tears to my eyes, beckoning the light and the blossom of the medicine to bring its gifts to each of the sojourners sitting in the room.

With each moment, I felt I was going deeper underwater and could hear only the distant strains of Panduro's sweet songs. I kept bobbing in and out, like a fishing lure waiting to be submerged when a fish takes the bait. I had no idea what he was singing, but he made me feel safe, allowing me to go deep while knowing I was still anchored to the physical world, and honored to be in the circle.

But everything soon changed.

It was as if I was sitting in a movie theater, watching different aspects of my life. For the first time, I felt the medicine and I were cocurating the experience. I surrendered and let the Doctor do the driving while I navigated, suggesting where I wanted to go and what I wanted to see.

Before long, I felt a deep sense of peace. Panduro had stopped singing, and the sounds of the jungle began to creep in. It must have been after midnight. The jungle was alive and awake, as though it was the middle of the day.

As I breathed peacefully, a warm presence gently emerged.

"You have come here to earth to serve the Grail," a godlike voice said. "You have come here to earth to serve the Grail."

"What?" I said, unsure what this meant.

"You have come to serve the Grail," the voice said, "and you are to go to Cusco in three days' time to receive further instruction."

"What? Serve the Grail? Go to Cusco?" I could repeat the instructions, but I couldn't understand them. Was I to trust this voice?

"Serve the Grail," the voice said again as it faded into the background.

The last time I'd heard this type of mystical voice was in 2003, when a palm reader kept repeating the word "separation" to me as she studied my hand. I became obsessed with the word. When I was alone, I asked out loud, "What does it mean?" a thousand times over. Was the word referring to my coming separation from my wife and my daughters? Did it have to do with changes in my business? Eventually, I heard the voice say, "You have been living in an illusion of separation from God." It was a statement of Truth that I was only beginning to understand.

Panduro marked the end of the ceremony by simply saying, "Finished." I couldn't wait to get out of there. I felt my heart pounding, and I needed room to breathe. "Serve the Grail, serve the Grail." I heard the voice resounding in my mind.

Over the years, I'd heard various versions of the legend of King Arthur and the Knights of the Round Table. The story of Percival, the Grail Knights, and the goblet that contained "the blood of Christ" was a tale of high adventure.

In the legend, the Grail Castle symbolized our true Home, the Christ consciousness within all of us. But as I made my way through the darkness with the cacophony of the jungle all around me, the Grail Castle seemed far away.

"Serve the Grail," I said to myself as I stepped back into my hut.

It was almost 2 a.m., and I had been up most of the last forty-eight hours. Still feeling the effects of the Doctor, I put my head down on my rock-like pillow. Just as I began calming myself, I heard a haunting howl from what seemed like a mile away. Before long, the howl became a pack of howls, echoing through the jungle canopy and finally drifting right over the hut. I felt goosebumps all over my body as wave after wave of screeches resounded through the jungle.

Howler monkeys. I'd heard them on other visits to the rainforest, but I'd never gotten comfortable with this aspect of Mother Nature. Her womb was warm and safe, yet she was always in motion, always incubating life. At night, I could feel the power of her Life Force, and I felt small and vulnerable in my tiny hut.

I stretched out on my bed, exhausted. With no more strength to think, reason, or function, I heard the voice repeating "Serve the Grail, serve the Grail," as I dropped into a dream state.

But this was not an ordinary dream. I was hovering above the bed, looking down at myself sleeping below. Suddenly I heard a slight creaking noise just outside the door to my hut, and the face of a jaguar flashed in front of my eyes. It was a big black cat with stunning yellow eyes.

He couldn't talk, yet I heard him. "Follow me," he said quietly. "You will be safe." He led me outside into the half-moonlight, slipping through the vegetation without a sound. I could feel the immense power in every ripple of his body, every silent pad of his footsteps.

After a hundred feet or so, we came to an opening.

"You have come to a choice point," he said. "You have two roads to choose from."

I took a deep breath, trying to focus on his voice. I felt safe with him but didn't trust him, all at the same time.

"The road to the right will take you back to the dream that you are currently living in your everyday life," he said. "Life will continue as it is with all the ups and downs, suffering, and moments of happiness. It will always feel hostile and foreign. This is the path of death."

"What other choice do I have?" I asked.

"The road to the left takes you to your sacred Home, the place in your heart and soul. Here the separate self will give way to an expanded sense of Self."

He swished his tail back and forth.

"So what road will you choose?" he asked.

"I don't know," I said. "Will I die either way?"

"Yes," he said. "All roads involve a form of death. If you take the first road, physical death will always be stalking you, but you will be birthed again into another life to explore and learn. Perhaps next time you can find completion and harmony."

It occurred to me that Men had spoken those same words to me early on. Maybe this was Men in disguise?

"And what about the second road?" I inquired.

"Yes, you will die an emotional and physiological death. Some say this road is far more difficult because you have to unload all your physiological baggage. But you will be left with the spiritual tools in which to hone your heart resonance and redesign your life according to your Divine Genius."

"So what's the catch?" I asked.

"You have to leave your ego identity behind," he said.

The victim within me tried to make an appearance, to no avail. "Why would I choose either of these roads? I asked.

"Because you have lived in a dream of opposites, a dream in which all choices are the lesser of two evils. Both are based in the separate design of the ego."

"I choose neither," I said, not knowing where that would leave me.

"Good choice," he said. I thought I detected a tone of respect. "There is another choice," he said, "a third choice. The direction you choose and lessons you learn will alter the course of your destiny."

The big cat was growing on me. I had worked with a shaman near my home in Santa Barbara some years before, and his name was Jon. In the Mayan Calendar he was the jaguar.

"So, Jaguar Jon—is it alright if I call you that?" I asked.

"Of course," he said. "Call me whatever you like."

"What am I to do?"

"Find a stick and draw two circles side by side," he said.

I used the illumination of the moonlight to find a stick nearby. Then, on a patch of dirt, I drew two large circles that had a tiny gap between them."

"If you look at the map you just drew, where are you now?" Jon asked.

"I'm right here in the exact center, in the gap between the circles," I said. I realized in a flash of genius that I was to take the middle road.

"That's it!" I said.

"Yes, that's it," he said. Then he quickly disappeared into the jungle.

In my lucid dream, Jaguar Jon was gone. But as I stood in the open space, I realized that I was in the middle of a treasure map. Was I to proceed right, left, or neither direction? Doing nothing was not an option. I gazed up from the treasure map, lifted my chest high, looked straight ahead, and stepped into the dense jungle brush, as though I was entering the jungle at the center point between the left and right roads. I shuddered for a moment, wondering what I would discover in the unknown.

There she was in all her beauty—the biggest and most stunning butterfly I'd ever seen. About the size of my hand, she was pale yellow. I thought of the name "Eb," an archetype in Mayan cosmology that represents the spiritual road. "I will call you Lady Eb," I said.

I followed her into the jungle as she led the way. Needing a rest, I found the shade of a giant kapok tree, which can grow more than two hundred feet tall and tower above the jungle canopy. I leaned up against the tree and took in the power and expanse of her limbs. Like the tree of life, was she offering a higher perspective? I knew from my shamanic work that the signs and wisdom of the natural world are instrumental on any quest, acting as signposts and markers along the way.

With Lady Eb ahead of me, I continued walking, taking in the wonders of the jungle. I saw more butterflies of all shapes, sizes, and colors. Birds sang the joys of life, and flowers radiated the hues of the rainbow. Everything was budding with life. I even saw a tribe of monkeys swinging their way through the upper canopy. But unlike my reaction to the howler monkeys I'd heard from my hut, I felt unafraid.

As I came upon a huge river, I had a flash of myself still asleep in the hut, but I felt compelled to keep going. The water flowed swiftly toward the Mother of God River, where the Lodge was located. As I came to the river's edge, I realized that the road had ended. My road. My middle road. If I was to cross, I would have to find a different spot, since the water flowed in torrents here.

Looking up and downstream, I noticed that the river came to a funnel about one hundred yards to the south. I bushwhacked my way through the dense brush to a spot where I thought I could safely cross.

As I looked into the river, I noticed something lurking near the top of the water in an eddy that had formed on the bank. It was a massive anaconda. Startled, I immediately withdrew from the banks, reminding myself to use extreme caution.

"Jaguar Jon said that the angel of death is present on all roads," I said. "Is that true, Lady Eb?"

"Yes," she said, directing my attention to several caimans sunning themselves on the banks. These miniature versions of the alligator looked like they were getting ready for breakfast. One even looked over at me and licked his chops.

"Lady Eb, what do I do?" I asked.

"This is a sign," she said with a hint of mystery.

Just then, we saw a flash of lightning and heard a roll of thunder. Dark clouds gathered, and a rainstorm roared to life.

I followed Lady Eb to a hollow in a tree trunk. "By the looks of it," I said, "the storm may last a while. I'm going to take a rest." With that, I sat down with my back against the tree. The droplets of rainfall from one leaf to another sounded like music.

Then I heard a door slam, briefly pulling me away from the lucid dream. *Was the* ayahuasca *playing tricks?*

"Lady Eb, is that you?" I said as she appeared from behind the fern just beyond a coconut tree.

"Yes," she said, clearly excited. "You cannot cross."

"What do you mean?" I said.

"You are not ready for the road that awaits you on the other side," she said.

"And why not?" I inquired.

"You will find out if you do what I ask," she said. "Your sacred soul Design awaits."

"Fair enough," I said. "What do I need to do now?"

"There is one last thing you need to clear from your past," she said. "It's a trunk full of emotional baggage."

"Am I going to die?" I asked.

"Yes, if you are lucky. You will not die a physical death, but an emotional one. Should you make it to the other side of the deep trauma you experienced, you will be given great treasures."

"You mean I will become immortal?" I asked.

"No, you will realize your immortality in this lifetime. You and all of your fellow humans are immortal, but you have not had the experiences necessary to make that a living reality."

"I am ready," I said with a sense of purpose. "Where shall I begin?"

"Do you remember the 'dreaded day?'" she asked gently.

"Do I remember?" I said. "How could I forget?"

"I will leave with your emotions," she said.

A flurry of feelings about the dreaded day poured through me. "But why?" I asked. "Why do I need to dig into the events of the past?"

"Because," she said clearly, "you need to make room in your 'cup' to receive the treasure on the road ahead."

6
Innocence Lost

Sitting by the hollowed-out tree, I revisited the dreaded day that occurred on April 1, 2005, when my three daughters were moving from California to Utah. Their mother and I had been going through the horrors of divorce court for the past fifteen months, and I had finally relented, allowing them to move away.

It was the most difficult choice I'd ever made, but I knew it was in the best interest of my girls.

My wife had chosen to take the route of domestic terrorist. Nearly every day for the entire fifteen months, she harassed, harangued, threatened, and laid waste to the entire life we had created together.

She was understandably hurt by my infidelity, but I never imagined she would wage a holy war, hell-bent on destroying me.

On that April day, sitting in a little beach shack in central Malibu, I heard my phone ring. I froze, not wanting to face the coming nightmare. Then I reluctantly answered, knowing karma had come calling.

"Adam, it's Gigi," she said, sounding out of control. "Where are you? The girls are waiting to say goodbye."

"I thought I was supposed to come by at one o'clock," I said.

"It's after one now, Adam. Get your ass over here!"

"I'm on my way," I said and hung up the phone.

They were at her parents' house, just ten minutes away. I had spent the previous night with a bottle of tequila and deep waves of sobbing, and I drove as if I was in a funeral procession.

The phone rang again. Lizanne. She had consoled me for the past few weeks, knowing what lay ahead for me.

"Adam, I love you," she said. "The girls will be fine. It's their journey as well." I could tell she was fighting back tears, too.

Beginning to cry once again, I pulled over. Looking out toward the ocean, I saw a family of four playing in the sand, triggering a new round of tears. But after a few moments, I started the car and headed onward.

I had created this mess and somehow, some way, with God's help I could make things right. *There is a crack in everything,* Leonard Cohen wrote. *That's how the light gets in.*

I was undoubtedly cracking open, or perhaps I was cracking up.

As I approached my in-laws' house, I could see my daughters sitting curbside, waiting for me. I didn't want them to know the depth of my sadness. I needed to be strong for them.

"Hi, girls," I said as I got out of the car. "Sorry I'm late." I put on a halfhearted smile.

"Oh, yeah, Dad," Morgan said. "You're always late, just like Mom says."

At eight years old, Morgan was the youngest. She was on the left, throwing small stones across the street. Sophia, twelve years old, sat poking at the street with a stick. Maya, fourteen, looked off in the distance, unwilling to meet my gaze.

I knelt down on my left knee a couple of feet in front of them, trying to find my balance.

Taking a deep breath, I mustered the courage to speak.

"Girls, I know this is hard to understand, but I came to say goodbye for now. Just because you're moving away doesn't mean we're not going to see each other."

The silence was deafening. Overwhelmed and fighting back the tears, I continued.

"Morgan, your mom and I worked so hard to bring you into the world. Please know I am so sorry for hurting you. I love you to 'infinity and beyond.'" My eyes met hers for a brief moment as I remembered all the times I'd tucked her into bed over the years.

She was our "miracle" child, the one Gigi and I had prayed for as we encountered back-to-back problems in having a third baby.

I turned to Sophia. "I heard you're going to join the soccer team at your new school. I look forward to coming and watching you play."

"Don't worry, Dad," she said. "You don't have to come." I felt an arrow penetrate my chest.

"Oh, I'm coming," I said. "I want you to know how much I love you, and everything will be alright."

Then I turned to Maya. "I'll never forget the night when you came into the world," I said. "Your face was and will always be one of the most beautiful things I've ever seen." She looked away dismayed, lost, and confused.

"From the beginning, I have always loved you from the bottom of my heart."

The girls glanced at me and looked away.

"I'm coming to visit in two weeks," I said. "Be thinking about what you'd like to do."

In turn, I gave them each a hug. But as I said goodbye, they looked down at the ground.

I got in the car, turned the key, and drove off a broken man. I couldn't help but imagine what pain they were feeling.

All I ever wanted was for the girls to live in the innocence and magic of being a child. But in that brief fifteen minutes, I lost it all.

When I was a boy, I said goodbye to my own innocence for different reasons. It was June of 1974 and my family was moving from Pasadena to Malibu, sixty-four miles westward. Malibu, a small beach community, was primarily known as an enclave for the rich and famous. The Who's Who of celebrities that included Cary Grant, Warren Beatty, and Steve McQueen.

The draw for my parents, though, was simply the beach. They found an amazing lot near Paradise Cove on a half-acre of land. The house was in the early stages of construction. I'll never forget the day that my mom and dad shared with me that we were moving.

"You're going to love the beach," they said. "You'll have so much fun." They knew they were trying to convince me of something I didn't want to do.

I had settled into a sweet spot with the local kids in our Pasadena neighborhood. Why would I want to move anywhere? Nevertheless, I resigned to the fact that I didn't have a choice.

On moving day, we piled into Mom's station wagon. Dad drove his new 1971 Datsun 240 Z, a sports car in the ugliest shade of avocado. It was stuffed to the brim, so we drove behind in the station wagon. My two oldest siblings were at college, and I envied them.

Off we went to Malibu. It was a hot early summer day in the San Fernando Valley, where the temperature on the freeway sign read ninety-four degrees. We took the 101 Freeway heading west, turning off at Malibu Canyon and traversing the road through the narrow canyon. It took us through a tunnel, and when we emerged, the big blue ocean popped into sight.

Maybe moving to Malibu wouldn't be so bad after all.

We drove five more miles north to our rental house, where we'd live until our own house was finished. Suddenly we heard the blare of a fire truck siren, and Mom pulled to the side of the road. Just as we were approaching Bonsall Drive, the traffic was stopped.

"Looks like there's been an accident," Mom said, craning to see around the cars ahead of her.

"Where?" my brother Ben asked.

"About seventy-five feet in front of us," Mom said. "I hope no one got hurt."

One of the firefighters started waving cars to move around into the other lane. As we neared two mangled cars, I saw an older man lying on the highway. Then a fireman draped a yellow tarp over his body.

"Is he dead?" Ben asked.

"I'm afraid so," Mom said.

I slouched down in the back seat, not wanting to see anymore. The man had been alive just a few minutes earlier, probably thinking it was just another day.

Now he was gone. And so was a piece of my childhood.

Just a week after we arrived in Malibu, Ben wanted to camp on the beach at our new house, even though we weren't living there yet. Dad was all for it, so we gathered a few essentials: sleeping bags, firewood, a tarp and most important, marshmallows, chocolate bars, and graham crackers. Off we went, the accident of a week ago seeming like a distant memory. The new house was five minutes down the road. We arrived, got everything set up and started the fire on the beach.

"Sorry, guys," Dad said. "I've got to go back and pick up my sleeping bag. I left it at the door."

"Can I come?" I asked. "I want to say goodnight to Mom again."

"Sure," he said. "We'll be back in fifteen minutes," he told Ben, who, at sixteen years old, relished the chance to hang out on the sand.

On the way home, I thought about how good the s'mores were going to taste. And before I knew it, we'd picked up the sleeping bag, given Mom another hug, and headed back to our campsite on the beach.

As we headed up the hill in the left lane of a four-lane highway, Dad suddenly screamed.

"Oh, God!" he said, swerving the steering wheel violently to the right.

In a flash, I saw a car coming at us in our lane. Quick thinking and an even quicker response by my dad saved us from certain death.

He pulled to the side of the road, trembling, and I began to sob. I was so terrified, I'd peed in my pants.

"I just want to go home," I said. "I just want to go home."

It had been a rough first few weeks in Malibu. I was longing to see my friend Brad Hall back in Pasadena. He lived a few blocks from our old house, and our last name was just one of many things we had in common.

For years, we rode our bikes all over town, organized games with the neighborhood gang, and built a fort in an old water storage tank in the mountains above the neighborhood.

After all the trauma of the past few weeks, my parents decided to let me visit my old friend. Dad dropped me off on a Friday afternoon. I had slept over at Brad's place in the past, but never for two nights and never so far away from home.

It took us no time to pick up where we left off, and we spent the evening playing Monopoly.

The next morning, we sat down with Brad's family for breakfast—big bowls of Cheerios sprinkled with sliced bananas. Tigger, Brad's older brother, joined in the conversation.

"Hey, you guys want to go over to the playground to try out a cannon I made?" He was excited to show off his latest invention.

"Tigger likes to build and tinker with all kinds of things," Mr. Hall said. "The other day, he made a wooden airplane that flew almost twenty feet."

"Sure, let's go," Brad said.

I followed the two Hall brothers out the door to the newly asphalted playground of Linda Vista Elementary, where I'd gone to school with Brad.

"Hey, Tigger, what's the deal with this contraption?" I asked as he tinkered with it.

"OK, it's made out of six Folgers coffee cans with the tops and bottoms cut out. For the bottom one, I only cut out one end so the compressed kerosene can collect in it."

Tigger reminded me of the Nutty Professor I'd seen in a movie not long before.

"What are the grapefruit for?" Brad asked.

"We put a grapefruit so it fits tight in the top of the cans. Then I add kerosene into this hole." Tigger pointed to a hole he had punched in the bottom using a can opener.

"Yeah, then what?" I asked.

"You shake it like this," he said, swirling the homemade cannon around and around.

"And then you light the match."

Boom. The sound was so loud we clapped our hands over our ears. The grapefruit shot out of the cannon and nearly went through the basketball hoop nearly a hundred yards away. We jumped up and down in sheer joy.

"Adam, you light this one," Tigger said.

"Sure," I said, lighting the match.

I placed the match to the hole, but nothing happened. A split second later it exploded, and the flaming kerosene lit my left leg on fire.

I screamed, trying to put the fire out with my hands. We had no water, and we were stranded in a sea of asphalt.

Brad and Tigger tried to beat the flames on my leg, but the fire only seemed to get bigger.

"Run to the dirt!" Tigger screamed.

I ran to a patch of bare ground about twenty feet way and rolled around to smother the flames. But the pain seared through me, and I felt like I was going to faint.

Brad ran home to get his parents, and they drove me to Huntington Memorial Hospital, the very place I was born. I spent the night in the Critical Care Unit with second- and third-degree burns, then visited the doctor every day for a month to have the bandages changed.

At such a young age, I felt traumatized by the death, near-death, and severe injury that had happened in just a few weeks.

In an instant, the magic of being a child was gone—a wounding that defined the next three decades of my life. I didn't know it at the time, but that summer marked the death of innocence.

"Innocence," I said out loud in my lucid dream, sitting in the hollowed-out tree. "Innocence." I said it slower this time, pondering each syllable.

It means so many things. The absence of guilt. An ignorance about life. Naivete. A lack of knowledge.

An innocent mind is curious, wanting to learn and explore. It's a beginner's mind, calling forth the spirit within.

And as I finished my dream in the jungle in Peru, with the words "serve the Grail" echoing through my mind, I remembered the innocence that had died within me and wondered if it could ever be reborn.

Wisdom Teaching 3
Death

"Life begins with Death. In the ego's separate mind, life and Death are two separate events. But in the genius Mind, they are the same. In other words, there is no Death. Death is merely a thought of the ego mind. All that dies is not authentic. Authenticity in the genius Mind cannot die."
—*Men*

Men's teaching on Death came to me as I was sitting in my sacred space at my home in Malibu. It was a peaceful spring morning. The sun had risen only moments before. I was in a deep meditation, resting in peace, feeling relaxed, and present to receive Men's next teaching.

At that moment, the true meaning of Death came to me. Indian yoga master Anand Mehrotra said that, "only the one who dies truly lives." In Men's teachings on Death, he reminds us that we do not die a physical Death, but our egocentric identity dies a psychological Death.

Death is the most feared aspect of being human. Death in the ego mind is an ending. It means the Death of a victim mentality. It fights literally to physical Death. Look no further than the current state of affairs around the world. If the ego does not maintain these fear-based emotions, it will cease to exist.

In contrast, Death in the genius Mind is a beginning. Men said that the genius Mind connects to the Life Force. Creating a genuine life experience means no longer getting caught up in feelings that create conflict and chaos. And living your authentic inner Purpose creates an experience of peace and prosperity.

The psychological Death of the ego forced me to transform long-held emotions of anger and sadness into a more compassionate and kinder version of myself. Most of the time now, I'm friendly. I smile and laugh more. I am okay sharing my deep fears and emotions, whereas before I would just repress them.

"A man with outward courage dares to die; a man with inner courage dares to live."
—Sun Tzu

Five Insights on Death

Here is what I learned and unlearned about Death from Men. I invite you to keep an open mind about your belief in Death. If you do, you can free yourself from the madness of inauthentic emotions of the ego, including the belief that you are a victim. On the genius path, Death reveals a secret.

1. **Death is a thought of the ego mind.** The ego identifies with the physical world. It believes that you are a body and will die. Not so. You are an immortal soul with a genius Mind that can never die.
2. **Change your thought of Death to a thought of life.** When your authentic emotions hide from your awareness, you are unable to feel peace, prosperity, and Unconditional Love. In the genius Mind, there is only life. The Life Force sustains the entire universe and flows endlessly through your heart, mind, and soul. Your soul is eternal and immortal.
3. **Accept your immortality.** Within you, there is a place called Home, the authentic Self. In this place that you never left, you will find the genius Mind. Here, life is eternal, infinite, and immortal. The Death of pain, suffering, fear, and unhappiness allows you to return Home.

4. **Eternal and immortal life is a thought of the genius Mind.** There is no Death. When this belief becomes true for you, peace and prosperity are given. As a bonus, compassion, kindness, and Unconditional Love become the norm.

Instead of the ego reacting in fear, the genius Mind—guided by your spirit—can move through life more gracefully and with ease. Authentic emotions are to be felt and expressed so long as they come from the heart and authentic Self.

Remember the difference between emotions and feelings! Emotions are universal—they run deep and can be unconscious—while feelings surge up from these emotions and are "unique" to each individual. When they run unchecked, these feelings feed the ego mind.

Two people can have the same emotion, such as anger, but can feel it, experience it, and express it differently. The ego translates all emotions into feelings of victimization, as in "Poor me," "Why me?" "It's everyone else's fault." In this place, there is no conscious understanding, and we choose our feelings based on our "story."

Becoming aware of that story helps us wake up to our unique unconscious drives that feed our ego's beliefs.

Also remember that anger, fear, happiness, and so forth are authentic universal emotions. It is the ego mind that translates them into feelings of victimization.

I would never have predicted that Death would be Men's third teaching; it seems like it belongs at the end rather than at the start. But that was the point. To learn about life, I had to unlearn what I understood Death to be.

In our culture, Death is still a taboo topic. It seems so final—the last goodbye, an end to a sometimes unfinished life, a punishment or mistake that robs us of life before we're ready.

But what if Death is just a thought? What if we never really leave? What if Death is simply a portal to rebirth and resurrection, a necessary precursor to awakening?

Men's teaching took me right back to the question Alberto posed seven years earlier, which I'd been wrestling with ever since: Could I get out of this lifetime alive?

To understand fully, Men said, I needed to understand the meaning of Life Force, which he defined as that infinite sea of consciousness I was navigating.

"Put your hand on your heart and close your eyes," he said.

I closed my eyes, took a few deep breaths, and felt the joy of my beating heart.

"Now put your hand on your belly," he said softly.

I put my right hand on my belly. My left hand began to vibrate with the beat of my heart, and my right hand released each beat into my abdomen. With each pulse, my heart sent the force of love into the belly of the ego beast within.

This was happening within my body, yet I was consciously sending and receiving love from the higher planes of consciousness to and from my body.

"What you're giving and receiving," Men said, "is a direct result of raising your vibration and expanding into your genius Mind."

And then he said something I could never have predicted.

"Adam, you are the grocery store of the Life Force."

"What?"

"Within you is a vast store that houses the Life Force in the physical world. That store contains the memory of all that has ever been."

Again, "What?"

"Your cells contain the memory of the entire evolution of humanity. Think of it like storing information in the cloud. The Life Force connects your human energy system with an unlimited source of vitality and the highest planes of consciousness."

"But how does the Life Force explain Death?"

"It means you are the keeper of life, and you and only you have the power to choose again and release all that no longer serves you," Men said.

"You, and all humans, can avoid or at least significantly reduce the occurrences of life-changing events like serious illness, accidents, and mishaps that could even cause physical Death. It only takes one choice."

"And that choice has to do with getting beyond the ego mind and choosing the genius Mind, correct?" I asked.

"Correct," he said.

As I looked back over my life, I could see that my ego mind—starting long before the traumatic events of my childhood—had kept me from being fully alive. The Death of innocence didn't happen because of anything that happened outside me. It happened long before, in the limitations of my ego mind.

When we unfreeze our authentic Selves, we became conscious of our emotions and the unique way our egos make us feel based on these emotions. We learn how to forgive and live our true Purpose. We become cocreators of our destiny by choosing feelings that serve the genius Mind, not the victim feeling fodder for the ego mind. Even with the Death of the ego mind, our job is to check our victim at the door consistently. It is a permanent job. With this wisdom, we can bring about the Death of the ego "victim" mind and its power over us. We are thus flooded with the Life Force!

"Death will stalk you until you choose again," Men said. "But when you do, Death will become your friend, and your life will become one of Destiny, yours to cocreate."

With Men's help, the Genius Processes of Forgiveness and Purpose rejuvenated my connection to what life was about: to be an active participant as a cocreator. Claiming one's Truth as a cocreator with God is not for the faint of heart. Speaking your Truth to power is the most courageous act anyone can take. For me, it was like sailing a ship into the vast sea of the higher planes of consciousness. Not knowing the outcome of such a quest did not matter.

The Genius Process on Death

This five-step Genius Process on Death will help to create experiences that will move you through the Death of dysfunctional ego feelings. Men's teachings on Death happen to be particularly challenging and require a constant reminder you are not going to die a physical Death. Going through the Genius Process on Death frees you of the burden of past events and the ego's emotions and feelings by experiencing the authentic emotions of the genius Mind.

1. **Ask the question, "What do I need to know about the ego?"** Choose the Death of the ego separate mind. Death of the body is real. Death of the ego victim mind is real, but the body and ego are not authentic. That which genuinely lives never dies.
2. **Listen for the answer, "Whom should I listen to?"** To receive, we must be open to letting inauthentic feelings and emotions die away. You choose the genius Mind in every moment by choosing kindness, acceptance, forgiveness, and love.
3. **Acknowledge the problem the ego caused in your life by asking, "What do I see that has yet to be seen?"** The ego mind may remain, but it will no longer prevent the authentic emotions and feelings of true peace, Unconditional Love, and abundant joy from being part of your life experience.
4. **Be open to the solution by asking, "How do I do things in life without doing them from the ego?"** When you choose the genius Mind as your identity, you never die. Because the ego identifies itself so fiercely with the physical world, it correctly thinks this also means the end of you as a body. You are not a body. You are an eternal and immortal soul.
5. **Activate your genius by asking, "How shall I be?"** When you choose the genius Mind, you remember your authentic Self and express your true emotions.

I was starting to get it. Men wasn't talking about a physical Death here, but the end of an old, limiting mindset. *A Course in Miracles* calls this mindset an illusion, a false belief system erected by the ego to protect itself from hurt and pain, but ironically causing hurt and pain in the process.

Could I taste infinity within my physical world? Could I welcome the Death of old belief systems as a portal to a new life? Could I live my life and expand the Life Force at the same time? And, ultimately, could I get out of this lifetime alive?

T. S. Eliot summed up the genius path on Death by saying, "We shall not cease from exploration, and the end of all our exploring will be to arrive where we started and know the place for the first time."

My exploration continues. Somehow, I knew the answers would become more explicit on my quest to serve the Grail and return to the inner castle of my Home.

7

Unsettling In

June 24, 2012

"Serve the Grail, serve the Grail," I mumbled as I awoke in my ten-by-twelve-foot Halcón hut.

I'd been in Peru fewer than forty-eight hours, and I was so thoroughly exhausted I could barely get out of the bed to pee. I lay still, listening to the morning sounds of the jungle. It was alive with birds chirping and monkeys chattering as they swung through the canopy of trees.

I had never been so completely wiped out after any of the previous medicine ceremonies. As a matter of fact, in all the other journeys with the Jungle Juice, I felt totally restored and refreshed. What had happened?

I decided to take a cold shower. Perhaps the jungle water would clear the psychic residue from my mind.

The pure water of the rainforest poured over my head in the shower in my hut. Letting out a sigh of relief and shock from the cold water, I began to come alive. I put on my lotion, combed my hair, and brushed my teeth. Every part of my physical being slowly came to life again.

As I became more aware, I suddenly remembered that I had forgotten to go to the sacred space at dawn to receive the day's wisdom from Men—the same ritual I'd been practicing for more than ten weeks straight.

Did my forgetting signal a change in my work with Men?

Knock, knock.

The sound stirred me out of my meditation. I opened the door to my hut and squinted at the bright sun.

"*Hola, Señor Adam,*" Fernando said with a smile.

"Hola," I said, feeling dazed.

"*Tu cuarto está listo,*" he said. My regular room was ready.

I followed Fernando out along a path that led away from the main lodge and huts. If I hadn't been impressed with Halcón, I was even less so with the exterior of this old and dilapidated hut. I could see why it wasn't in use. Maybe they'd hidden it away on the edge of the jungle as a place to banish employees, isolating them in the wilds for punishment.

Unlike the other huts, it didn't have a name. I immediately decided to call it "Serpent," thinking I might feel one slithering across me in the middle of the night.

Fernando opened the door, releasing the stench of death and mold. It felt ominous, but I caught myself and remembered to not let my mind play tricks. However hard I tried to deny the reality of what I was experiencing, I couldn't help but think I was being put to the test.

"*Bueno? Bueno?*" Fernando asked. Clearly he knew the hut was below par.

"*Sí, muchas gracias,*" I said politely.

"*Adios,*" he said, then hightailed it out of there.

I sat on the edge of the bed. The mattress felt like springs covered by nothing but a sheet.

Just breathe, Adam. Just breathe.

Just as I started to relax, I heard a knock at the door. Maybe it was Fernando again, coming to tell me they'd found a nice, clean room for me in the lodge.

"Who is it?" I asked.

"Señor Adam," Fernando said through the door, "your baggage will arrive in two hours."

I stood and flung open the door. "That's great news!" I said. "Please find me and let me know when it arrives," I added.

"I will," he said, fleeing once again.

What a relief. Maybe things were looking up after all. I tried to remember the contents of my bags, as though I'd left Santa Barbara months before rather than hours. The clothes, snacks, books, and various amenities of life didn't matter. But one item did. The treasure.

After my children and Lizanne, this was the single most important thing in my life. But right now, sitting alone in my Serpent hut on the edge of the Amazon, it was my first priority. Two hours. I'd be reunited with the treasure in just two hours.

With a sudden burst of energy, I felt a flood of hunger roll through me. So much for the meeting with Men, I decided. I closed the door on Serpent and nearly ran to the kitchen.

At the main lodge, a few other travelers on the quest were in the dining area, chatting over cups of tea. The large open space accommodated dining tables in neat rows, with buffet-style service. Most of the guests had already gone out for the day's adventures. Marcela was sitting in the corner writing intently when she looked up and waved me over. I scooped up some fruit, hard-boiled eggs, and bread and went to sit down with her radiant light.

"*Hola, mi hermano,*" she said with a bright smile.

"*Hola, mi hermana,*" I said, feeling brighter myself.

"So, how was your work with the medicine last night?" she asked.

I paused for a moment, wondering where to begin. "Well, the journey really began when I got back to my room and laid down," I said.

She put down her pen and took a sip of tea. "Tell me," she said.

"While I was in the ceremony I kept hearing a voice saying, 'Serve the Grail, serve the Grail.' When I got back to my hut, I asked, 'How can I serve the Grail if I don't know what it is or where to find it?'"

She nodded, encouraging me to go on.

"I heard the howler monkeys, and they scared the living bejesus out of me," I said.

"Ah," she said. "They always do that to me in a weird way as well."

"Once I settled into the sheets, the second wave of the medicine came flowing into my psyche," I said. "A black jaguar came and knocked on my door."

"Really?" She sounded as excited as a child. "Tell me!"

"I followed it into the jungle, where we came to an opening—a fork in the road. I was faced with two options, and each posed a question."

"Okay…" she said.

"The road to the right was the one I'm living in my everyday reality with business, family, friends, money, and everything that comes with the territory. The jaguar said it meant certain death."

"Really?" Marcela said again.

"And the death was stalking me," I said, "seeking my surrender. It was strong masculine energy in all respects."

Marcela nodded.

"If I continued on that road, I was subject to fate. Life would live me instead of the other way around."

"Well," she said, "you do have to die to truly live."

"But I was told that the world would remain separate, hostile, and foreign to me. I'd never find completion or harmony. And I wouldn't die, but I'd have to forego all the hard work and treasures I've found on my spiritual path."

"Ah," she said. "I get it."

"On the brighter side, I'd keep my identities, and the world would continue to evolve around me. I'd get to keep living as me, myself, and I."

"That doesn't seem like a good choice," she said.

"The other choice wasn't much better," I said. "It involved a death of sorts as well."

"What do you mean?"

"A death of my ego, the ego world, and the entire ego system. An emotional and physiological death, if you will. The second road veered off to the left. It offered an opportunity to return to my sacred Home by living in my heart."

"That sounds much better," she said.

"My separate self would give way to an expanded sense of Self. I'd dump the *me* and replace it with *we*. More feminine energy, less masculine."

"So what's the problem?" she asked. "The choice seems like a no brainer."

"There's more," I said. "The left road would mean I'd disconnect from the world. I'd live a life of solitude. Somber, quiet, peaceful, and many other splendid things, but I'd never quite belong in the world."

"Oh, I see," she said. "That works, yet it doesn't."

"Right," I said. "Like the first choice, it's missing completion and harmony."

"It sounds like you'll be spending some time here over the next couple of days contemplating which road to take."

"I already made my choice," I said. "I chose neither."

"Really?" she said.

"Neither one worked for me," I said. "I realized the return road Home was the middle road, so that was the one I chose."

I took a sip of tea and found myself saying something I hadn't thought about in quite the same way before.

"I didn't come here to live in the Garden of Eden," I said. "I came here to *be* the Garden of Eden. And to do that, I desire to serve the garden and all of humanity."

I knew the Buddhist way is the middle way. The middle road offered hope, at least for now.

Marcela smiled. "What's the middle road all about, Adam?" she asked.

"When I find out, I'll let you know." *Perhaps that's where I'll find the Holy Grail.*

"Well," she said, "I hope you find what you're looking for, because I sense it's looking for you."

I started to tell her about Lady Eb, about reliving the dreaded day and my loss of innocence, but I decided I needed a break from it all.

"I think I'll go sit by the Mother of God River and do some deep listening," I said. "Perhaps she'll share some of her wisdom with me."

"Thanks for sharing, Adam," Marcela said.

I made my way out of the dining hall and headed out to sit on the dock. The luggage would be here soon, and I wanted to be right there to welcome it as it arrived.

Just before I headed down the steps of the riverbank, I bumped into Maestro Panduro.

"*Hola, Maestro,*" I said warmly.

"*Hola, mi amigo,*" he said, giving me a once-over.

"*Muchas gracias por la noche,*" I said with appreciation.

"*La medecina es muy importante.*" It felt like he was saying, "Good work."

"*Si, muy importante.*" I said.

I headed down the steps and found a seat on the dock. The muddy river must have been a couple hundred yards wide, and it was moving swiftly. It smelled of earth—a rich, pungent smell. I felt called to pull out my journal and jot down some notes.

As I drifted off into my thoughts, the hot sticky air of the jungle began to drip off my brow. I thought of ancient alchemists who knew that change requires heat, energy, warmth, fire. It felt as though something in me was enlivened, expanding. I was simmering, turning on long-dormant Spiritual DNA.

I had a funny feeling I was being baked from the inside out, with the themes of life and death swirling through the past, present, and future.

8

Deception

When my father died in December 2007, I walked into the crematorium, where I stood next to his casket. The undertaker, a man in his sixties wearing a black suit with a white shirt and black tie, asked, "Would you like to see him?"

"Yes," I said, catching my breath. I sank into the final moments of saying goodbye. With the undertaker there as a witness, I shared a few last words I'd written in honor of his journey and to thank him for being in service to my soul's growth. Then I gently laid the note on my father's heart.

When the time came to push the button on the conveyor belt that would carry the casket into the furnace, I paused and wept. Death seemed to be the totality of the human experience—the end of our physical world.

My father had been a gentle, handsome man with bright blue eyes. My relationship with him growing up embodied the light of those eyes, but also the shadow, which was the most challenging part of my life's journey.

When I was a boy and we moved to Malibu, my dad and I spent Saturdays on the beach, which was just fifty yards outside our back door. While we were in close proximity to one another, I can't say we spent the time together. On fall days, Dad sat in his beach chair with the radio tuned to the USC football game and his earphones on. My brother and I swam in the clear ocean, tossed a Frisbee to our golden retriever Bijou and, when we got hungry, headed back to the house for a snack. Dad was oblivious, inhabiting his own world. He was there, but he wasn't present.

By the time I was a teenager, I started acting out to get his attention. I was louder than my siblings, more demanding. He took it in stride, and we maintained a pleasant relationship. But every time I tried to get closer, he pushed me away. He provided well for us financially and was well liked in the community. But he was never able to be what his soul was meant to be. Deep within him were the shadows of his own cloaked father. He carried his own wounded self within him, just as I carried mine.

My father was a wounded king, seeking his own Holy Grail. But I knew that after he died, with a perspective from the other side, he could see the wholeness of his own journey, including the wounds that he passed on to his children.

And this—this—is the marvel to me: in his death, I felt more supported by him than I did when he was living. If he could, I think these are the words he would say to me now: "I'm proud of you. Your courage is something I wanted but did not find. I love you."

When I did the ayahuasca ceremony in Peru, I didn't take the prospect of death lightly. I could feel it stalking me even through the lucid dreams, even with the shapeshifting entities I met through The Doctor.

In the shamanic world, "shapeshifter" is the name we give to beings that appear to be something they're not. Some can change their physical appearance, such as a wolf turning into a human, or a man shapeshifting into a robot. It's the stuff of folklore and legends, and it's also linked with sorcery and witchcraft.

My dad had been a shapeshifter, just as we all are, adapting our ego selves to get what we want, protect our family, and feel safe in the world.

But sometimes people come into your life who are more deliberate tricksters, even when their physical appearance stays the same. In my life, at a vulnerable time, two shapeshifters showed up back to back. At the time, I didn't realize that their sorcery would cause a death I needed to experience.

At one time, Zach was a successful real estate developer in Texas. In his mid-forties, he had played with a lot of money. I was looking to build my business with more capital and needed to raise money, so I was referred to Zach by a Colorado mortgage broker.

"He has a lot of baggage," the broker told me. "He built a luxury condo tower in Denver, and there are lawsuits all over the place."

"Yeah, yeah," I said, not wanting to listen. "In real estate, people will accuse you of all sorts of things."

"Like fraud," the broker said. "This guy misrepresented all sorts of things. He told buyers they were getting GE appliances when they were a cheaper brand. Stuff like that."

"He's got money, though, right?"

"Not so much anymore," the broker said. "He ended up filing for bankruptcy."

Still I didn't listen. I knew Zach was a brilliant, talented guy, and I convinced myself that everybody deserved a new beginning, a second chance. So I ignored the warnings, overlooked the circumstances, and hired Zach as a consultant to help me build my business.

An everyday kind of guy, he stood about five foot nine, with brown hair and a few extra pounds. I flew him out to New York to meet with investors and spent $40,000 on lawyers, getting a partnership in place to bring in large capital. But before long, it became evident that Zach was damaged and troubled, trying to be something he was not.

The Denver Business Journal did a story about his fraudulent practices. People called and asked me what I was doing, associating with him.

And then things got worse. Zach had two young children in another state, and he didn't have a home in Santa Barbara. He traveled around with a printer in his car. I could feel the desperation.

And finally I had to ask myself a powerful question: Why am I so desperate that I'm hanging onto a partnership that doesn't serve me? Why was I hanging on to death instead of life?

One day, Zach came into my small office in downtown Santa Barbara and closed the door behind him.

"What can I do for you?" I asked. He looked haggard, as though he'd slept in his clothes.

"I need a favor," he said.

By this time, I no longer wanted to have him around, but I heard him out.

"I'm behind on my child support," he told me. "My ex won't let me see the kids until I pay up." I knew this story all too well. I felt like I was looking in a mirror, and instead of feeling compassion, I felt anger, angst.

All I'd wanted was to take my business to the next level, and this is what I had attracted. A drowning man trying to save himself. It was the same old story I'd lived through—was still living through.

The Law of Attraction had worked like a charm. I'd just forgotten to ask for what I wanted from my higher mind and had attracted from my frightened ego instead.

Zach had done exactly the same thing, with a much more tragic ending. A few months later, he was indicted for fraud on the building in Denver. And weeks later, he was found hanging from a tree in Georgia.

Death was the stalker, trying to prove that, no, we can't get out of this lifetime alive. At least not with the baggage of our past still in tow.

Not long after my partnership with Zach, I met Kurt, a real estate broker in Phoenix. In his fifties, he was a gentle guy who loved to talk about his father and growing up on a ranch with his dad in Texas. He told me how he played college football and about the success he'd had as a stock market speculator.

I was introduced to him at a "salon" in Malibu, where we were both part of a group reading *The Lens of Perception* by Aldous

Huxley. We connected right away through our shared interest in conservation. What he didn't know was that I'd reached a low point financially.

"Let's get some real estate deals we can do together," I said. I still didn't know much about him, except he was living in a nice place in Malibu, and he'd read my book. Plus, I liked the fact that he was a big-hearted guy, genuinely concerned about the environment.

And then the red flags started showing up. He would rent cars for a month at a time instead of buying a car, which meant spending twice as much money in the end. He rented a cottage on my property. And he wanted me to write checks to him and buy into his stocks.

Then there came a pivotal moment when Kurt brought an investor and his wife to Santa Barbara to potentially make an offer on an industrial building we were selling. Kurt made the arrangements, flew them in from Phoenix, and put them up at the Four Seasons Biltmore, one of the most expensive places on the water. Then he never showed them the building. He'd started to unravel. He seemed anxious and desperate, much like Zach had been. And again, I realized I was looking at my own reflection.

He moved out of the cottage. Disappeared. Told the woman he was dating that he'd meet her in Italy, then never showed up.

And then I got a call. It was from the investor who came out to Santa Barbara.

"Where's Kurt?" he asked, clearly upset.

"I honestly don't know," I said. "He's disappeared."

"Well you'd better find him," he said. "He showed me a property in San Luis Obispo, and I gave him $400,000."

I felt a heaviness in my chest. "What property did he show you?" I asked.

He described the same property that Kurt and I were looking at buying and conserving. Just weeks earlier, we had gone to inspect it. Kurt had set up me and the investor with a bait and switch.

I sat back in my chair, stunned. Kurt had swindled the guy for almost half a million dollars. And there I was, a party to it all. Déjà vu all over again.

I realized I'd been swindled, too, but I knew better than to think I was a victim. My ego had wanted to take a shortcut to building what I thought was success and had been willing to ignore the warning signs once again. I'd used Kurt as much as he'd used me, seeing him as a means to an end.

What was I seeing in the mirror this time that I couldn't see before? I wasn't sure, but I was determined to get a different mirror. This time I wanted to see a reflection of my soul's purpose, not my ego's fear.

Apparently an aspect of my wounded small self needed to be healed and let go. It looked to others for money and comfort. I had hoped that something or someone else would have come to the rescue, but my ego called for Zach and Kurt instead.

Despite the darkness of that time, I felt blessed that Spirit took care of me through it all. The universe will send you things and people and events when it's time to let something go. Kurt and Zach weren't bad people. In fact, they were gifts, helping me finally wake up to the lessons these shapeshifters had come to teach me. It was time to turn to Spirit and create from love rather than fear.

Clearly, I'd been actively choosing a path in conflict with my soul direction, and it was time to let Spirit lead the way. Before long, I started changing my business model to incorporate both real estate and conservation. I'd seen them as separate, but when I realized they were one, I could feel myself stepping into a higher purpose. I felt aligned with the Holy Spirit instead of separate from Him.

I had learned the meaning of "letting go."

Life, it turns out, can be found in death.

Life, in fact, is all about a thousand little deaths, which allow us to gently, gracefully, and consciously evolve into our true nature of God's light in the world.

My ego tried to convince me that letting go meant loss. But fortunately, my soul had a different perspective.

"Why," it asked, "would you want to hold onto that which no longer serves your greater good and the oneness of all things? Why would you want to keep a tool that isn't useful anymore?"

I thought about the moment when I let go of drinking alcohol. I'd had a dream in which a voice said, "It's time to stop drinking." In that moment, I experienced the death—the letting go—of the emotions that drive drinking: a desire to be separate and alone out of guilt or shame, to numb pain or past traumas, to self-punish. Without those emotions in the way, I was free to feel joy and Forgiveness and Purpose. I never drank again.

We can choose to believe in loss and live out that story. Or we can choose the gift of peace instead.

In the process of release is rebirth. The Life Force. The unifying whole.

"With each little death," Men would teach me, "you come into a deeper, more meaningful relationship with everything and everyone."

I'd experienced exactly that with my father. Now, could I make it happen with myself—and still get out of this lifetime alive?

Wisdom Teaching 4
Divine Life

"When you are living a Divine Life, the Life Force is like your umbilical cord. It feeds the unborn within you. And it continues to feed your authentic Self throughout your lifetime."
—Men

I recognized that all the wisdom teachings Men had shared so far—Forgiveness, Purpose, and death—were foundational as I reawakened to life. Men taught me that my authentic Self overcomes the thought of death. He added that the death of my feelings of pain and suffering would birth an eternal and immortal life.

The timeless and everlasting nature of life mirrors the universe. No wonder my ego mind wanted to block them. With each step toward awakening, my ego's domain shrunk and became more impotent.

"The Divine Life is like art," he said. "You are returning to your spiritual Home and becoming an artist of consciousness. In the lower planes, art comes from the ego mind. It reflects life that dies. But when art is birthed from the higher planes of consciousness—your genius Mind—it reflects the eternal, immortal aspect of life," he said.

It takes time and hard work to master anything, and Men's teaching reminded me to be patient. Before learning and unlearning about Men's teaching on Forgiveness, Purpose, and death, I struggled to be my authentic Self. With the guidance and support in the wisdom teaching on the Divine Life and Life Force, I was equipping myself to live the Truth of my authentic Self.

Five Insights on Divine Life

These five critical insights put forth by Men can help you become an artist of your consciousness. Each will help you discover your authentic Self, the genius within. Of all the teachings, the one on life helps me to manifest what I would like to see happen in my relationships, with my work, in my health and mind. They will help you on the path to genius to get beyond the ego's thought of death as a body. Once you complete this teaching, life will reveal a hidden power that is unique to your genius Mind.

1. **The Life Force harmonizes the body and soul and inspires a Divine Life.** Your genius Mind can be experienced in relationships, at work, and in your health and mind when you harmonize the body with the authentic Self.
2. **The Divine Genius Mind flows through the Life Force into your authentic Self.** The separation created by the ego mind creates an imbalance between body and soul. The Divine Genius Mind can only flow into your life experience when you are centered in the heart of your authentic Self and in balance with the body.
3. **The Life Force is a life-giving energy that expands Consciousness.** Light makes up everything in the universe. Light is energy. This infinite source of light and energy creates the Life Force. Allow the Divine Genius Mind of the universe to flow into and through your genius Mind.
4. **You are an artist of consciousness.** When you choose the genius Mind, you become an artist of consciousness. Instead of being the victim of life, you become the cocreator of the life you want to live. The genius Mind has a hidden power to manifest the heart's truest intent when aligned with the authentic Self.

5. **Energy can be directed toward the will of the ego mind or genius Mind.** By directing the energy toward the genius Mind, you are sure to live the Divine Life of completion and harmony. In all that you do, peace, prosperity, and love will be given.

The weeks leading up to my trip to Peru were as much a part of my adventure as the trip itself. Men's teachings were preparing me—for what, I didn't yet know. But I kept track of where we were within my eighty-one-day quest. Something powerful was sure to be revealed.

As we neared the fortieth day, I thought of the significance of the number: the forty days and forty nights that Jesus fasted, the period of gestation for a human baby, the cycles of days tracked by early astronomers.

I knew from my discussion with Men about death that life is not just a matter of being in a physical body. I had confused living in the physical world as life when, in fact, our physical being is only one aspect of life.

"The life that emerges from the genius Mind expresses itself in the manifest world as beauty, grace, peace, love, compassion, cooperation, cocreation, transparency, and service," Men said. "All come from Source and the Divine Universal Genius Mind. You uncover them by removing the obstacles to your authentic Self and experiencing the abundance of each of those God-given gifts. Lack does not exist in the genius Mind."

"And how do I do that?" I asked. I knew he had told me before that I could choose the genius Mind at any time, but I sometimes forgot the path to my genius.

"When doubt arises," he said, "attune to the Life Force. Begin by looking around in the outer environment. See and feel the Life Force within the natural environment. Listen deeply to the wind, songbirds, and the magical voice of stillness. Feel into the rhythm and harmonic flow of Mother Nature's grace. These frequencies are access points or portals into the higher planes of Consciousness."

This made sense to me. How many times had I felt my soul uplifted at the ranch at Big Sur or looking out at the ocean?

"So I can become an artist of cocreation, tapping the creative Source of the Divine Genius Mind in the universe, by returning to my genius mind?"

"Yes, Adam," he said. "The dawning of the light has begun to shine in your soul."

A Course in Miracles calls this the reawakening from our false alignment with the ego mind. "The journey to God is merely the reawakening of the knowledge of where you are always, and what you are forever," the course says.

My experience of life in the ego mind blocked aspects of my genius from fully expressing themselves. It was as if my genius had fallen asleep. I had forgotten my true Purpose and had no clue of my authentic Self.

One of my limiting beliefs was created when I was attending University at UC Berkeley. As a freshman, I was required to take a basic English test. I didn't pass the test and was required to do a remedial course in English. My spelling and grammar were particularly weak. I did not pass the remedial English course, but eventually I retested and passed. As a result, I never felt confident that I could write a paper or story, much less a book.

To this day, I remain challenged by my writing skills. But as time passed, I developed a passion for writing. I had a strong desire to share the journey to my authentic Self with others who are walking the path to genius. I began making notes in my journal and sharing stories with friends. Yet I held on to the belief that I could not write.

Eventually, with the help of *A Course in Miracles*, I began to forgive myself for judging myself. Eventually, a creative impulse inspired me to write what became the first book in the trilogy of my spiritual journey to genius. The more I forgave, the more I realized that I had a purpose of sharing my creative self with the world. As I shared my authentic Self, I was able to let go of my limiting belief.

Now I feel the flow of my authentic Self, my genius Mind, which connects me to the Life Force. It ignites the sleeping passion of the wordsmith within, my inner genius Mind. It put me on the path to true Purpose. As I remembered my authentic Self, I became aware of the Life Force and connections of my inner genius to the Divine Genius of the Universe.

The Genius Process on Life

This five-step Genius Process on Life will help you move beyond the death of the dysfunctional ego feelings back to the genius Mind. As you navigate through the ego mind to a reawakening of the authentic Self, Men encourages you to listen deeply to your heart and soul. The journey to genius is challenging and requires a strong will and unwavering diligence, but it's worth it. Reawakening your genius Mind will help you manifest a new life as beauty, grace, love, compassion, cooperation, cocreation, transparency, and service. Peace and prosperity will become commonplace.

The idea of death to the ego will induce fear and conflict. Men's teaching on life shows us that there is only life, and that life is peaceful and full of love.

1. **Ask the question, "What do I need to know about the ego?"** Harmony and lasting peace happen when you awaken to the authentic Self, the genius Mind, which is life itself. The ego mind will do everything to prevent that awakening.
2. **Listen for the answer, "Whom should I listen to?"** In the ego mind, death stalks you. In the genius Mind, infinity claims you. The ego speaks loudly, whereas the authentic Self of genius listens quietly.
3. **Acknowledge the problem the ego caused in your life by asking, "What do I see that has yet to be seen?"** When you acknowledge the ego mind for the separation it creates, you will come back to the genius Mind. When you do, the authentic emotions and attributes of the Divine Universal Genius Mind—including infinity, immortality, bliss, grace, peace, prosperity, and love—flow through you.

4. **Be open to the solution by asking, "How do I do things in life without doing them from the ego?"** When harmonizing the genius Mind, you will mirror the sacred design of the Divine Genius Mind. It will reflect the eternal, immortal nature of life and flow into all that you create and do.
5. **Activate your genius by asking, "How shall I be?"** When you choose the genius Mind, you're the artist of consciousness and you cocreate with the Divine Universal Genius Mind. You will live the Divine Life.

To recap, the map to cross the bridge from ego and separation to the authentic Self and genius Mind began with Men's four foundational teachings: Forgiveness, Purpose, death, and life. These are the pillars that uphold the bridge to love and the genius Mind.

1. **True Forgiveness** asks you to forgive yourself and others for what did not happen. You forgot that you are one with others, and they forgot they are one with you. Both parties simply made an error, and your Forgiveness dissolves the painful grip the event or person has over your present life experience.
2. **True Purpose**, as taught by Men, shifts our belief that we are here to do something in the outer world. Of course, we are here to do great things in the world, and the purpose of everything we do is to remember our authentic Selves. Events and people in the outer world are signposts to point us Home to the genius Mind. Ask yourself in all you do, "What is this person or thing for?" Your purpose is to express authentic emotions from the heart.
3. **Death**, as taught by Men, does not entail physical death. Men teaches us that surrender of old ego mind patterns of behavior awakens us to the authentic Self. "Only those who die truly live."
4. **Divine Life**. Men compared his teaching on life to becoming an artist of consciousness. The Life Force that gives life

> to all things flows through our genius Mind. What we do with it is a matter of choice. Do we use it to serve the ego's need to separate and create conflict and chaos, or do we use it to create peace and love as cocreator with the Divine Genius?

"When you balance those seemingly opposing forces as one, you allow for the optimum life experience," Men said. "Only life includes the totality of consciousness."

Men faded away, and I sat by the fire. I instinctively turned to the east to see if the sun had broken the horizon. There was a sliver of gold poking its head to greet the new day. I smiled as I returned to the sacred space within my Home.

I realized I was on a journey—to what, I didn't know. Like a loaf of bread in the oven, I felt half-baked.

What I did know was that Men's teachings on Forgiveness, Purpose, death, and life laid the foundation for what was to come.

If the remaining forty-one days were similar to the first, I did not doubt that my quest to serve the Grail would be filled with unexpected treasure. What on earth could be next in the ever-turning spiral of conscious evolution?

9
Waiting

June 24, 2012

Where is that darn boat with my luggage? It's been over two hours.

I'd been sitting on the dock for what seemed like forever. I'd journaled about my adventures with Jaguar Jon and Lady Eb, feeling propelled to something I didn't yet understand. In journaling over the years, I'd noticed the subtle—and not-so-subtle—dance of being pushed forward toward growth from behind, and pulled toward evolution up ahead. In this way, everything and everyone in my life played a role, including the unseen forces that beckoned to me and sparked my curiosity to understand a bit more in the next moment, and the next.

Now I sat in the sun, staring at the river and trying to *will* the boat to come.

"Hello, excuse me," I shouted to a young man standing a hundred steps above the pier. "Do you know when the boat is going to arrive?"

"No hablo ingles, señor," he said.

I remembered the feeling when I stepped off the Miami-bound flight in Los Angeles and realized my bags and I would be traveling on separate planes. *Oh my god, what did I just do?* I took one step into the gateway connecting the plane with the boarding ramp when the magnitude of the decision struck like a bolt of lightning.

I stopped, did a one-hundred-eighty-degree turn, and looked at the plane door being closed and locked into place. *There it goes.* I didn't care about my bags. But the treasure in the guitar case. It was priceless. Irreplaceable.

I walked up the ramp and immediately walked to the window and watched the plane moving down the tarmac. I was going one direction, and the treasure was going another. Giving in to the power of surrender, I realized that this was part of my activation process. It always began with surrender, and this was another experience of letting go. The attachment to the material world—even the treasure—was nearing its end. It was all part of my quest for the Grail.

The morning I left for Peru, I'd awakened to a bright sunny day in Santa Barbara and realized that, for the first time in seventy-one days, I was not enthused about seeing Men.

Lizanne was already up, dressed, and making a cup of Earl Grey tea. Normally she would be launching into her interior design work for the day. But she and I were leaving for the Los Angeles International Airport in a little over an hour. My flight departed for Miami at 12:08 p.m. Fortunately, I'd finished packing my bags the night before, so I only had a few details left. I made sure I had B-12, which gave me energy and drove away mosquitos; grapeseed extract for stomach parasites; and grapeseed drops that I used to cleanse and purify drinking water.

Knowing I needed to show up to receive Men's wisdom of the day, I sat down in front of the fireplace, dropped into meditation, and felt the household energy fade away. For the first time, I wasn't looking forward to this time with Men, simply because mentally I was already on the plane to Peru, and I knew I couldn't be fully present with my teacher.

Still, I tried. In my mind's eye, I followed the same path that had led me to Men over and over again. I first saw myself walking in Manhattan's Central Park. Then, after treading slowly and gently on the earth, I was transported to a mesa in the desert Southwest. Men was nowhere to be seen.

I looked as far as I could toward the horizon. Finally, after scanning the landscape, I noticed a glint of light reflecting from off in the distance, like a mirror catching the sun.

In my meditation, I hiked down off the mesa and worked my way through the desert sage and granulate of blooming cactus. There, sitting in the cool shade of the high canyon wall, was Men.

When we'd begun this journey together, we'd sat at the fire for forty nights. That was followed by twenty days at the water's edge of a creek. And for the last ten days, we'd met high upon the mesa, feeling the gentle breeze of destiny's call.

Now we were in the earth, resting in a canyon a few hundred feet below the high desert terrain.

"Catalyze," Men said, looking me straight in the eye.

"Catalyze?" I said, curious.

"Catalyze your Being," he said.

That's all. Three words.

Then he dematerialized into a pile of earth before my eyes.

I sat on the canyon floor, staring at the small pile of red sand and soil in front of me. It pulsated as though it was radioactive, radiant, and vibrant like blood. I had heard that indigenous cultures of the Southwest were people of the Red Earth. Now I understood why—but I wasn't to fully understand Men's words for days to come.

With several deep breaths, I left the canyon in my mind's eye and returned to the living room in our home.

"Are you ready to go, Adam?" Lizanne called out from the kitchen.

"I'm ready," I said, hoping my words were true.

Now, here I was staring at the Mother of God River, unable to catalyze anything without my treasure. I couldn't sit on the dock a minute longer, so I hiked back to the dining hall, where Marcela was visiting with her son.

"We're heading across the river to Monkey Island," Marcela said. "Do you want to come?"

"Sure," I said, "but the baggage still isn't here. Can you wait?"

"We're not going until after my students arrive," Marcela said. She was waiting for an additional contingent of students, who were joining her and the ones who had arrived the day before. "Your bags and the students will be on the same boat."

"When do you think that might be?" I said, feeling snarkier by the minute.

"Should be in about twenty or thirty minutes," she said.

"Okay," I said. "I'll be back at the dock."

I felt like a yo-yo, headed back down the steps to my familiar seat looking out over the brackish water of the Mother of God. I trained my eyes downriver again, waiting. Every time I saw a boat, I did a double take. And every time, I slumped back on my elbows, waiting once more.

Suddenly a boat appeared from around the bend at a high rate of speed. It was heading right for the dock. I stood up, my heart pounding. *Yes! The treasure is here. And a clean pair of underwear won't be a bad thing, either.*

The boat was a twin to the one that brought me to the lodge two days earlier. It pulled up to the dock, and workers jumped off and tied it in place. It was full of students, many of whom had never ventured into these wild parts. Most had no idea what was in store. All had the look of anticipation—a mix of excitement and anxiousness.

I quickly scanned the boat for bags. There on the back was a pile of luggage—and one beautiful guitar case.

Thank God. It made it!

I grabbed it, pulled it up to the dock, and carried the precious cargo as quickly as I could back to the privacy of my humble hut.

10
The Treasure

Two years before my trip to Peru, I'd been studying different indigenous traditions and their achievements in math, science, and engineering long before they had advanced tools. As others have wondered and researched over the years, I asked the unanswered questions: How did these ancient civilizations build the great pyramids and temples? How did they move vast quantities of water up and down hillsides? How did they harness the cycles of time by watching the sky? And most of all, what message did they leave us about the future of the planet?

Clearly they had access to information that scientists even today don't fully understand. As I studied the precise creations of these ancient people, I realized that they understood and were working in concert with the Divine Genius. They got "it," whatever "it" was.

I wanted to get "it," too. And so I began seeking a way to unlock the code that civilizations were privy to thousands of years ago.

As I studied, I discovered that the original technologists were all connected via some sort of grid or network. What connected them was unknown. However, they all had access to information that moved through the galaxy as light.

The pyramids and temples also acted as "recharging centers"—places where ancients could align their energy systems to the transmissions of light energy moving out into the galaxy.

Since they didn't have telescopes, radios, computers, satellite dishes, and the like, they had to become the instruments themselves.

In other words, the mind became the tuning fork to the universe and transmitted energy into the body, where the supercomputer known as the brain could assimilate the information and use it to build the wonders we still marvel at today.

If I were to access that same information, to be the same kind of tuning fork, I needed to go deep. Not deep into my work or my ego desires. But deep into my connection with something greater. I needed to get into a place within my own being that could take me beyond my mind and body.

And, on top of it all, I needed the help of a special tool. Then I would see if it was even possible to understand "it" the way our predecessors did.

In February, 2009, I had a near-fatal ATV accident in the mountains of Big Sur, California. I'd traveled a dirt mountain road about 1,500 feet above the ranch house I owned at the time. When I headed off the road to explore the hillside, the ATV slipped on the wet grass. I jumped off, knowing it was going to flip over. But when I landed, I felt my right shinbone snap and the ligaments and nerves below my knee rip apart. When I tried to move, I realized my collarbone was broken as well, and I couldn't move my right arm.

With no cell phone, laying in the grass off the main drag and in a race with the setting sun, my only choice was to drag myself back to the ranch house. For what seemed like hours, I slithered through the grass like a snake, trying to focus on my goal rather than the unbearable pain. When I was still far short of the house, my neighbor miraculously—and I use that word intentionally—drove by and heard me yelling. That was the beginning of a recuperation that took months and led me to deep insights about my own hubris and ego.

At one point during my long rehabilitation, I received a message from Spirit.

"Pick up your staff of power," the voice said.

The message made sense to me because, in my studies of the Mayan civilization, I took a liking to a staff that was used by the ancient WisdomKeepers and EarthKeepers. It was shaped like a labyrinth on top, then spiraled out into a question mark, symbolizing the need to question the intelligence of the human design.

Staffs were used by other ancient people to receive "downloads" of information traveling as light waves. The staff connected the Great Central Sun to the Milky Way Galaxy and into our solar system, extending to the earth and all living things. The journey was all about returning to the center of the galaxy and the source of eternal light.

I became enamored by various images of tribal elders who wielded a staff. Some were used for healing, others as symbols of leadership. But in the mythology, the one who carried the staff also held the conduit for cosmic communication. I wanted a staff that would act as a lightning rod, a channel for receiving and transmitting information to and from earth and the center of the Milky Way.

Perhaps the real question was this: What did the staff want from *me? If I am becoming an instrument of God, my mission in the world is less about me and more about how I can serve that which is greater than my self.*

To honor the image I saw in one of the books on the Mayans, I laid out a design for the staff that incorporated several ancient and powerful symbols. Not long before, I had reconnected with Peter, an elderly master metal sculptor in Big Sur. Back in the 1970s, my parents had commissioned him to create a weathervane to put atop our house, and he created a magnificent whale spouting water.

I knew he was the right man for the job. There was only one problem. He had a method to his genius. He agreed to accept the commission for my staff under one condition: no deadlines or time constraints.

More than three years later, I received the call to go to Peru, and I knew the staff would be essential to the trip and the future of who I was becoming. I decided to call Peter and check in.

"Hi, Peter, it's Adam," I said over the phone.

"Hey, Adam, how are things in Santa Barbara?" he said.

"Things are going well," I told him. "I'm heading off to Peru in ten days, and I'm getting ready for high adventure."

"That sounds like you," he said.

I paused, not sure how to bring up the subject of the staff.

"I have some good news," he said.

"Really?"

"I'm nearly done with your staff."

I felt the delight all the way through my body, marveling at Divine timing. "That's fantastic," I said. "When do you think I can pick it up?" I was already envisioning the guitar case I'd need to carry it on the plane.

"I'm guessing in about a month or two," he said.

Oh. I took a deep breath.

"How about in a week?" I asked. "I'd like to activate it in the jungle."

Silence.

"I'll see what I can manage," he said. Then, as though he'd already had time for second thought, he said, "Why don't you come and pick it up in Big Sur next week?"

I smiled. "That would be fantastic, Peter, thank you for doing this. How does next Wednesday around two sound?"

"Sounds good," he said. "I'll see you then."

A week later, I made the three-hour drive to Big Sur, feeling as though I were in a high-speed vacuum. The slower evolution of my physical reality was miraculously catching up with the high-velocity evolution of my soul. I pulled into Peter's driveway, nearly hitting his dog Rapunzel, and almost leapt out of the car in my anticipation.

Peter answered the door, almost as excited as I was. "Great to see you," he said. "Come on into the shop."

"I've been looking forward to this day for a while now," I said, although I wasn't complaining about the time Peter had needed to complete the staff.

"Thank you for your patience," he said, almost apologetically. "I knew it wouldn't happen fast."

"No worries," I said.

We walked into his shop, a large warehouse space that must have been several hundred square feet with twenty-foot-high ceilings. Smelling of oil, it was piled floor to ceiling with miscellaneous scrap metal pieces. He was like the mad scientist of the metal artist world, a master of heavy machinery. And in the midst of the chaos lay the staff. It shone like a gilded treasure.

Peter picked up the staff with great care, treating it with the honor it deserved. "Here you go," he said, handing it to me like a baby.

I stared at it, momentarily speechless. Peter had executed my design in ways that were far beyond my expectations.

The staff was almost four feet long and looked as weighty as it felt. At the top, the metal curved into a classic question mark with the sun in the center, surrounded by ancient symbols. Along the length of the staff, double helixes, representing intertwined masculine and feminine energy, twisted upward in a sweep of power.

The double helix was sculpted to look like snake skin, culminating in two snake heads, the intertwining of the masculine and feminine. Peter had inlaid rubies for the eyes of one snakehead and emeralds for the eyes of the other. The green and red precious stones gave a wild, penetrating appearance. Together, the elements symbolically connected heaven, represented by the circular portion at the top, and earth, the bottom of the staff.

"It's stunning," I said, overwhelmed. "What metal did you use?"

"It's a red silicon bronze," he said. "Do you like it?"

Liking it was an understatement. It looked like red gold.

"I love it," I said. "It was well worth the wait." As I said it, I realized how much tension I'd been holding about it during the past three years.

"I'm happy to hear that," Peter said.

I kept turning the staff over and over in my hands, exploring every inch of its beauty and symbolism. But something sitting nearby caught my eye.

"What's this?" I asked, nodding toward a six-inch-high block of metal that had a round hole in the center. Flat on one side, it bore three pillars on the other three sides, and the top formed a funnel of concentric rings.

"That's the counterweight," Peter said. "It goes on the bottom of the staff. I took you up on your idea to create something that represented the three-by-three symbol."

I was awed by his artistry, and the way he'd interpreted the conversation we'd had three years before. I'd told him that the ancient Mayan, Cabalist, and other cultures shared the power of three and the middle way. Three also is a powerful number in the Vedic tradition, representing the gross, subtle, and causal bodies that form the totality of the human physical and nonphysical experience.

Peter had taken the power of three and embedded it in gold with the columns or pillars on three sides of the counterweight, honoring sacred mathematics.

It was the perfect representation of the ferryman's staff. Representing star gates between worlds, it symbolized three different paths toward cosmic consciousness. The one on the left is the path of the mind, with knowledge unfolding. The one on the right is the path of the heart, with its celebration of feelings, passions, and nature.

The central pillar is the way that unifies heart and mind through Divine devotion and service. Unification. The central path. The middle path, as the Buddha would say.

"The three-by-three columns establish the determinant of the matrix," I shared.

Peter looked at me with a blank expression.

"Well, I can't fully explain it," I said, thinking about the study I'd done of staffs as tuning forks. "But the determinant establishes the value of the energy that flows in and out, and the center line holds it all together."

"I'm going to do a little research on that one," Peter said.

Despite the fact that I didn't understand it, I felt like Peter's representation of the all-powerful three held important information.

Maybe it could help explain how the finite and infinite worlds, vibrating at different velocities, can function as a whole.

"Keep me posted," Peter said.

"I will," I told him. I ran my hand along the fine craftsmanship of the staff, appreciating the texture of the snakes and the engraved symbols of the sun.

"When are you taking off to Peru?" he asked.

"Three days," I said. "I'm going to activate the staff in the jungle."

"Have a wonderful time," he said, "and may your adventure bring you joy."

I gave him a hug of gratitude, then I carefully set the staff in the passenger seat of my car, where it would ride shotgun with me. I wanted the treasure close, where I could reach out, touch it, and feel its mighty power.

Peter's masterpiece existed because I had accepted my sacred duty to "pick up your staff." It was the mythic call to return to the castle, to the kingdom, to Christ consciousness. Even though I hadn't fully grown into that duty, I knew the staff was a mystic transmitter, a spiritual warrior in its own right. It would be a formidable ally and guide on my journey.

As I climbed into my car for the drive back to Santa Barbara, I propped up the staff in the front passenger seat and buckled it in, knowing it was an extension of a powerful and ancient technology. It became my copilot, a sidekick on my journey to genius. I felt peaceful in its company, sensing only time would tell what destiny had in store for us.

"Welcome," I said to it. "Your presence is felt and duly noted, and I'm of service to your Divine wish."

Wisdom Teaching 5
Peace

"Peace is an inner knowing that you are safe, secure, and loved, no matter what happens—even death. It is an element of True Love. Without Peace, you will have love, but not Unconditional Love."
—Men

I was following Men's guidance daily and trying to stay in the moment rather than anticipating what was to come. I was like a sponge, soaking up his teachings and wondering what wisdom he would impart next. His teachings on Forgiveness, Purpose, Death, and Life laid the foundation for my next steps on the path to genius. Because of Men and the wisdom he imparted, I felt more safe and secure stepping into the unknown.

The next teachings on Peace, Love, and Function would complete what Men called the "development of the primary being." Once we reawaken to the authentic Self, "the foundation of Self," and unlearn the patterns of the ego mind, we can go into the soul with lasting Peace, Unconditional Love, and our outward expressions of these two unforgettable qualities of being. Function completes the trinity of the soul.

I started to get a glimpse of this when I asked Men, "What could follow life?"

"Peace," he said. "Fear prevents everlasting Peace from being a constant in your life. It comes from the decision to accept the ego mind and its identification with the body. The ego wants you to fear everything because, if you did not fear, you would experience unconditional Peace."

Peace is a precondition for Unconditional Love and all else. Men made it clear that the foundation of Forgiveness, Purpose, death, and life would have little value if it didn't rest in lasting Peace. Life in the ego mind would continue to create conflict and chaos.

"The Peace of God is my one goal."
—*A Course in Miracles*

Five Insights on Peace

These five critical insights put forth by Men about Peace will help you find the Peace of God. Each will help you discover your authentic Self, the genius within. Of all the teachings, the one on Peace helped me to relax. I felt safe and secure in a world that can seem dangerous.

On the genius path, Peace prepares us for Unconditional Love.

1. **Fear of Peace creates conditional relationships.** Lasting Peace to the ego mind means the end of its identity. The ego fears Peace, and it fights ruthlessly to create conflict. When you choose the Peace of the genius Mind, you will not die. A new identity will emerge along with your genius Mind. Your true, authentic Self remains. A new perspective on life will come into your consciousness that will create Peaceful relationships in all areas of your life.
2. **Only the people and things that are Peaceful will remain in your life.** Choosing the inner Peace of the genius Mind will align you with others who want to do the same for themselves. These relationships are centered in the heart and create Unconditional Love.
3. **Fear reminds you to be forgiving.** Fear helps you practice true Forgiveness and to remain on Purpose. Paradoxically, fear tells you to restore a life of Peace and let go, let die away, a life of conflict.

4. **You need do nothing to find Peace.** "What do I need to do to obtain lasting Peace?" I asked Men. "Nothing," he said. "Just choose your genius Mind."
5. **Lasting Peace requires taking action from the authentic Self.** The ego mind, the inauthentic self, reacts. It creates conflict and chaos, whereas the authentic Self acts from a place of Peace in the genius Mind.

I was showing up to learn and unlearn the various aspects of my life, yet Peace remained elusive. Fear was still a regular occurrence in my life, and fear created conflict. Although my ego mind desired Peace, I feared the Peace and love of God. My ego mind knew that if I chose the genius Mind of my authentic Self, it would disappear.

The ego fear of being forgotten and or destroyed by God was proving to be the greatest obstacle to lasting Peace. Men's teachings taught me that it was the ego mind that wanted me to forget God. The ego sought to destroy my authentic Self at any cost to maintain its identity.

Men's wisdom teachings were being taught from a place beyond the ego mind. I was beginning to understand that authentic learning comes from within and not from a book, teacher, or anything outside of myself. Men was teaching me to unlearn the ego mind, my inauthentic self, to learn about the genius Mind, the authentic Self.

I was beginning to see parallels between my study of *A Course in Miracles* and the training I received as a shaman. In the course, Jesus shares his wisdom from the genius Mind that transcends the world of form and duality. Men, as a shamanic master, was doing the same.

I was seeing that any actual wisdom teaching must share in the world of form and the body, yet it must emerge from the genius Mind of Spirit. Men was teaching me to bridge these ostensibly two different worlds, integrating the two into One.

"What does it take to make Peace appear?" I asked Men.

"Nothing," he said. "You need to do nothing because Peace already exists in you, everything, and everyone."

His wisdom was hard to swallow. How could Peace exist in the business partners who had duped me? Or in my ex-wife, who created havoc? My ego thought it was the victim of other people's actions and acted out of fear.

In truth, my ex-wife and ex-business partners served a compelling purpose on my path to genius. The circumstances surrounding my business and the divorce created fear of abandonment. My ego was pointing me back to my true Purpose and authentic Self. My fear of being abandoned by my parents, God, and others kept showing up in all that I did. The fear of abandonment, like that of death, humiliation, and failure periodically created life experiences and relationships of the very thing I feared. Until I learned to find the Peace of God in my genius Mind, I would remain in the conflict and chaos of the ego.

"You do not feel the Peace because you are still living according to the ego mind," Men said. "This will allow you only fleeting moments of Peace. Lasting Peace can be found only in your genius Mind that reflects in the Divine Genius Mind of the Universe. Look inward, not to the outer world."

I began to understand the frustration I'd felt over the years, seeking Peace in relationships and business deals. I'd been trying to draw water from an empty well, which created nothing but an undercurrent of pain. This pain, says *A Course in Miracles,* is another tool of the ego as it creates obstacles to Peace. The harder I tried to find Peace outside myself, the emptier I felt, and the more fearful I became.

My ego mind was walling me into a lack of Peace, thinking it was protecting me when it was only defending itself.

"Yes," Men said. "You no longer need to seek anything. Just remove the filters of the ego mind, and everything you've sought will be present."

Could it be that easy?

The next day, before I met with Men, I transported myself in my mind from my home in Santa Barbara to Central Park in New York.

There I took in the beauty of the spring, blossoming in all its glory. Joyfulness was everywhere.

As I walked by a playground, I saw a little boy giggling so hard he could barely walk. He looked up, smiled, and laughed even harder.

"Hey there, what are you laughing at?" I asked, smiling.

"I don't know," he said, then he giggled again.

At that moment, I saw little Adam. He was free, boundless, and living in the joy of not knowing. Why did I have to see or hear something to laugh? Why couldn't I just feel tickled by life and smile for no reason at all?

Because of the undercurrent of fear that persisted in my life, I was unable to feel the unbounded magical child within. I knew that healing my fear of emotional abandonment was essential if I was to find lasting Peace. My work with Men was helping me explore the fear that prevented the memory that the Peace of God lies within.

"My, you look so much younger today," Men said with a smile.

"I am feeling young today," I said.

"Today will be our last day discussing Peace. And it will be the beginning of lasting, permanent Peace in your everyday life," he said.

I marveled at that promise. Was it possible?

"What would you be without the fear of death, failure, humiliation, Peace of God, or even Unconditional Love?" Men asked. "How would it be if you identified with something other than your body and an ego mind that invokes guilt, fear, and pain? What would that be like for you, Adam?"

I could feel myself choking up. "It would be like the little boy I just saw, playing and laughing with abandon."

"Abandonment. How beautiful," Men said.

"I never thought abandonment was a good thing."

"When you abandon your identification with the body, you can return to the Peace of being you," Men said. "And the world you knew in the ego mind will end."

"But it's all I've ever known," I said. "What about my friends, my family, my work, my belongings?" I asked.

"It will all remain, and it will all be gone," he said.

The Genius Process on Peace

This five-step Genius Process on Peace will help create experiences that will move you through the fear of the dysfunctional ego mind.

Men asks you to explore the question, "What are you afraid of?" Reconnecting with the inner Peace of your genius Mind will help you overcome fear and manifest a life of harmony in all your relations.

The Genius Process on Life uses the same formula as the previous teachings. Ask the question, listen for the answer, acknowledge the problem, and be open to the solution. Yet it focuses explicitly on creating Peace of mind beyond the ego. Remember, the idea of Peace to the ego induces fear because Peace in the genius Mind spells the end of ego's intent to create conflict and chaos. Be aware of these feelings as they arise. Know that they come from the ego mind.

1. **Ask the question, "What do I need to know about the ego?"** You're not leaving the world; you're shifting the place in which you see the world. Your body will be where it always was, but the way you feel about it and the rest of the physical world will change. The Peace found in your genius Mind creates fearlessness.
2. **Listen for the answer, "Whom should I listen to?"** Choose to be a cocreator of your evolution. Choose to come Home to the Oneness of God. You will want to practice being in silence. Listen to that which does not even speak. That is Peace.
3. **Acknowledge the problem the ego caused in your life by asking, "What do I see that has yet to be seen?"** Only those people and things that reflect the Peace of the Divine Genius Mind will remain in your life. Those seen in the ego mind will be felt and experienced differently. As a result, you will feel Peace because you'll be sharing it from your genius Mind and loving heart.

4. **Be open to the solution by asking, "How do I do things in life without doing them from the ego?"** Everything other than the genius Mind will hold no value other than to remind you to live in Forgiveness and stay on Purpose.
5. **Activate your genius by asking, "How shall I be?"** When you are in the genius Mind, you become the Peace you want to see in the world. Foster Peace in all relations.

The Genius Process on Peace, along with that of Forgiveness, Purpose, death, and life, has helped reawaken my genius Mind. I began by asking questions like this: "Why do painful and conflicted events keep happening in my relationship and at work?" When I acknowledged the problem that was being created in my separate genius Mind, I was able to look inward to see what other alternatives might be available. The solution became clear when I accepted the genius Mind.

I discovered with Men's help that the answer to life's challenges is found with a straightforward choice: the Peace found in the genius Mind. As I ventured further into the unknown to discover how to serve the Grail, little did I know how important Men's teachings would become.

I began to realize that Men had no intention of making me uncomfortable. He was remarkably adept at reducing my fear and evoking Peace. At times, though, he saw me squirming about and let me know that everything would be okay. I was riding the edge of my conscious evolution.

"Life will be simple," Men said before he faded away.

Simplicity. Peace. At that moment, they felt like the same thing. I only hoped I could reach for them again as I walked into the jungle of my fear of emotional abandonment, which was more profound than I'd ever felt before. Could it be that in the depths of my fear, I would discover the Grail? And maybe I would find the answer to getting out of this lifetime alive.

11

ACTIVATION

June 24, 2012

When I got back to my hut with my oversized duffle bag and guitar case, I laid them on my bed and quickly changed my underwear and clothes. Then, one by one, I flipped open the latches on the guitar case and slowed myself to a pause. I'd been in such a hurry to get the case back in my possession that it felt sacred, and I needed to approach it that way—with reverence, the same etiquette with which I entered a holy place.

As I opened the case, I saw the treasure for the first time in what seemed like weeks, even though it had only been a matter of hours. Sitting on the red velvet lining of the case, the staff glittered like gold. The ruby and emerald eyes of the intertwining snakes caught the light, and the rich bronze patina shone.

I let out an involuntary sigh.

I'd felt such trepidation when I relinquished the staff at the Los Angeles airport and climbed onto another plane. Seeing the guitar case brought back my inner thoughts about detaching from it.

Let it go. The power is not of the staff or you. It doesn't belong to you. You're simply its steward.

But I couldn't deny the relief I felt as I opened the case and saw the staff safe and unharmed. Now that it was back in my possession again, I felt a sense of responsibility to care for it so it could fulfill its purpose.

I looked in the eyes of the snakes, at the symbols circling the golden sun, then I sat quietly and asked, "How should we activate you?"

After a moment, I heard, "In the jungle tonight."

Perfect. I was in the Garden of Eden, after all, the home of the serpent, and it was fitting to leave the staff in the wilds of Mother Earth's womb.

But at the same time, the jungle was not the kind of place you wanted to roam at night. The king of the jungle, the jaguar, comes out most often at night. On previous trips, I had ventured toward the jungle to explore what it felt like to be under the canopy, in the mystery of it all. But I had never gone more than a few hundred yards or so, for fear of getting lost.

I'd gone far enough to know that everything looked the same once you stepped a few feet off the path. Besides, at night, the silent creatures were all around. The spiders, the crawling things, the ones that could end your life in an instant with a single bite.

But the staff had spoken, and I was duty bound to follow instructions. Perhaps this also had something to do with what Men had told me earlier in the day.

"How was your date?" Men asked as I sat in meditation.

"What date? Do you mean with the medicine?" I asked.

"No, with the butterfly," Men said.

"Oh, you mean Lady Eb. She was delightful," I said.

"Good to hear. Are you ready to cross the river into your sacred soul Design?" he asked.

"Am I?" I asked.

"I would say yes, you are ready," he said.

"Then I am ready," I said, feeling confident yet humble.

"Do you remember what I last shared with you when you were flying into the jungle?" Men asked.

"I remember everything. You said, 'You will soon arrive. Follow the butterfly.'"

"Yes, and what did I share the morning of your departure from Santa Barbara?" He seemed to be testing my memory after my exhausting couple of days.

You said, 'Catalyze your being,'" I answered.

"Correct. You are here to activate your staff, are you not?"

"Yes, among other things."

"Your soul requires that you activate your Divine Genius," he said. "You, Adam, are the staff that connects the dew of heaven with your Divine earthly nature."

This took me by surprise. I *had* the staff; I didn't think I *was* the staff.

"The red bronze staff is only a symbol," he said. "Don't confuse the symbol with the content of your being."

I realized he was spot on. Once again, I had defined my identity by an outer symbol rather than my own sacred soul.

"The complete reversal of your old design and its thought system will take some time," Men said. "For now, let's cross the river and activate."

"The Mother of God is a big river, Men," I said.

"There you go again," he said, as though he were talking with a child. "You are thinking of the river literally rather than as a symbol. You will cross the river with one small step."

I felt frustrated since I'd heard the metaphor many times before. "I've been crossing river after river on the spiritual road," I said. "What makes this different?"

"This will be the last crossing until you take your last breath in physical form," he said, then he dissolved into a pile of Red Earth.

I sat for several minutes, trying to absorb what he'd meant. I began to sense that on the eighty-first day, in just a few days' time, I would mark a completion in my life. But the idea of my "last breath in physical form" felt foreboding.

I had a sense that this was a big moment and honored myself for having gotten to this place. I saw myself bowing and touching Mother Earth. "Thank you, Mother," I said.

I knew that the only baggage I could carry across the river was all that I could not leave behind. To get here, to the river's edge, I had to unload the karma debt, the trauma, and let go of the ego's thought system. Or at least be deeply committed to the Holy Spirit, the inner voice, the soul sage that had guided me along the path.

Now, the staff was with me. God willing, I would activate it and get out of the jungle alive.

I headed back out to the dock to see what everyone was up to. The new arrivals were buzzing, excited by their new surroundings. Marcela was standing at the top of the steps.

"Everyone who wants to head over to Monkey Island, please gather around," she said. About twenty of us clustered in a circle around her.

"We're going to head over to the island, just over there," she said, pointing to a small landmass in the middle of the river.

"When we get there, please do not feed the monkeys. Please do not touch the monkeys, and at all costs please do not get close to them," she was as stern as a schoolteacher.

"They may strike or claw at you," she said. "They carry parasites and who knows what else. So, heads up."

I hoped the new arrivals would heed Marcela's warnings. But I had a feeling that, like me, the novelty of the situation would get the better of them. When I'd first come to the lodge seven years earlier and visited Monkey Island for the first time, I didn't think much about the cautions, and I got closer than I should have. A fairly large monkey jumped out of the canopy, right onto my back. Of course, I was thrilled at the time. It made for a great photo op.

But on a different level, that monkey was symbolic. I'd come to Peru with a lot of baggage on my shoulders, and now I literally had a monkey on my back. The monkey is the fool, the master artisan, and the keeper of playfulness in the jungle. It also—if we're attuned to the messages animals bring us—can be a great teacher.

This time, I kept my distance from the monkeys, enjoying seeing the students' reactions to their new surroundings. I was preoccupied with thoughts about where to go that night to plant the staff in the jungle.

I knew one thing for sure: I was not going to wander too far off the path. Like the monkeys, everything in the jungle was bigger than life. The spiders were the size of my hand. And who knows? I could bump into a jaguar for real. If so, then so be it.

I headed back to the Serpent Hut and lay down for a rest. Before I knew it, I awoke from a deep sleep in total darkness. As I slowly came back to life, I heard generators humming in the distance and the screeching of the howler monkeys that had haunted me the night before. No matter how many times I heard them, the shrillness of their collective howls gave me goose bumps. Knowing I was headed into the jungle, that was the last sound I needed to hear.

The time had come. The sun had set not long before, and the jungle was moving into night mode. It was profound to feel the shift from day to night, as though a new crew had arrived, coming on duty to care for Mother Nature and deliver her to a new day.

I picked up the guitar case with the staff carefully swaddled inside and stepped out the door of the hut. Overhead, in the clearing around the lodge, the stars created a dense canopy of light, brilliant and sparkling. Looking both ways in hopes no one would see me disappear into the jungle, I decided to head out the back of the property toward the path leading to a distant lake.

I switched on my flashlight and followed the path, walking as slowly and methodically as a jaguar. The path was well defined, and I felt safe as long as I stayed on it. But if I was to leave the staff in the jungle overnight, I couldn't leave it on the path.

I proceeded a few hundred yards, then decided to stop and sit on a fallen tree. I turned off the flashlight. Tiny droplets of rain dropped to the ground from the tops of the trees. It was as if they had bounced from leaf to leaf on their way to the jungle floor.

I heard the stirring of nocturnal animals, well aware that they had night vision and I did not. Were they studying me? Did my presence disturb them? It felt as though everything was alive and in motion, far beyond what my five senses could absorb or understand. I was the one intruding upon their space, and I could *feel* the silence and their eyes upon me as I walked further into the jungle.

Clicking the flashlight back on, I began scanning my surroundings for a place to plant the staff, where it, too, could stir to life. I walked softly and breathed even more so, aware that my slightest movement would ripple out through the ecosystem. It was as if I could hear the breath of the moon.

I was as far into the jungle as I was willing to go. About a hundred yards off in the distance, I noticed, was a massive tree trunk lit by the rays of the moon. I picked up the case and headed that direction. Rain droplets were finding their way to earth from high up in the canopy. *They must be the dewdrops from heaven.* No sooner had I taken one step than a loud voice in my head said *STOP! Do not wander off. Mark your course.* I immediately froze in my tracks and began to look around. I marked nearly every step from where I had left the fallen tree at the path until I reached my destination. The plant life was so dense it nearly came up to my waist. Every step was a conscious one. Every breath felt as if I was being called to breathe in unison with the jungle.

Shining the flashlight up into the upper reaches of the tree, I was awed by its sheer size. The light didn't even reach the top. I had clearly found the right place to leave the staff for activation.

I walked around the side of the tree so as to hide it from any direct line of site from the path. Although I intended to come back first thing in the morning, I didn't want to take any chances of the staff falling into the wrong hands.

I lifted it high over my head. Then, with one forceful heave, I thrust the staff into the earth. I drew in a deep breath, then stood next to it, praying.

May the soil of our Divine Mother activate the full power of this staff.

May its birth into the world serve to better guide my journey and that of all humanity.

May its power and beauty serve the Grail.

Silently, I took in the power of the moment. The soft light of grandmother moon barely filtering through the thick canopy of the jungle. The moist smell of the freshly disturbed earth. The buzzing energy of the creatures and the air itself. And the strength of the staff, connecting heaven and earth.

Reluctantly, I turned around and retraced my steps back to the path, feeling very alone. Before the staff was out of sight, I looked back and shined the light upon it. It was beaming with life already. In the mist of the darkness, a thin ray of moonlight reflected off of its sacred center.

I left it there, and marked its location as best I could. Yet again, just like at the airport in Los Angeles, I was relinquishing the staff, knowing its energy was coming alive with the powers of the universe.

I felt assured that I had come to the right place at the right time. I found the way back to my hut, tucked myself in and fell fast asleep, knowing that tomorrow would bring an entirely new me.

12

Conception

A couple of years before my separation from Gigi, I began the quest for completion and harmony. I wasn't sure exactly what those two words meant, except that they had something to do with enlightenment. But as I glimpsed the fullness of who and what I was becoming, I began to explore shamanism and the different modalities of Eastern and Western traditions. This led to experimenting with wisdom teachings that would offer clues as to which way to proceed.

These teachings were not just inspiring words. They were frequencies that activated my movement along the evolutionary path. I became fascinated with astrology, mysticism, Gnosticism, shamanism, Mother Naturisms, and other nontraditional teachings of the native cultures of North, Central, and South America.

Eastern traditions shared wisdom that supported deep presence and mindful expressions of thought. And *A Course in Miracles* tossed out my old patterns of thinking and opened me up to a perspective free of the judgment and projection I'd lived with all my life.

While I gained wisdom from all the teachings, the earth-based traditions resonated with me because they're grounded in what I needed to change old patterns of thinking: less left brain, more right brain. Less masculine, more feminine.

The feminine energy became key, as I saw that native teachings from around the globe offered a deep connection to Mother Earth, Mother Nature, and the natural world.

Within this work, I began to understand a broader meaning of the word "mother," a perspective that helped heal my trailing "little Adam" wounds, thinking I would never win my mother's love, no matter what I did.

After my father's death, my mother moved to Santa Barbara. She lived just ten minutes from my house, and I felt a responsibility as her son to "step up" now that my father was gone. I was dutiful yet still raw and emotionally tender from my relationship with her.

One day, I'd spent several hours working on my new web site and shooting a video for it. I was on a high, feeling excited and eager to share.

We sat down to dinner at my mother's house, and I started describing my day. I did it out of pure joy. The enthusiasm poured out of me as I described the video shoot and how much we'd accomplished.

My sister, who had joined us for dinner, sat expressionless as I spoke. This didn't surprise me, since she has always felt comfortable in the archetype of the damsel in distress. But after I was finished, my mother passed the salad to my sister, looked at me and said, "Adam, you've consumed our dinner with your stories."

No congratulations. No encouragement. No motherly pride. Just a verbal slap on the hand for monopolizing the conversation.

My sister looked at me with an expression that was close to gloating. "See?" she might as well have said. "You've always wanted to be the center of attention, and Mom doesn't like it any more now than she did when we were little."

I was a grown man, but I felt the sting of my mother's rebuke as clearly as I had when I was ten years old. I felt the shame of not doing it "right" or being good enough to get her attention—only this time was different. I was watching my mother's reactions from a more objective place, recognizing that my external world reflected my own thoughts about myself. She wasn't shaming me. *I* was shaming me. Was there any wonder I'd worked so hard to try to please women—and why I'd failed at it so consistently?

I took full responsibility for being a brat when I was growing up. It's true that I needed to be the center of attention and sometimes was disrespectful to my mother, who carried the burden of discipline in the house. My dad was more of a soft touch. If I acted out, he'd take me into another room. "Don't disrespect your mother," he'd say. Then he'd let me go. Until the next time. And the next.

My mother had been a fashion model in her youth. Then, before most women entered the workforce, she got into the clothing business and taught design and merchandising at the Fashion Institute. Always stylish and elegant, she was also the taskmaster, ordering us around as kids. It was not lost on me that often when I entered the room, she didn't seem happy to see me. At dinner when I was a child, it felt as though my brother Ben and I didn't exist.

She rarely encouraged me, which made me savor the times when she did. Her love seemed conditional. But when I was honest with myself, I saw that my love for her was conditional, too. We had constructed a special relationship, both expecting the other to make us happy. Any honest feelings on my part were not allowed if they violated that unspoken agreement.

I knew that my mom's younger sister had contracted polio as a child, absorbing the attention of her parents. No wonder my mother interpreted my actions as attention-getting, and why she reacted so strongly against them.

As *A Course in Miracles* says, special relationships are built on ego fear that we're not enough. And no one—not even our own parents—can fill that void for us.

Before my trip to Peru, in one of my meditations with Men, he asked me if I experienced peace.

"Sure," I said. "Usually with meditation and being in the stillness of Mother Nature."

"And when you left those moments and went back into your everyday activities, did the peace stay with you?"

"Yes," I said, "at least for a while."

"So, when was the last time you felt absolutely peaceful?" he asked.

"At night, when I sleep," I said, although it didn't feel like an adequate answer.

"I want you to return to the time in this life that you *were* peace," he said.

Hmm. This was very different from feeling peaceful or serene. What did he mean by *being* peace?

"When you are peace, nothing needs to happen in the outer environment to create peace. Peace just is. Until you return to that peace, you will need to create the conditions that help you remove the obstacles to it. So, I ask you again. What was the last time you were peace?"

I was quiet for a moment. "I guess never, Men, unless when I was in the womb. Now that was a peaceful place."

He smiled, as though I'd come up with the right answer. "For the vast majority of humans, that was the last time they felt the peace of who they are. Go back to that time and feel into what that peace was like."

"But how do I remember that?" I asked.

"Just feel the peace of the loving and nurturing womb," he said. "And one little hint. Imagine the moment you were conceived in your mother's womb. You may discover a hidden secret of peace."

He was cryptic as ever, with one final message before he disappeared.

"Do it for yourself, Adam. Your life depends on it."

As I sat with his instructions, I heard an inner voice.

"You are synchronizing with Divine Time," it said. "You are now redesigning what was in the past to what has always been in the future. You are going to the place where you will end up anyway. So why not go now?"

Pausing for a moment, not sure what that meant, I remembered something I'd learned in my study of indigenous people and shamanic traditions in my quest for completion and harmony.

The ancient Mayans were, among other things, masters of time, and everything was about cycles. The cycle of fifty-two years marked an end to the first complete cycle of life.

I would complete my first grand cycle of fifty-two trips around the sun on March 30, 2013. I knew that I was born with something called the Galactic Signature, which imprinted certain soul characteristics. That exact imprint was scheduled to occur again on March 30, when I turned fifty-two.

When Men suggested that I meditate on my conception in the womb, I realized I had not gone back to that moment in time. As I sat with the date, I saw that the anniversary of my conception in the womb must be coming up in late June or July 2012.

I pulled out the Mayan calendar and began searching for what was going on nine months before I was physically born. I discovered that nine months before my birth date was the exact same imprint I had when I was born. *That must have been the day of my conception.*

The date was June 30, 1960. And then it hit me with all the force that awakening can sometimes summon.

The fifty-two-year cycle would be complete on my *eighty-first day with Men.*

Hardly able to sleep from the excitement around my conception day, I awoke to a new day and a new Adam.

We don't often think about the day when the light seed came into the womb, the day I was planted in my mother's body. In all of Mother Nature, is there any greater peace than this?

As I reflected on that moment, I felt I was returning to the inner sanctum, to the time when I was closest to love without fear. My Galactic Signature had been determined, and during my gestation, my relationship with my mother was already taking shape.

I had no burdens then. I was the seed of love in its purest form. And as I did what Men suggested—journeying back to that moment in my mind—I experienced one of the greatest loves I've ever felt. Love of Self, love of Spirit, love of all that is.

While I was in the womb, I had none of the ego barriers or blocks that make us feel separate and alone. And while I could feel the hurts that my mother had endured in her life, I knew that underneath it all, she remembered this pure love, too.

Now, with all the history between us, could I return to this love of my mother? Could I love myself as deeply as I did before I became fully physical? Or would I be part of the walking dead, closed off from the spark of light that settled in my mother's womb June 30, 1960?

I wasn't sure. But I knew that, as a seeker, this was the core of my quest.

Wisdom Teaching 6
Love

"True Love is an omnipresent force of the natural world that accepts all things as is without any preconceived notions or conditions. Love, being abstract and nonspecific, is beyond the physical world. However, it can be known by all humans."
—*Men*

As I reflected upon Men's words about peace, "Peace is an element of True Love," I felt lifted into a new place, a new way of being a loving presence in the world. There is fear or love. Once you transcend the fear of the ego mind, only the Love of God remains.

The Love of God that flows like the Life Force ignites our hearts. It cannot be found in our outer environment, only from within. When we are in touch with our authentic Selves, our higher heart nature, we become a mirror of God's Love. As Men shared, peace creates the condition in the ego mind for Unconditional Love to emerge.

"Do everything in Love."
—1 Corinthians 16:14

Five Insights on Love

These five critical insights put forth by Men about love can help you remember what you already are: Love. Each will help you discover your authentic Self as a loving genius. Of all the Thirteen Wisdom

Teachings, the one on Love helped me find intimate and authentic relationships at work, with my body, and with my authentic Self. They will help you on the path to genius to get beyond the ego's unloving conditional thoughts that create conflict and chaos.

On the genius path, there is only Unconditional Love.

1. **By shifting your perspective on the body, love will birth a new reality.** The ego mind uses the body and everything in the physical world as a tool to project separation and conflict. The ego's purpose is to create an experience of separation. The genius Mind uses the body and physical world to communicate the Unconditional Love of the higher heart.
2. **You can live from fear or live from love.** You can make and do things from a place of concern in the ego, or you can create something from a place of love in your higher heart. When you walk into the world with an open heart, you will remember that you are love. And your life will be unconditional. It will help you build meaningful and authentic relationships in all that you do. You can do this by remembering that you are a soul being, not a body or mind.
3. **When you love yourself, you are creating unconditionally and rejecting the ego's belief that you are not lovable.** Self-love feels like the innocence of a child. Tender, nurturing, compassionate, and kind, authentic love is rooted in peace and expressed from a loving heart. Love the part of yourself that feels most unlovable.
4. **The ego's sole purpose is to remind you that you are love.** On the genius path, God's love is the end. Forgiveness is the means to return to love. We can remember God's love by looking inward with the eye and ear of the higher heart. The ego, in turn, will look outside itself to other people and things to find love. It creates a veil of forgetfulness.
5. **Unconditional love resides within you. Your genius Mind finds this love.** Earthly love, as expressed by people and things in your outer environment, most often puts conditions

> on its love. When Self love experiences love in others, they become One. In True Love, there is no other.

So how do you remember your authentic Self as Unconditional Love? Men's Wisdom Teaching on Love teaches us to unlearn the ego mind's idea of love and remember our authentic Selves. When we do, we can then experience our authentic Selves as soul beings.

Because the soul is abstract, formless, and nonspecific, it can be hard to discern. Like love and God, the soul just "is." At the level of the soul, we are closest to God's love. And beyond all levels, we are one with God. We can return to the peace and love of God as a soul. The popular saying that we are spiritual beings having a human experience could just as well be "we are soul beings having a human experience." Soul beings experience their outer lives from the heart, not the mind or the body.

Unconditional love can be tough to open our hearts to. Conditional love we can control and share as we see fit. Unconditional love overwhelms the ego and turns its world upside down. The conditional love shared by the ego mind always separates and requires others to act according to the ego's needs and wants. In the genius Mind that sees with the eye of the heart, everything and everyone becomes One, thus creating fear in the ego mind.

The ego mind fears Unconditional Love because it no longer has control. It loses the ability to create fear, and as a result, the ego no longer has the power to create conflict or chaos. The ego mind does not exist when Unconditional Love reflects our hearts into the world we live in. Pure love is to be in the light; it's blinding to the eyes of the ego. And as a result, the eye of the heart sees a whole new world of peace and Unconditional Love.

Before experiencing Men's teachings, I had sought this understanding for years. Now I had my private tutoring sessions with a master who was committed to helping me reach the completion and harmony and find the Unconditional Love that I was seeking. He was my guide, the hermit, on my return to the Grail Castle.

Without him, I doubt I would ever have known what it meant to "serve the Grail."

My feeling of being left alone in the world has persisted throughout my life. My mom and dad provided a beautiful home, good food, and more. Yet, I did not feel the emotional connection of love. There would be times at the dinner table when I wasn't sure they even knew that my brother and I were present. I could not come home to share my hurts and pains of growing up.

Knowing now that I was not the victim of my early years, much less my parents' lack of emotional connection and love, I realize they were mirrors to the abandonment of my authentic Self. My soul being Self knows only of love. I had abandoned love and adopted the fear of the ego mind. I had left the part of me that felt most unloved, the little wounded Adam. That all changed when I got on the genius path some years ago. And now Men brought his wisdom on love home to my heart.

The Adam and Eve myth in the Garden of Eden tells a story that we left heaven and God's love. We were thrown out of the garden by God for eating the forbidden fruit from the tree of knowledge. Some stories say that God did not see us, and we left the Garden. Nothing more could be further from my Truth. I was the one who abandoned God with my free will. We were never thrown out of the garden. I had a tiny mad idea that I could be separated from God's love. That one idea led to the ego mind and subsequently to the world in which we experience conditional love.

With Men's teachings, I remembered that love had not abandoned me at all. It was the other way around. Love was always present. I was not showing up with the loving magical Self that I now know myself to be.

"Did you have any trouble finding love when you wanted it?" he asked me.

"Come to think of it, no," I said. "Love was always there, and all I needed to do was show up," I said.

"And when you showed up, love found you, didn't it?" He was pleased with himself and with me.

"It did," I said, realizing that a miracle had just taken place in my thinking. "And it still does. I've forgotten to show up from that place of peace and innocence."

"Not to worry," he said. "Now, you have returned to love."

This new definition of love propelled me into my past to reevaluate all my relationships. I had thought that having a trophy wife was love. I called it love when I measured my worth by the size of my bank account.

I sought love in all the wrong places, expecting someone or something outside of me to make me happy. *A Course in Miracles* calls this the "special relationship," which is simply the ego's desperate attempt to believe that it has value, even while it's blocking true peace.

According to my ego mind, if my mom took care of me, I must be okay. If my wife had sex with me, I must be okay. If other people looked up to me, I must be okay.

How much of my life had I searched outside myself for something I had all along?

"How can I know it more deeply?" I asked Men.

"Remember these five things on a soul level," he said.

The Genius Process on Love

"If I love myself, I love you. If I love you, I love myself."
—Rumi

This five-step Genius Process on Love will help create experiences that will move you through the death of dysfunctional ego feelings. Reconnecting with the inner peace of your genius Mind will help you manifest a life of love.

1. **Ask the question, "What do I need to know about the ego?"** You experience True Love because you are love. You are not your body. Your body is simply a vehicle from which you extend the love that you are. The body communicates love

through you. Are you a savior, victim, or perpetrator of fear? These ego projections disappear when you return to the heart and the love that you are here to share.

2. **Listen for the answer, "Whom should I listen to?"** The ear of the heart hears at the same sound frequency as love. Because you are love, you receive and feel love from God, who created your authentic Self as love. Listen with your higher heart to the beat of love. You can discern actions and reactions that are from the heart as opposed to the ego. Own your actions because if you try and blame them on others, Unconditional Love will never find you.
3. **Acknowledge the problem the ego caused in your life by asking, "What do I see that has yet to be seen?"** To see with the eye of the heart takes the courage to get beyond the ego's need to create fear. To fully feel the love of Self from God, who loves, you must be willing to heal the parts of yourself that feel unloved. You can do this by shifting from your ego to your genius Mind. In the genius Mind, your heart and soul come into union with God's love. The original wound of humankind and our fall from love can be healed with this one simple choice.
4. **Be open to the solution by asking, "How do I do things in life without doing them from the ego?"** To choose the love of your Self and that of God shifts the place within your mind where you experience life. To heal the parts of yourself that feel most unloved, you must surrender your attachment to the outer world and remember the love within. When you follow your heart, it automatically chooses Unconditional Love over fear and separation. What relationships over the years have caused you heartache? Properly perceived, they reminded you of your purpose to forgive and return to the inner love of Self.
5. **Activate your genius by asking, "How shall I be?"** To walk in the world as Unconditional Love, you must remember that fear is the absence of love. When you follow the eye and

> the ear of your heart, being love will become part of all that you do.

The Genius Process on Love, along with that of Forgiveness, Purpose, death, life, and peace, has helped reawaken my genius Mind. With Men's help, I discovered that the answer to life's challenges can be found by consciously selecting the love of the genius Mind.

"Ah, so it's a choice then," I said.

"Yes," Men said. "It is a choice. In every moment, choose love, then choose again."

13
Summons

June 25, 2012

I awoke after such a sound sleep, the howler monkeys could have been in my hut and they wouldn't have disturbed me. Daylight was breaking across the jungle, and the night sounds transitioned to the buzz of the day. I could see the light through the screens off the porch of my hut. All of a sudden I shook off the sleep with a sense of urgency.

The staff.

The sun was beginning to shine on the staff. My ego mind immediately jumped to concern. Would it be where I left it the night before? I imagined a jaguar pulling it out of the ground or howler monkeys playfully touching the sun symbol and texture of the snakes, curious about this foreign addition to their jungle home. Was its activation complete? Would it carry the power of connection between heaven and earth?

I would check on it after my morning session with Men to make sure a trickster hadn't stolen it in the night. Or, better yet, I would go to the jungle first, find the staff, and meet with Men on that sacred ground.

I quickly put on my jungle gear, comprised of insect-repellant pants and shirt, hiking boots, and my Indiana Jones-style hat. Even though I felt a sense of urgency to find the staff, I stopped in my tracks when I left the hut.

The moist, fertile smells of the jungle overwhelmed me. The sun was breaking through the canopy, casting a golden glow upon the ground. And the sounds—that incessant hum of insects and unseen activity—reminded me of the intense Life Force of which I was a part.

I was standing in the Amazon rainforest, one of the most magnificent places on the planet. A Garden of Eden, giving life and taking it all at the same time. I took in a few deep breaths and, with gratitude and humility restoring me to a sense of peace and trust, went on my way.

Retracing my steps from the night before, I followed the path to the jungle and easily found the spot where I'd left the staff. When I saw it, I felt a moment of relief, just as I had when I saw it arrive on the boat the previous day.

The sun glinted off the sun symbol, and the bronze ironwork gleamed. It still stood straight and undisturbed, just where I left it, and I wondered what it had experienced during the night. It felt alive to me, as alive as another human being.

The staff was made of silicon bronze, a hard metal. In Eastern traditions, metal is the fifth element, joining with fire, water, earth, and wind. For indigenous traditions, the first peoples of the earth, everything was valued and alive in its own way. Even the stones and clouds were revered as "people."

In this way, I knew the staff would help me claim my clarity of intent, my power, my willingness to show up and serve the Grail, which is God's light and love in the world.

Activating the staff was not simply an act of magic. Planting the staff in the most fertile soil on earth was like planting a seed into the rich, moist, fertile soil of a vegetable garden. The jungle symbolically represents the womb of Mother Earth, generating about 6 percent of the oxygen produced by photosynthetic organisms. The weather patterns of our planet are affected by the delicate balance of the rainforests, oceans, and deserts.

From a metaphysical perspective, the jungle and I were flipping on the power switch so the staff could begin to receive and send vibrations and frequency.

In truth, I was being activated along with it. In and of itself, my intention to honor an ancient symbol allowed me to claim more power and authority in my life—not in the sense of having power over others, but by living within the power of a higher authority. Like the staff, I was becoming an instrument of God. *All I need to do is serve the Grail.*

I looked into the eyes of the snakes and felt a sense of kinship and oneness, sensing that the staff and I were being activated at the same time. It was being attuned to the highest frequencies as a transmitter, And, thanks to my work with Men and my intense spiritual study over the past seven years, I was activating my conscious evolution to become a cocreator with Spirit.

It was time to see what Men had to say.

I got in a comfortable seated position and dropped into the sacred space of being in the womb of Mother Earth for this morning's session. I took the imagined walk in Central Park, where the day was as glorious as it was along the Mother of God River. Everything seemed to be singing a hymn of joy. It didn't take long to arrive at the doorway in the alley and find my seat on the red earth.

"You look radiantly activated, Adam," Men said with a smile.

"Why thank you, Men. I'm feeling it," I said. Then, as usual, his next comment seemed to come out of the blue.

"Activating your being requires that you return to the time of your conception on earth," he said.

I felt an opening in my psyche, that now familiar feeling as Men opened another door in my mind, a looking glass of my third eye.

"How so?" I asked, knowing it was not physically possible to do such a thing.

"You're on a quest to return Home to completion and harmony, correct?" he asked.

"Correct," I said.

"You have chosen to choose again so you can have a direct experience of your Divine Genius, correct?"

"Correct," I said again.

"Because you are in human form and have an ego mind, you have to go *through* the ego to get to your soul Design. You cannot work around it or circumnavigate it. Instead, you must transcend it and include it in your unique soul Design. Are you following?"

I said yes, knowing there was more to learn.

"This process, which you have referred to as the Genius Process, ensures that you do not get stuck in your ego patterns on a perpetual basis.

"That is helpful, Men, thank you. And how do I transcend it?" I imagined myself like the staff, being planted in the ground to receive higher vibration frequencies. There was some higher intelligence. In order to access its vibration, I too must active my own intuitive intelligence. But I knew it wasn't that easy.

"Allow yourself to be," he said. "Accept and celebrate this joyful playground you know as the world of form. When you do this, you can fully function and celebrate your humanity, while not being trapped within its walls and structure."

And then he said something that made me feel like a big piece of the puzzle had just fallen into place.

"That's what your friend Alberto meant when he suggested the idea of getting out of this lifetime alive."

I sat in silence, feeling what he had just said on the deepest level of my being. Could this truly be the answer I'd been looking for?

"And if I allow myself to *be*, what do I *do*?" I asked. As appealing as the prospect of *being* was, I wanted to contribute to the evolution of Humanity 2.0, not simply stand by as a witness.

"Doing and being are One," Men said, grinning.

"And cause and effect are One," I said playfully.

"And we are One," he said, continuing the game.

"And the worlds are One!" I said, laughing out loud.

"And human evolution has come to an end."

What? I stopped laughing.

With that, Men dissolved into a pile of Red Earth, and I was suddenly ejected from the sacred space back into the Amazonian Garden of Eden.

Stunned by the sudden shift of mindset, I took a moment to rebalance. I looked at the staff, still standing strong and shining in the sun. Then I heard Men's words echoing in my mind.

Human evolution has come to an end.

I looked at the staff. "I don't know about you," I said, "but I don't think I'm ready for that quite yet." I took hold of its shaft and pulled it from the earth, then knelt down to wipe the dirt from it with my hand.

As the staff and I headed back to my hut together, I could feel the central sun of the staff picking up light and reflecting it back to the world.

So this is what it means to be, I thought.

Maybe it *was* possible to get out of this lifetime alive after all.

I left the staff safely in my hut, then headed straight for the commissary to see what everybody was up to and get a bowl of fruit. Marcela waved to me across the room.

"Adam, how are you doing?" she said. "I didn't see you last night. What are you up to?" She was in a joyful mood, as always.

"I'm doing great, *hermana*," I said. "I was in the jungle last night."

Her mood turned more serious. "The jungle at night?" she said. "Not a good idea."

"I know," I said, remembering the warnings she and Alberto had given me about the dangers of nocturnal creatures and losing my way, "but I was instructed to activate the staff I mentioned to you."

"By the looks of it, *you* have been activated," she said. "You're beaming energy."

"I feel it, *hermana*," I said. "I'm in it." There was that word "it" again.

"Do you want to come to the lake with me and the students?" Marcela asked.

"No," I said, looking forward to some reflective time on my own. "I'm going to explore the jungle and do some writing. But thank you."

"Enjoy," she said. "See you tonight. Are you coming to ceremony?"

"I am," I said. "See you later."

The Garden of Eden was calling, and I felt compelled to answer. I got my backpack and headed off to explore some of the trails that meandered around the area.

Even though I'd been to the rainforest before, I delighted in each new experience. The butterflies were as big as my hand. Monkeys swung from the trees. Deadly snakes slithered nearby. I saw brilliantly colored birds, insects of all description, and mysterious footprints that reminded me of Jaguar Jon. I was in the womb, the garden, the place of conception of life on earth. What had Men said?

Activating your being requires that you return to the time of your conception on earth.

I wasn't sure about my own conception, but I felt connected to the primordial beginnings of everything around me.

Before I knew it, the sun was getting low over the horizon. Almost five o'clock in the afternoon. I thought of the long days back home in Santa Barbara and the duality of the short days in the Southern Hemisphere. Everything about this experience challenged my long-standing "norms" and perceptions.

It was time to return to my hut and prepare for the next round of medicine. With so much activation taking place, I wondered: *What would be my intention tonight?*

I remembered the mantra from two nights before, when the Doctor of Death planted the words "Serve the Grail" in my mind. *Maybe the good Doctor could give me more information,* I thought. *What is the Grail, and how can I serve it?*

"It." There was that word again. Men had been referring to "it" for months, and it had remained a mystery to me. But now I knew what it was.

"It" was the Grail.

After a couple of hours of restless "relaxation," I headed off to the ceremonial space. With the arrival of the students, it was a full house—a contrast to the few of us who had gathered two nights before.

I managed to claim a space, sat on a mat on the floor, and waited for the ceremony to begin.

The maestro started promptly at nine o'clock. As always, he circled the room, energetically checking in with each of us individually, then said his Incan prayer and handed us a cup of the medicine.

Unlike my earlier experience, forty minutes went by, and I hardly felt anything. Another thirty minutes passed, and I felt the effects of the medicine had gotten only marginally stronger. In the meantime, I was aware of others in the group vomiting, groaning or in stillness. They seemed to be deep in their process.

I decided to let it be and simply drifted off into the cosmos, attuning to the stillness that precipitated deeper listening.

While I had no sense of time, it didn't seem long until I heard the same voice that had spoken to me two nights before.

"The Grail Temple has summoned you," it said. "You will receive the message of the Red Earth in just a few days' time."

As soon as I heard those words, my energy shifted. I thought the moment of many lifetimes was soon to arrive. What would it bring? Death, rebirth, illumination, initiation? Over the years on the shamanic path I had stepped into the unknown, yet something told me that the coming few days would be one of the biggest moments of my fifty-one years. It was as if a vacuum was sucking me out of what was into what forever has been and will always be.

I knew the red earth had something to do with red blood. Aahh, Red Earth, red blood, Grail Castle, the kingdom, the goblet, the blood of Christ. I rested on the mat contemplating what I'd heard. Finally, after a couple of hours, I decided to disentangle myself from the energy of the group and return to the privacy of my hut.

With a cold jungle shower, I felt cleansed physically and energetically after an easy night of journeywork. I stretched out on my bed, which was damp with the humid air, and laid my head on the lumpy pillow. Despite the distractions, I intended to more deeply contemplate the message I'd received.

The ubiquitous sound of the howler monkeys faded into the distance. I looked over at my companion, the staff, which leaned against the wall by the bed. It was attuning itself to the heart of the rainforest. Once again, I had the sense that I was being attuned as well.

As I drifted off into dreamtime, I whispered the words of the medicine.

The Grail Temple has summoned you. You will receive the message of the Red Earth in just a few days' time.

14
Gone Missing

While in Peru, I had plenty of time to reflect, and my thoughts kept carrying me back to my three daughters. It had been seven long years since my divorce, enough time for healing to take root and start to grow. But it had not been easy. Not by a long shot.

The first few years after the divorce, the geographical distance between us amplified the emotional rift. I flew to Utah every month, if possible, to see my daughters, but communication in between those visits consisted mostly of cards, texts, and an occasional phone call. And typically, when I called, I got the answering machine, with a message that was accurate on more than one level: "Sorry we're not available at this time."

I envisioned Gigi listening to the phone ringing and seeing my number come up on caller ID. "Don't answer the phone, girls," I imagined her saying. "It's your dad. He can leave a message."

Sometimes, though, she did answer, and I felt the vitriol shower over me like a hard rain.

"What do *you* want?" she'd say, spitting out the words. I tried not to take it on, to have compassion for the fear that kept her frozen in so much animosity. But to be honest, it got to me. At least I had spiritual tools and teachings to get back on my feet when I was at my lowest point. But Gigi didn't. Anger was her default, and my greatest concern was for the psychological violence she was inflicting on our daughters. At their vulnerable stage of life, what were they absorbing? Would they ever be free of their mother's resentful voice in their heads?

My girls simply didn't have much to say to me. And when they did speak, I heard the virulent refrains of my ex-wife in their words.

"Hi, Maya," I said when I talked with my oldest daughter on the phone before one of my visits. I felt my heart wanting to open, but guarded from years of rejection. Maybe this time would be different.

"Hi, Dad," she mumbled. I could hear her sisters and her mom talking in the background.

"Can't wait to see you this weekend," I said, hoping for an equally enthusiastic response.

"Yeah, well… I'm going to a friend's birthday party," she said. "It's a slumber party, so I probably won't be around much."

I willed the tears in my eyes to go away and tried not to let her hear my disappointment. "Sure, of course," I said. "I'm glad you've got good friends there."

My heart ached, feeling exiled from my own family. What I would have given to sit down with Maya after school and hear about her day, to wait up for her when she came home from a date, to be part of all the small moments in her life that I would never know anything about.

I heard my ex-wife's voice in the background. "Tell him you've got to go," she said. She sounded angry as ever.

"Yeah, gotta go, Dad," she said. At this point in our conversations, I always wondered when I'd hear her voice again.

"Okay, see you soon," I said, trying to sound upbeat. "I love you."

"Yeah, see ya."

Click.

I closed my eyes, feeling the defeat all the way through my body. "Keep going," I told myself. "Keep choosing love. Things will change someday."

But more often than not, I remembered when my daughters were little, filling the house with their giggles and teasing. I thought how much I wanted things to be different, bowed my head and cried.

Over and over, I got the message *you're not welcome here* loud and clear. It wasn't much different when the girls came to see me in Santa Barbara, which rarely happened. I welcomed them with open arms, but they didn't hide the fact they were counting the minutes until they'd be back home.

When Morgan, my youngest daughter, was fifteen, she came to visit me. I've scaled mountains, swum in deep oceans, explored caves. But that weekend with Morgan led to one of the most terrifying experiences I've ever had.

From the moment she landed in Santa Barbara, she was on the phone with her mother. And most of the time she was acting out emotionally and crying hysterically.

"I don't want to be here, Mom," she said, obviously aware that I was hearing her entire conversation. "I want to come home."

While I took full responsibility for my part in the end of my marriage, I also knew that I had tried to be the best father possible. Morgan's feelings didn't make any sense, apart from knowing her mom had painted me as the villain.

"You don't care about us at all," I'd heard each of my girls say. "You like my sisters better than me. You're always playing favorites. You act like you love us, but we know you don't. You abandoned us."

I could hear the parental alienation in every word. Despite the fact that we lived apart, I'd done everything I could to show my girls how much they meant to me. I used every tool in my spiritual arsenal to be positive, to send love and prayers, to affirm the girls, and to feel compassion for what they were experiencing in an unstable home with their mom.

I could only hope they'd see the truth eventually, but during their teenage years, they were being fed a steady diet of acrimony against me.

So when Morgan came to visit in such a highly emotional state, I figured the best I could do was to be patient and even-keeled, and not mention her mom.

On Saturday evening, I took her to State Street to do some shopping. We'd checked out the Apple store, and I sat down on a bench to wait for her as she finished up a purchase at a boutique.

I checked my email and sent a couple of texts, passing time until she came out of the store. Several minutes passed, and she didn't show. *Maybe she's trying on some other clothes,* I thought. I walked into the store to check on her, but I didn't see her. I looked through the entire store. Nothing. *She must in a dressing room.*

"Excuse me," I said to one of the clerks. "My daughter was just in here to buy a sweater. Five foot six, brownish hair, about shoulder length. Wearing jeans and a T-shirt. Could you check and see if she's in a dressing room?

The clerk glanced over at the wall of rooms.

"I'm pretty sure no one's back there, but I'll see."

I started to feel a slow wave of anxiety rolling through my chest.

"Nope," the clerk said as she came back. "No one there."

The wave started to gain momentum, moving from anxiety to panic.

Did you see where she went?" I said.

"Sorry," the clerk said. "I was busy with customers."

Lord, no.

I ran back to the street, looking in all directions, but Morgan had disappeared.

My heart started racing. *Calm down, it's okay. I'm sure she's nearby.* But all the worst-case scenarios started playing in my mind. Kidnapped by sex traffickers. Running away with nothing but her cell phone and a few bucks in her pocket. *Where could she be?*

I tried calling her. No answer. I stood on the sidewalk and turned 360 degrees, unsure which way to go or what to do next. Where would I even begin to look for her? *Should I go searching? Should I stay here since she knows where I am?*

In the back of my mind, I knew what I needed to do, no matter what the consequences. I took a deep breath, said a prayer, and called her mom, knowing the hailstorm of anger this would unleash.

"What do you mean you can't find her?" Gigi shouted. What the hell, Adam? What did you do? I knew I shouldn't have sent her there. I told her she wouldn't be safe with you."

"What do you mean she wouldn't be safe with me?"

"You don't pay any attention. You never have. I've had to raise these girls all by myself."

I wanted to tell her how wrong she was. That it was her choice to take the girls away and turn them against me. It took everything in me to say, "I can't talk about this now. I need to look for Morgan. If you hear from her, call me."

Once again she was directing all her fear at me rather than talking about her daughter. I hung up just as I heard the word "asshole."

I ran to the car and started driving up one street and down another, scanning the sidewalks and storefronts for any sign of her. *Keep it under control, Adam,* I told myself whenever the wave started to overtake me. *Keep your head on straight. You'll find her.* But in the next breath, I could feel sobs starting to rise from that dark wave.

While I scanned the sidewalks for Morgan, I pulled out my cell phone. "Lizanne," I said, when she picked up. She heard the distress in my voice immediately.

"It will be okay, Adam," she said in her soothing voice. She had her own history dealing with volatile relationships, and she provided the grounding I needed. "Just stay calm, take deep breaths, and you'll find her. Morgan doesn't know how to handle her feelings, so this is her way of acting out. But she's a smart girl. She can't be too far away."

Carrying Lizanne's reassurances with me, I kept driving, praying with every breath. *It will be okay,* I repeated to myself. *It will be okay.*

Thirty minutes had passed. A lifetime. Long enough for a kidnapper to drug her and drive her … where? To do what? Every time a scenario started to play out in my head, I prayed again, more fervently than I'd ever prayed in my life. *Please, God, please let her be okay. Please help me find her.*

A full forty minutes after she went missing, I was about to call the police. And then I saw her, walking down the street a few blocks from where she'd disappeared.

Thank you, God. Thank you. Thank you. I couldn't remember ever feeling such relief. The pain I'd felt when I was a boy, when my leg was on fire, had been nothing compared to the emotional pain of thinking I'd lost my daughter.

I pulled over to the curb, jumped out and ran after her.

"Morgan," I said. "Stop. Where are you going?"

"None of your business," she said, refusing to look at me. She had stiffened at the sound of my voice and put her head down, as though she wanted to disappear.

"You worried me and your mom sick," I said. "Come with me. Come back to the car and we'll go home."

"No," she said, still walking. "I'm not going back with you."

I reached out and put my hands on her shoulders to keep her from walking away.

"Please," I said. "We can talk about this."

She squirmed to get away, defiant.

"Leave me alone!" she shouted.

I let go of her, seeing people on the street looking alarmed.

"I can't make you get in the car," I said. "But you have to be someplace safe. What do you want to do?"

"I want to go to Lynn's," she said, referring to one of her mom's old friends.

"Okay," I said. "Okay. That's what we'll do if it's alright with Lynn. But first you need to call your mom and tell her you're okay."

While she called Gigi, I stood close, continuing to thank God for her safety, feeling the tidal wave of fear in my entire being subside. *Thank you, thank you.*

Despite Morgan's protests, her mother convinced her to get into the car with me. I was grateful for that.

On the drive home, Morgan was incoherent and angry, but she was alive. She was safe. "I'll call Lynn right now," I said. "It'll be okay."

Back home, Morgan slammed the car door and went in the house to pack her things. She was ready by the time Lynn arrived.

"She's had a pretty emotional night," I said to Gigi's friend. "Thank you for doing this."

"No problem," she said as Morgan brushed past her and got in the car. "We'll take good care of her."

Again, I was grateful. For Morgan's safety, for her well-being, and for friends who seemingly could do what I couldn't.

I spent the rest of the evening in deep reflection and humble gratitude, feeling the shock in my body fade one cell at a time. A single question lingered in my mind: *How did I help create this situation?*

A Course in Miracles teaches that we project our own ego wounds onto others. If we've been hurt, our egos learn not to trust, and we see the world as a threatening place. We isolate ourselves and blame others. Our egos see people and situations for their potential to hurt us.

This is exactly what Morgan was doing, and I saw myself reflected in her anger and anxiety. While it was easy to make my ex-wife the perpetrator in Morgan's life, I knew she wasn't the only one. I, too, had taught Morgan to function in the world with fear. We'd both been in the grips of it that night, and I'd seen more clearly than ever how dangerous and divisive it is.

It wasn't what I wanted for my girls, or for myself. As *A Course in Miracles* says, "My only function is the one God gave me." I knew God didn't intend for any of us to live with this kind of drama and chaos. Morgan was safe at Lynn's. Now I needed to feel safe in my own mind and learn a new way to function in this world.

Wisdom Teaching 7
True Function

"In the finite world, you measure function by how you operate in your body. This function is in the mind of the ego. But in the genius Mind, function reflects the gifts and genius given to each human. Those gifts and that genius include but are not limited to peace, love, abundance, joy, and creativity."
—Men

"Function happens within the context of your authentic Self," Men said. "The source of your purpose originates from the Divine Genius. It emerges from the infinite into the finite world of your genius Mind."

When you think of the body most often, it is about how well it is functioning. "Am I feeling well?" "My shoulder hurts." When you are Functioning as your authentic Self from the genius Mind, you're Functioning as an extension of the Divine Genius. It expresses itself through your genius Mind and subsequently into the body and out into the world.

Purpose, as taught by Men, differs from Function in the sense that your Purpose in the genius Mind is to reawaken your authentic Self. The Purpose of everything and everyone in the world is to help you remember your authentic Self.

Without knowing our true Purpose, we cannot know our true Function. And as a result, the body will function in a state of dis-ease.

"My only function is the one God gave me."
—A Course in Miracles

Five Insights on True Function

These five critical insights put forth by Men can help you Function as your authentic Self in your genius Mind. Of all the wisdom teachings, the one on Function reminded me that I am not a body that functions in the world. Instead, I am a heart and soul who has a genius Mind and shares this in the world through my body.

On the genius path, your Function reflects the genius in you.

1. **The ego mind functions separately from the authentic Self.** It seeks to find meaning in the outer environment. As a result, the ego mind becomes cluttered with ideas about what you should be and do. It keeps you in fear, separation, and conflict. The ego mind functions at a lower vibration, whereas the authentic genius Mind Functions in the high vibrations of peace, prosperity, and ove.
2. **Your true Function in the world extends from the Oneness of Peace and Love.** Your genius Mind Functions by being in the authentic Self. It creates from Peace and Love. When you Function from this place, life feels boundless. You, as Love, reveal fear to be powerless.
3. **True Function expresses itself through the body as limitless potential.** The body in and of itself does nothing. Yes, it's amazing, yet without the Life Force and Love of the Divine Genius, its function remains limited. True Function helps remind you that the body is here to express the authentic Self and genius Mind as Peace and Love.
4. **Your limited potential resides in the ego mind and acts out in the body.** Separation from the Divine Genius Mind and its limitless potential creates limitations on who you are and what you can be and do when you're in the authentic Self. By choosing to Function in your genius Mind, your limitless potential can express itself through the body. Your work,

gift, and genius then become aligned with your heart, soul, and the limitless potential of the Divine Genius.

5. **You need do nothing.** Being authentic requires nothing of you. Being nothing but Love and Functioning from the genius Mind is everything. When you abandon the ego mind, you become an un-abandoned genius Mind. When you reawaken your authentic Self and genius Mind, work becomes a vocation. When you are expressing your Self in service to Peace and Love, it becomes about serving something greater than yourself.

The Function of our authentic Selves is merely to extend God's Peace and Love. The body's sole function is to communicate Peace and Love. Through it, you can mirror this aspect of your authentic Self and the genius Mind with others.

When I stepped on the path of remembering my authentic Self, I found that I had cluttered my inner spiritual Home and life experience with ego needs that I thought would make me successful in this physical world. The love I felt and gave was conditional. It was a projection of the ego mind. I was functioning in the world as a wounded, emotionally abandoned child in need of salvation. I was functioning in the body.

But the more I became conscious of the Divine Genius, the more I began to experience my body and genius Mind as One. These insights helped me unlearn the ego as the source and learn the Divine Genius as the only true Source. My true Function and that of all humans has begun to feel natural. I needed to remove the ego as an obstacle to this natural state of being.

As I embraced Forgiveness, purpose, death, peace, love, and function, I began to realize that I no longer needed to hold on to the ego mind that lives in the past but rather could grab onto the Divine Genius's Function of the future. The trick was to live in the present moment because that is all there is. This required me to vigilantly discern my thoughts. Were they being sourced from the ego, or were they coming from the true Source, genius?

I thought about how I was unforgiving, lacked a true purpose, hung onto anger, and was unwilling to embrace the Life Force. Peace and Love were fleeting, and I functioned as a slave to the ego's bodily needs. My deep inner wound of emotional abandonment influenced nearly every move. I was either living in the events of the past, or I was living in the future from the past. As *A Course in Miracles* says, I was projecting my inner fears onto the world and the people around me. Because my ego felt like I wasn't enough and didn't matter, I tried to form relationships and business successes that would prove I had value.

When that began to break down, a complete redesign of my life began to take hold. As I forgave myself, my old patterns of guilt were being healed, and I no longer felt I deserved punishment for my "sins." Men had given me a new perspective on Purpose, Death, Life, Peace, and Love. I was starting to see how they were stacked intentionally and in precise order, like one building block upon another, creating a new structure in my life.

Within that structure, the ego was no longer in charge, and I could see its insanity more clearly. For instance, I discovered that the ego belief in punishment could be so strong, we may unconsciously believe we deserve to die. That, says *A Course in Miracles*, is one of the ego's most significant obstacles to peace.

By choosing Love instead, everything from family and friends to my work and life experience began to be wholly redesigned according to my authentic Self.

I began to function in the Oneness that *A Course in Miracles* describes as our true nature, one with the mind of God. However, I couldn't have explained it that way until I met with Men in early June, just three weeks before I left for Peru.

"If each human is given various gifts and genius, then why are we not living them in our everyday lives?" I asked Men. I suspected that I already knew the answer, based on his previous wisdom teachings.

"In the ego mind, your gifts and genius are revealed, but the ego's fear limits your experience of them."

I thought about my daughters. I knew I had gifts as a father, but my fear about letting them down, not being good enough, and not loving them enough kept me trapped inside a wall, no matter how much I wanted to reach out to them. I could see how my gifts and my genius were stymied. They couldn't function at their optimal level within those limitations.

I knew Men was tuning into my thoughts.

"You see, Adam," he said, "everything in the genius Mind originates from your centeredness as a being of Peace and Love. Function comes from that center and acts as a pillar to support your authentic Purpose. Are you following?"

"I think so," I said. "So our Function is not our actions. Our Function is the capacity for us to Love. Is that right?"

"Yes," he said. "The ego design has been dominant, but that is changing. As more people become aware of the Genius Process and the higher levels of consciousness, they will activate the energy of the Divine Genius within their genius Minds. The closed operating system of the ego is like old hardware. To run the new software of the Genius Process, humans will need a whole new operating system."

"Like Humans 2.0," I said.

"Yes, that's it. A human experience based on the soul nature of each of you and the Divine Genius. Remember, this happens in the higher whole mind and soul, which are connected directly to Source."

"So, how do we make this work?" I asked. "How do we install new hardware and software?" I asked.

"They are found in the heart." Men said.

"I have been feeling the heart a lot of late, Men," I said. "What else do we need to do to find our true function?"

The Genius Process on True Function

This five-step Genius Process on Function paves the way on the path to the genius Mind for Unconditional Love. This process will help move you through the death of dysfunctional ego emotions and into Peace and Love. Know that Love will be the guiding light.

Reconnecting with the inner peace of your genius Mind will help you reawaken your authentic Self. To Function in the genius Mind as Love, you must continuously Forgive the ego mind.

1. **Ask the question, "What do I need to know about the ego?"** Go beyond your physical body by imagining the genius Mind as your Home. You can expand your mind by removing the separation of the ego mind, thereby lifting the veil that keeps you separate from the authentic Self. Connect your heart body with your genius Mind, and you will Function as a reflection of the Divine Genius.
2. **Listen for the answer, "Whom should I listen to?"** Know that the Home you're returning to is one you never left. It has no separation. Feel how boundless it is. When you Function at this level, your limitless potential reveals itself.
3. **Acknowledge the problem the ego caused in your life by asking, "What do I see that has yet to be seen?"** The amount of space you create within your mind is directly related to the functionality you bring. If you do not bring function from the Divine Genius, space will be limited. If you have limited space, you will not be able to move very far on your path to the genius Mind.
4. **Be open to the solution by asking, "How do I do things in life without doing them from the ego?"** You only need to choose again. Instead of the ego's thought system of separation, you can choose the thought system of the authentic Self and the genius Mind.
5. **Activate your genius by asking, "How shall I be?"** The authentic Self just is. You need do nothing, just be. The restoration of the peace of God and the ensuing love ensures that your genius Mind will shine upon all that you do. That is your Function.

These exercises will help you unlearn the ego's function. What remains is the Function of authentic Self as Love.

In the past, I thought projects, responsibilities, and deadlines defined my function. I thought function was about being a body. The idea of spirituality was utterly foreign. No wonder I'd felt so stressed for so many years, so out of tune with my own life. I thought my actions were my gifts. Now I knew that my Function was simply to express my Love, gifts, and genius from the Divine Genius.

Men, through his teachings, was helping me deconstruct the life that I had lived. And at the same time, he was helping me reconstruct the life that I was meant to live. Taking something apart and putting it back together in a new and improved way resonated with me. The seemingly complex and confusing puzzle of my life began to come together.

To recap, the map to cross the bridge from ego and separation to the authentic Self and genius Mind began with Men's four foundational teachings: Forgiveness, Purpose, Death, and Life. These are the pillars that uphold the bridge to Love and the genius Mind. They continued with these teachings:

Peace. Peace, as taught by Men, was simple. "I need do nothing" other than be authentic.

Love. When I show up in the world in my authentic Self, Love finds me.

True Function. Men says when we Function as Love, we are in a perpetual state of reawakening our authentic Selves and sharing the genius Mind. We need do nothing other than be Peace and Love.

"When form manifests from the function of the ego mind," Men said, "life becomes an endless search for completion and harmony. When form manifests from the Function of the Divine Genius Mind of the universe, the totality of the human experience can be realized as lasting Peace, Love, and Prosperity.

Before long, I would need to Function that way more than ever.

15

Moving Day

June 26, 2012

Indigenous cultures use the term Red Earth in much the same way we think of the Holy Grail. The blood of Christ is the Red Earth, representing a return to the Kingdom of God, communion with the Christ mind, a return to our Divine Genius.

The Grail Temple has summoned you. You will receive the message of the Red Earth in just a few days' time.

After focusing on those words as I went to sleep, I awoke the next morning with a flurry of thoughts. It was moving day. When I planned this trip to Peru—or, rather, when Spirit outlined it for me—I split it into two parts. The first, in the jungle, served to activate myself and the staff. And the second, in the Sacred Valley, a region high in the Andes Mountains that encompasses Cusco and Machu Picchu, would help me discover what was next for me. I looked forward to returning to the Philosopher's Stone, a place of wisdom that Lizanne and I had visited on our trip to Peru in 2005.

The Stone is believed to hold the wisdom of the ancient alchemist—one who takes the trauma and burdens of life and turns them into gold. As an alchemist, I was invited to transform my life and its existing design. No wonder I heard the Philosopher's Stone calling to me while I was in the jungle. Maybe it would help me understand my assignment and how I was meant to fulfill it.

The boat would leave the lodge just after ten in the morning to take me back to Puerto Maldonado, where my flight to Cusco would depart shortly after two in the afternoon. As much as I wanted to lay in bed, focus on the message, and listen to the sounds of the Garden of Eden outside my door, I had to get in the flow.

The session with Men was first. I carefully packed the staff in its guitar case, grabbed my backpack, and headed out into the glory of another jungle morning, coming to life after a good night's slumber.

The staff had been activated, and so had I. *Mission accomplished. Or was it?* I decided to go back to the place where I'd activated the staff and plant it firmly in the soil once again. Once it was standing erect, I found a comfortable seat at its base.

Just as I was about to close my eyes and drop into sacred space, I glanced skyward. There, sitting high in the canopy, was Men.

"Your walks in the park are no longer needed," he said. "You are walking in both worlds now, Adam . . . simultaneously."

"Wow," I said, realizing that my feeling of being activated was real. "I'm in awe, Men."

"Get used to it," he said. "You are fully tapped into the creative force of the universe. You have un-earthed your soul." I could tell he was pleased with his play on words.

"My heart feels wild," I said.

"Yes," he answered. "You have un-leashed your wild heart to run freely with your un-tamed soul."

Obviously there was a lot of un-doing involved.

"Your spiritual renewal is just like the sun," he said.

As usual, he was full of surprises.

"How's that?" I asked.

"The sun explodes and implodes, which means it can self-regulate and self-generate energy. No outside energies required. You will be the central sun in your own soul Design, exploding and imploding in much the same way.

"That would be a truly remarkable feat!" I said, sensing the impossible.

"No, it would not," he said, grinning.

"Why not?" I asked.

"One word," he said. "Involution." Then he dissolved into the Red Earth.

I shook my head and looked over at the staff, wondering if it understood my conversation with Men any better than I did.

Now I had another word ringing through my mind, joining with the messages about the Grail. Involution.

Maybe in the Sacred Valley, I thought. *Maybe in the Sacred Valley, it will all start to make sense.*

I hurried off to pack and get down to the dock to catch the boat. All went according to plan. As I left the lodge behind and headed toward the second leg of my journey, I was grateful for the medicine and honored to have been in the womb of Mother Earth. The immense beauty, grace, and flow of the natural world had helped me cast off what no longer served me and open up to a powerful and mysterious message. What was next? I had gone deep into my unconscious to untether my soul from my ego thought system. I was more determined than ever to create Adam 2.0. Nothing was going to stop me from finding and fulfilling my mission, from doing God's work in the world.

Riding on the boat leaving the lodge to head back to Puerto Maldonado and the airport was a mixed bag of emotions. On one hand, I was excited to take the next step of discovery in my adventure. On the other hand, I could have stayed another day in the jungle. All and all, I was ready to find out what lay around the next corner of my destiny. Not knowing if I would ever come back to the Eco Amazonia Lodge, I blessed the land and thanked it for holding me in the sacredness of its medicine and magic. Then I found Marcela to say goodbye and give her a gift—a T-shirt from Thailand that had the image of an eagle spreading its wings.

I arrived in Cusco, the capital of the Incan Empire, caught a cab, and took the ninety-minute ride to the hotel in the Sacred Valley.

Through the windows of the cab, I tried to take in the towering mountains of the Andes in all their majesty. They rose twenty thousand feet or more into the heavens, with clouds floating in rings around them and occasional rays of the sun illuminating them with refracted showers of light.

I had been on this drive several times over the years on various pilgrimages, yet this one was different. Not because there were only five days left until my conception day, but because I was going to see an old friend who by all accounts was dying.

How strange, I thought. *I've come for rebirth. Has he come for death?*

I checked into the well-appointed hotel in the Sacred Valley, appreciating the soft bed and smooth pillow and my first night without the howler monkeys. When I awoke the next day, June 25, I thought about Javier.

The last time I saw my friend was a couple months earlier in Los Angeles. Unlike the person I had met years before, he was nervous and full of anxiety. About sixty years old, he looked fairly well, but his mindset was not. While he could carry on a conversation with me, I could tell he wasn't present emotionally. Although I couldn't explain why, I sensed that my coming to the Sacred Valley at this time of my conception, the birth of my soul in the mother's womb, corresponded with Javier's process to hold onto life.

Was he dying? Or was he evolving? Had he had simply reached the end of his evolutionary journey? Was he preparing to receive life—or death?

As I thought about him that morning, I felt the death of my own physical, emotional, and physiological human experience. I kept playing the phrase in my head, "Only those who die, truly live." I was to meet with Javier later in the day. I also was looking forward to seeing Alberto, who was hosting a group of sojourners on his annual Via Illuminata high adventure trips. I didn't consider it an accident that I would soon see the man who had posed the question of whether I could get out of this lifetime alive.

It was day seventy-six, and only five days remained until day eighty-one. The finality of my journey would be realized, or so I hoped. I awoke from a wonderful night of rest and dreamtime. The moist, sticky sheets of the jungle bedding get old very quickly. I lit the portable candle that I carried on the journey, rested my head on the cozy pillow, and set off for my morning walk in the park. Even though Men had told me I no longer needed those walks, I did it out of habit. Originally this was the way I connected in and out of time with Men, but I was beginning to always be connected with him now.

I arrived at the designated place at the designated moment around sunrise and found Men sitting in his usual position on the Red Earth.

"You have arrived on the soil of one of the most ancient wisdom peoples of the millennium, the Incans and your ancient soul tribe, the Laika. How do you feel?" Men said.

"I feel clear and strong, Men. I still have a lot to process after the amazing journey into the jungle."

"That will fully emerge in time, Adam. I see by the look in your eye that the activation of your light body has reached a new maturity. And without that, we would not be able to proceed."

"Why is that?" I asked.

"Because the quantum wave of energy that you're riding requires that you activate your entire Spiritual DNA. Over our remaining five days together, we will be concluding the activation process with Universal Fire. However, today we began with the end of your evolution."

"End of my evolution?!" I knew that I had come for my conception day, so perhaps it was not an ending at all.

"Yes, the end of evolution. You see Adam, you and many others have been selected to participate in the coming evolutionary miracle. You have been selected to undergo a radical transformation, to return Home to your unique soul Design. Then you can help transfigure not only your own Design but also that of humanity."

This was the first time Men had given me a glimpse of the role others and I might play in the collective Divine Genius, and I was surprised and humbled.

"What does all this mean in relation to the end of evolution and the coming miracle?" I asked.

"It means that the evolution process that worked so well for humans over tens of thousands of years has been redesigned according the Divine Genius. The primary force of the creative wave will no longer be evolution. It will be involution."

"Are you saying that humanity will no longer ascend to the higher plane of consciousness?" I asked.

"No, humans will continue to spiritually ascend and evolve. But what is radically new is this: the evolutionary wave will be matched by the 'de-evolutionary' wave of the incoming Divine Genius. This will require the dissolution of certain aspects of the current human design. So, Adam, simply embrace the involution."

"That would be a miracle to jump from an evolutionary spiritual human to a Divine Evolutionary human, guided by the Will of the Divine to fulfill our own unique planetary mission," I said.

"Humans have reached an evolutionary retrograde. It may feel as though everything outside has sped up, and simultaneously everything inside has come to pause or may even be going backward."

I nodded, having felt exactly that. Over the past few years, I had paid particular attention to climate change. My work as an EarthKeeper was dedicated to large land conservation, or what I called undevelopment. However, I noticed that the outer climate change was nothing in comparison to the inner climate change.

"This is what we want you to make known to every human," he said. "Don't fear the push of the past or the pull of the future. Instead, embrace the uniqueness of the Divine Genius in the present."

With that, he disappeared.

I headed off to breakfast at the hotel, trying to process the magnitude of Men's teachings. As I was walking to the dining room, I saw Alberto.

"Good morning, brother." Alberto said.

"Good morning to you, brother," I said, giving him a big hug.

"Let's meet in the garden just behind that building in a couple of hours. Does that work for you?" He pointed to the building just off to our left.

"That would be great," I said. "See you then."

I went for a long walk to soak in the beauty of the valley. The air was crisp and clear. Situated at around five to six thousand feet, the Sacred Valley was high, but not high enough for altitude sickness.

I labored a bit to breathe as I walked up a dirt road to foot of the Andean Mountains. Streams of water flowed from the mountain, steered into small channels that were used to irrigate the fields of wheat, quinoa, and other grains. It was rich and fertile land. The valley always seems to feed the body and soul.

I got back to the hotel with fifteen minutes to spare before connecting with Alberto.

Acknowledging the significance of our being in the Sacred Valley at the same time, I hoped that Alberto would bless the staff. Carrying the guitar case, I found my way to the flower garden where we were to meet. I sat on the lawn and soaked in the warmth of the sun.

When he arrived, we settled down on the lawn.

"It looks like you've got another good group of spiritual travelers," I said, thinking about the tens of thousands of lives he had impacted. "Well done."

"Yes," he said, "we have a great group of eighty-one initiates coming this year for the mountain journeys."

Did he say eighty-one?

Then he glanced at the guitar case. "I didn't know you play an instrument," he said. "Is that a banjo?"

I smiled, reached for the case, and unzipped it.

"Wow, amazing," he said. I gave him the staff, placing it carefully in his hands.

"I had it commissioned some time ago, and it made the journey to Peru. I began the activation process in the jungle, and now I'm hoping you will give it your blessing."

"It would be my pleasure, Adam." He ran his hands along the textured skin of the snakes and felt the smooth curves of the sun symbol at the top. "Exquisite," he said.

As he held it in his upturned palms, he closed his eyes and took a deep breath.

"May this staff, this instrument of Divine Will on earth, be fully received," he said. "May its power be fully activated so that Adam can receive the messages of the coming era and serve others and humanity during these times of great change."

His words were perfect, infused with the grace, Love, wisdom and understanding from the lineage that our EarthKeeper community represents.

I was deeply touched, feeling that the staff had been christened with Alberto's light.

"Thank you," I said. "May we share the magic and be the keepers of the wisdom, and may the ancient ones be with us."

"Beautiful, Adam," he said. "Thank you for sharing this." He pulled the staff closer to him, holding it as if it were a guitar.

"I feel like I'm in a band," he said with a smile.

"You are," I said. "We're called The Cosmic Messengers."

He grinned. "All will be well so long as you sing your note in the cosmic song of eternal life."

"Ahh, yes," I said.

"Remember two things," he continued. "I am here for you, and you have important work yet to do on earth."

"Bless you, brother," I said, feeling grateful for his magic, medicine, and gift.

Alberto left to join his group, and I sat in the garden a while longer, soaking up the beauty of the moment. Before long, I heard a familiar voice.

"Adam?"

I looked up and saw Javier. He looked frail and thin, so much so that I hugged him gently, afraid he might break.

"It's so good to see you," I said. "How are your travels going? This land is powerful, is it not?"

"Yes," he said. "I've been meeting healers and feeling the earth." He paused for a moment. "I am not well, brother," he said. "I don't think I have much time left."

"Hey, one day at a time, alright?" I said, trying to lighten his fear.

"If it's okay with you," he said, "I'm going to take a rest. Can we catch up later?"

"No problem, Javier," I said. "Take care."

I watched him hobble away, an old man before his time. I felt stunned by the intensity of his decline. Yet I wasn't sure that death was imminent for him. A deep knowing told me that he was ready for a childhood wound or karma from another lifetime to be cleared away. A death of sorts, but it wouldn't take his life.

Quickly my attention turned to my spiritual companion, the staff. What did this all mean in relationship to the quest that I was on? More clearly than ever, I knew the answer was coming.

And it had everything to do with the words *Serve the Grail.*

16
POVERTY OF RICHES

When I wrote my book *Undeveloping the Future,* my agent dubbed me the "Millionaire Jerk." I didn't deny it. In fact, thanks to years of spiritual inquiry and inner work, I knew exactly what he meant.

Over the course of twenty-six years in business, I had accumulated a net worth of a few million dollars. I was focused on making money, and that I did. But much of that wealth went away through my divorce and financial irresponsibility.

I was a reckless borrower and spender. My relationship with money was about making more and spending more. While I did make some good investments, I made bad ones as well. I was ruthless in the pursuit of financial wealth. My lessons around money in this earth school came hard and fast.

By 2012, I was well into a journey of inner growth that had me reevaluating my need for financial wealth—and what I would do to get it. I started each morning sitting by the fire, drinking tea, and studying *A Course in Miracles.* I added to that astrology, my inquiry into the teachings of the ancient Mayas, and my shamanic and metaphysical practices. The spiritual growth spurt within me had started shifting my relationship with money. But, as I was soon to learn, big lessons still lay ahead.

I enjoyed the work I was doing with land conservation, but the commercial aspect of real estate had become unfulfilling. Simultaneously, I was working on book edits, as *The EarthKeeper* was in the queue to be released by Hay House in June of 2013, a year after my quest to Peru.

A part of me was all in for the book launch, but my ego held me back. Releasing a book into the world for the first time—or any time—often comes with a deep feeling of vulnerability, of standing naked and baring your flaws and mistakes to the world. It's as though you've been in a closet for a very long time. And when you peek out, you see that there's so much light, it's frightening. You have to take it slowly.

When my agent called me the Millionaire Jerk, he was referring primarily to the stories I told in *The EarthKeeper* about my marriage and children, and about my once cavalier attitude toward the earth and my associates.

I put on a good face whenever I talked with him, but he reminded me that I was revealing myself to the world, warts and all—and, at the same time, that I was a nobody.

"What are you doing to build a platform?" he'd ask while we drove our golf cart to the next green. "You're unknown as a commodity, a voice," he said. "How are you going to promote yourself?"

I tried to sound like I had a plan, but deep down the whole idea was intimidating. *Who am I to think I can write a book? Why do I think I have a message people will want to read?*

I felt my ego grasping for grandiosity rather than Spirit. According to *A Course in Miracles*, grandiosity is the ego's need to puff itself up with false importance in a veiled attempt to feel worthy and valued. I vacillated between ego and a half-hearted reach for Spirit, which is a sure sign of self-sabotage. If I had committed to Spirit, I would have felt true empowerment. But instead I chose the ego's false attempt at power, a residual representation of the Millionaire Jerk, thinking fame and fortune were my destiny.

Years earlier, I had a different encounter with destiny when Maya, my first daughter, was born. It happened at Cedars-Sinai Medical

Center at 3:33 a.m., when my initial glimpse of her grayish blue eyes overwhelmed me with the magnificence of her being.

As I recovered my composure, I stared at the suppleness of her skin, the glow in her face, the bit of auburn hair that was just enough to attach a pink bow when her grandparents came to see her.

A nurse put her in my arms, and I fell deeply, irrevocably in love. She was radiant. Pure light. A precious, delicate being who changed my destiny for good. This little spirit was not a product of fate. Her existence wasn't happenstance. She was the result of collaboration, a cocreation not just between her mother and I, but with Spirit, the Divine forces that bring pure light into being.

In the moments after Maya's birth, when I sat by the window and introduced her to her first sunrise, I felt a deep trust of Spirit, an impulse to do good in the world. That's the thing about destiny. It invokes the question, "What am I serving that's greater than myself?" Of all the things in this world that can nudge us closer to that question, nothing is more powerful than new life.

At a time in *my* life when I wasn't conscious about the earth, Mother Nature, my relationships, or myself, Maya reminded me of wonder and God's grace in the world. I still felt the wounds of my own childhood and felt inadequate to be a father. But now there was no turning back, and I felt a glimmer of emotion that I'd never gotten from my business deals or expensive cars.

"You are destiny," I whispered to Maya, gently rocking her to sleep. "You give me hope."

The year 2012 brought plenty of mystery to people around the world, as some believed the ancient Mayan calendar predicted that the world would end. While I didn't worry about the end of time, I knew in my own way that it was a year of great change.

Cosmologically for me, it was a time of more light emerging, which would be marked by the contrast of darkness. My old way of functioning in the world was coming to a demarcation point. As if I was crossing a bridge, I stood equidistant between darkness and light, fear and love, but I was moving into a lightness of being.

While I intensified my spiritual studies, I let go of much of the business model I'd operated under for years.

I moved my office to a bland stucco building on Garden Street in Santa Barbara with parking in the rear. Located on the second floor, my two rooms were not well lit or ventilated. But my space had windows on the west and north sides, with a view of the mountains. I tried to put my own stamp on it with a teak desk and filing drawers, a seagrass rug, and aerial photos of my ranch in Big Sur.

I'd sold that ranch to my business partner, making a substantial profit from it. He wanted it for his own family to use, and I needed the money. It was a win for him, for me, and for the land, since it conserved the entire ranch and a mile and a half of pristine California coastline.

Inspired by that success, I worked on new land conservation projects, including one just outside of Telluride, Colorado, and one in the forests of Northern California. In both cases, my conversations with potential investors focused on negotiating conservation easements and reducing the intensity of development of the land. I traveled to meet with land planners and conservation groups. But since the economy was still emerging from the depression of 2008, it was a difficult time in the real estate world.

In the end, neither project came to fruition—a disappointment, but also an acknowledgment that the timing wasn't right.

I was committed to my work as an EarthKeeper, and I was beginning to feel it was not simply about land conservation, but about a key passage from *A Course in Miracles*: "Seek not to change the world, but choose to change your mind about the world." I wanted to believe I could bridge my work with the land and my spiritual lessons, but that intersection had not yet fully emerged.

On the personal front, the turbulence with my ex-wife and my daughters continued. Frequently I wasn't able to get my legally allotted time with the girls. And even when I did, I'd arrive in Utah and find they weren't there.

The alienation from their mother continued. Even though I kept showing up, the challenge was as intense as ever. Often I came home from a business trip or my little Garden Street office in tears, suffering from a pervasive inner turmoil.

"Adam, are you okay?" Lizanne would ask, filled with compassion for my ongoing struggles.

"Sometimes I just feel like giving up," I'd tell her, meaning that I didn't know how much longer I could subject myself to my ex-wife's anger and my daughters' apathy.

Masterfully, Lizanne guided me through that part of my journey, speaking from the wisdom of her own difficult experiences.

"Just keep doing what you're doing, Adam," she'd say. "Stay on the path, keep doing your inner work, and continue showing up. Things will get better in time."

With her encouragement, I adopted a teaching from *A Course in Miracles,* combined it with my shamanic studies, and put it in practice with my daughters. The idea was to create a meeting place—not an actual place in the physical world, but a virtual "location" of energy and acceptance.

I created the meeting place so I could spend time with the girls—not in the old story of their mom and dad, but in an intention of neutrality. I cultivated this place as a field of peace and love. In that peace, the girls didn't need to choose between me and their mom. It was a safe zone, and I would invite them there in my mind, then hold the space for us to come together to heal.

Sometimes in this safe place, I simply felt peace flowing through me. I asked for it to bless my girls so they could know how much I loved them. Other times, I saw my daughters in my mind's eye. In these spontaneous visions, we were laughing, sharing details about our day, walking together. Nothing momentous. Just soaking up the delicious feeling of harmony and ease.

In that place, I surrendered to the depths of the darkness I'd been in, and to the depths of love. Little by little, I lived out the Joseph Campbell quote: "It is by going down *into the abyss* that we recover the *treasures* of *life.* Where you stumble, *there* lies *your treasure.*"

Until I started down my spiritual path, I didn't know that when you stumble over a rock of relationship or business failure, you stop and own it, then allow it to teach you. You allow the person or experience to be your master teacher.

In this presence of forgiveness, of the light of love and the Holy Spirit, I was attuning myself more deeply to my true nature. I recalibrated from the grandiose author of *The EarthKeeper* to a humble and cocreative steward, asking Spirit how I could best do the work of supporting humanity's relationship with the earth.

I let go of my limiting beliefs about money, realizing I had to lose my wealth to align with my destiny. That didn't mean I couldn't have money. It simply meant I had to realign my relationship with it. As a result, I surrendered the sense of lack within myself, which had kept me in a constant spiral of needing more. In its place, I developed a deep faith, knowing that if you trust in Spirit, Spirit will trust in you.

At the same time, I realigned my priorities to heed the call of my soul. I continued to meet my daughters in our safe zone, slowly rebuilding my relationships with them through the power of energetic intention.

In short, I stepped into my destiny. And as I did, I embraced a new operating system, returning to the magic Maya brought into this world, and leaving the Millionaire Jerk behind.

Wisdom Teaching 8
Destiny

"You are actively involved as a cocreator in Destiny, consciously evolving your existence into being. When you activate Destiny, you become a cocreator of the Destiny of humanity."
—Men

I was beginning to function more on the level of my authentic Self, with greater awareness of Men's teachings in my life. Strangely, it was as if years of growth were happening all within this eighty-one-day period. I began to visualize the future. What was I to become? And how could that serve the greater good of all?

Men's teaching on Destiny reminded me that Destiny does not just happen. Fate happens. When you're ready, the Divine Genius will cocreate with you as an artist of consciousness to manifest a life of Peace, Prosperity, and Love.

Destiny is not a destination to arrive at; it's a journey to become your authentic Self and unleash your limitless potential as a genius Mind. The Divine Genius of the universe cocreates along with our genius Mind. Unlike the ego mind, the genius Mind cooperates to foster cocreation. What makes this collaboration so exciting is the fact that when we are cocreating with the Divine Genius, we're connected to the Quantum Field. Here, everything already exists. By connecting your genius Mind with the "field," everything becomes possible.

Men's teaching on Destiny helps you realize that Destiny requires you to show up in your daily life authentically. To show up in my relationships, I needed to remember that Forgiveness leads to Purpose. And Purpose leads to Death and Life. And they point to Peace, Love, and Function.

Five Insights on Destiny

These five critical insights put forth by Men about Destiny can help you remember that you are the artist of consciousness. Of all the Thirteen Wisdom Teachings, the one on Destiny reminds us that we are not a body subjected merely to fate. We are all souls who have genius Minds. Each of us can cocreate the life we want to live.

On the genius path, you cocreate your Destiny with the Divine Universal Genius.

1. **The ego mind cannot see your true potential.** Being separate and disconnected from the Divine Genius of the universe, the ego mind experiences the world as a place of conflict and chaos. It dictates fear and defensiveness instead of Love and expansiveness.
2. **Align the heart and genius Mind with what you want now.** The authentic Self experiences the present moment. In the now, you can feel those emotions of the heart and imagine the Destiny you're meant to cocreate. Listen to the heart, and you shall receive. The separate ego mind experiences the past and feels guilty. It also experiences the future and feels fear.
3. **In stillness, you can choose the ego mind or the genius Mind.** In the present moment, "now," you quiet the mind. Even the busy mind can experience short moments of the now. It only takes thirty seconds or so to hear and see with the ears and eyes of the heart.
4. **Fate happens to you. Destiny happens through you.** The Life Force flows into the human body. It carries the seeds of your limitless potential. The ego mind, being separate,

constricts the flow of the cocreative Divine Genius of the universe.

5. **You need do nothing except be still and let creativity flow into all you do.** The ego mind will do everything to block the flow of the cocreative Divine Genius from being remembered. Peace, Love, and stillness are its enemy, and it will do what it takes to keep you in fear of your genius Mind.

As I wrote *The EarthKeeper* and prepared for it to be published, I felt I was accomplishing a dream. I might even have said it was my Destiny. As I zipped around Santa Barbara feeling full of myself, I couldn't help but boast to myself that "I was destined to write this book, to be a published author."

It was a statement of ego, thinking my creation was more special than that of most mortal souls. My "destiny" put me a cut above. I was special. I was to be seen as wiser and more erudite than those around me.

By the time I experienced my fifty-seventh session with Men, even I could see through that kind of thinking. The reason, I was soon to find out, was my limited ego definition of "destiny."

In meditation, I arrived on the mesa to find Men sitting with his eyes closed. I took a seat and closed my eyes, leaning into stillness.

Men didn't waste time getting to the subject for the day. "The great master Lao Tzu once said, 'To the mind that is still, the universe surrenders.'"

"I am feeling the power of stillness in being centered, Men," I said.

"This center just so happens to be the center of the universe. From here, you can be the co-sculptor and not merely the stone."

I smiled. "That's good to hear," I said. "I was beginning to feel as if I might remain the stone of the ego."

"The ego judges itself by how it appears on the outside. But you are crafting your unique spiritual/Divine Design on the inside. When you do that, you become an artist of consciousness," Men said.

"Remind me again, what do you mean an 'artist of consciousness?'"

"Consciousness is like an assortment of paints, colors, and brushes," Men said. "You are the canvas, paint, and the painter. When you access the higher planes of consciousness, you have an unlimited selection in which to create the masterpiece you are becoming."

"I see. How is this different from fate?" I said.

"Fate is not a creative force," Men said. "Fate is mired in the fears of the ego mind, which believes it is subjected to the whims of the universe."

I thought about this in the context of writing my book. Part of it came from an ego desire to be seen. But it also emerged from a more deep-seated need to be of service to the greater whole. This awareness was a significant change.

"I have no intention of simply recreating the same old Adam 1.0," I said.

"Yes, because you have answered the call of destiny," Men said. "But destiny is for all of humanity and not just yourself."

Men's wisdom was overwhelming at first. It felt as though I'd been given responsibility for the future of the planet and everyone on it. But the feeling was momentary as I recognized the fear behind it and saw my ego trying to distract me from peace once again.

By living from the love that we are, we remind others of the light within. This knowing is our highest service to all of humankind because it comes from the well of joy and peace, not from sacrifice.

"Life has become about serving something larger than myself," I said.

"Yes," Men said. "And that destiny requires a continuous and active engagement of the higher planes of consciousness."

"How can I best do that?" I asked.

The Genius Process on Destiny

This five-step Genius Process on Destiny will help you open to the creative force of the universe. Your connection to the Divine Genius and your genius Mind builds a bridge between a life based on the past and fate to a life based on the present and Destiny.

1. **Ask the question, "What do I need to know about the ego?"** Take yourself to high places that have expansive views. Center yourself in your body and stay in your joy. Observe what comes into your mind's eye, then think of it as a hint or clue that will get you beyond the ego mind.
2. **Listen for the answer, "Whom should I listen to?"** Look again to the horizon and imagine what your soul yearns to become. Let yourself feel the full experience of what you want to be. Feel your heart. Merge your vision with that feeling.
3. **Acknowledge the problem the ego caused in your life by asking, "What do I see that has yet to be seen?"** When you find the stillness in the universal mind and surrender to it, the Divine Genius will find its way into all that you create.
4. **Be open to the solution by asking, "How do I do things in life without doing them from the ego?"** You can choose to experience a life of fate, karma, and death as a finite being—or you can live life as Destiny, dharma, and deathlessness as an infinite being. If you choose the latter, you become a cocreator of your Destiny with the Divine Genius. Fate happens to you; Destiny happens through your genius Mind.
5. **Activate your genius by asking, "How shall I be?"** The artist of consciousness experiences his or her every moment as if it were new. From stillness, the creative genius Mind from within flows through his or her body to reveal its brilliance.

I sat by the rim of the mesa wondering *why*? Why me, why now? Why was I receiving this wisdom and information? While the answers would likely reveal themselves over time, I knew on one level that I was part of the Divine Genius Mind and that I was fulfilling my role to help humanity evolve its Destiny. I was being guided by that which is far higher than us all. I needed to keep showing up and listening to its wisdom and guidance.

Little did I know that the creative power of the Divine Genius would be my guide back to the Grail Kingdom.

17

Feet on Earth

June 26, 2012

When I awoke in the hotel in the Sacred Valley, I felt as though a fairy had visited me in the night and sprinkled magic dust over me. I detected a shift in my energy since my conversations with Alberto and Javier. It was if the unknown and mysterious had evolved into something known and certain.

This I knew for sure: I was being summoned to the Grail Castle to receive the message of the Red Earth. And it was unfolding moment by moment.

Like Percival, one of King Arthur's Knights of the Round Table, I had set out on a quest for the Holy Grail, facing obstacles in my way. While many versions of Percival's story have been written through the centuries, the quest iconically involves healing, restoration of peace, the keys to the kingdom of God—and questions. Unanswered questions that lead to the next clue and the next.

I had an abundance of those unanswered questions. Would the message instruct me on how to serve the Grail? Would I go through an initiation of sorts? Was it the end of my evolution? Would it be destiny or fate? No longer did I fear that I might not make it out alive. I felt more alive than ever.

More than likely it was all of the above, and I felt at peace with what was to come. I felt confident that the universe and I were cocreating my destiny, and I was in flow with its Divine course. I opened my eyes to the light seeping into the room.

Perhaps the morning session with the all-seeing eyes of Men would offer a deeper insight into what might emerge. I moved to the small brown outdated couch in the corner of my hotel room. After lighting a candle, I began my familiar morning walk and arrived in the canyon to meet Men.

The afternoon sun had heated the earth and rocks to such a degree that it was unbearable to sit in our normal spot. Men had moved into a creek-side cave that had been carved out by thousands of years of water flowing downstream. It was cool and still.

"What message did you receive from our meeting yesterday?" Men asked. As usual, he got right to the point.

I paused for a moment. "That we are cosmic messengers?"

"Yes and no," Men said. "Take a moment, close your eyes, and feel into this word: *descend.*"

As I did, I began to feel as if the cave was crushing me. I tensed and drew back.

"Allow the feeling to unfold," Men said. "Do not react."

As I began to observe the feeling, I felt as though I couldn't breathe. Everything went black.

"Let go, surrender to the feeling," Men said. "When you hold on, the lens of perception becomes black. When you let go, it becomes white."

I let go, and a rush of light flooded in. It was thick, yet fluid and milky. And it imploded in gentle bursts of energy. It flooded my physical being, filling me with a sense of euphoria.

"Wow!" I said. "What *is* that?"

"That," Men said, "is the center of the new human operating system. It's not new. "It" no longer remains in the shadow of the ego design."

"Oh my god, Men, was that the Divine Genius?"

"Yes," he said. "It happens when you move beyond the problem of the ego design and open into the higher planes of consciousness."

I could still feel my body attuned to the light. It felt pure and nourishing.

"Today I suggest that you find a place on this sacred land, in this fertile valley, to receive a Divine transmission," Men said. "Find a place to plant your feet and feel the Earth Force and its intelligence. Soon it will merge with the universal creative force and intelligence."

Then he disappeared into the Red Earth.

Earth Force, I thought as I emerged from the meditation. Up until now, Men had spoken of attuning the human energy system—body and all—to the Life Force.

Now I was to connect with the Earth Force. In all my shamanic training, I had long ago connected with Mother Nature. Aligning with the Earth Force, I figured, would be no problem.

I thought it was early morning, but when I glanced at the clock, I saw the morning hours had all but disappeared. That's what happens when you step out of time. Things aren't always what they seem.

I headed to the hotel dining room, soaking in the cool, crisp day. I felt the sun on my face, grateful for my latest assignment from Men. *Find a place on this sacred land, in this fertile valley, to receive a Divine transmission.* How was I to do that? I trusted that I would be guided to the answer.

When I walked into the dining room, I saw Alberto having tea.

"Good morning," I said with a big smile.

"Good morning," Alberto said. "You're beaming, Adam. What's going on with you?"

"I just had a wonderful morning of meditation with an ascended master," I said, knowing that Alberto would understand and sense the magnitude of what had just happened, even if I couldn't fully describe my experience of the light.

"How are you doing, brother?" I said. I could feel a vibrant energy radiating from him as well.

"Feeling good today," he said. "Perhaps it was your staff that got me into a good groove today. Or maybe it was the vitamin B-12, or maybe it's the tea, or maybe it's that I feel so grateful for this Sacred Earth we all share."

"It's probably all of the above," I said, feeling as though we were riding the same wave of pure joy.

"What are you up today?" he asked.

"I'm not sure yet," I said. "The ascended master told me to find a place in the Sacred Valley and receive a transmission. It feels like I'm to connect with the vitality of the earth, but I'm not sure where. Any suggestions?"

Without hesitation, Alberto met my gaze. "You are to go to the Temple of the Serpent. I will arrange for a driver to take you there immediately." There was no doubt in his voice, and I trusted him completely.

He jumped on his cell phone before I could say a word and arranged for a driver to pick me up in front of the hotel in thirty minutes.

"Thank you, brother," I said. "I'll go pack up my gear for the day."

"Take lots of water," he said.

I remembered the harrowing hike up the mountain with Lizanne in 2005 when I could barely make it down at the end of the day. "I'll never be without water again," I said.

"Hey, by the way," he said, "how was your trip to the jungle?"

"Powerful as usual. I'll fill you in on that later, but I received a message that keeps repeating itself. Serve the Grail, Serve the Grail."

"Wow," he said, "your trip today may have something to do with that message. Let me know. Enjoy."

"Love you, brother," I said, giving him a big hug.

I quickly headed off to my room to organize my backpack. Nuts, water, the staff, and my mesa. The mesa was a cloth, about two by three feet. It had magnificent colors and patterns that symbolically represented the shamanic path and connection with the elements of earth, fire, water, air, and ether. It held a bundle of sacred stones that I had collected or received as gifts. Each of the twelvc stones held a specific significance and purpose in healing, visions, and transformation. Like the staff, the stones had been activated with power. There were three for each of the four directions.

By the time I got down to the lobby, the driver was waiting for me. Carlos drove a shabby 1980s car that had no seatbelts. It was so old the brand of the vehicle had fallen off. Even though I'd sworn I'd never ride in a car without them, I took a deep breath and climbed in. Alberto had recommended him, after all. As Carlos headed out of the Sacred Valley north toward Cusco, I could breathe exhaust fumes through the floorboards, but I tried to relax and focus on the moment.

I had visited the Temple of the Serpent years before, but I knew that this time would be different because *I* was different. As Carlos drove up the valley, he chatted in his broken English about the villages along the way.

I asked about the golden fields of quinoa stretching out on either side of the road, the crude irrigation systems that captured the flow of water from the peaks of the Andes, and about Carlos's family.

"*Bueno, bueno,*" he said over and over. Despite the rough road and the knock in the engine of his car, life was good.

About halfway up the mountain to the temple, I saw something so staggeringly beautiful that it proved *bueno* indeed.

Towering one thousand feet almost straight up from the road was a waterfall shooting through the middle of a mountain. The water wasn't flowing over the top, but from *inside* the mountain itself.

In awe, I watched the water rushing out—a pure, cool stream cascading onto the rocks below.

"Can we go there?" I asked Carlos.

He shook his head. "No way, no way," he said. He was talking about the logistics—there simply was no access. But I vowed to myself someday to come back and swim in the pool of that waterfall, immersing myself in the pure, holy water of the sacred Andes.

After about forty minutes, Carlos pulled off onto an ancillary dirt road, the final approach to the Temple of the Serpent. I felt purified simply by seeing the waterfall and recognized that the drive to the temple had been a journey in its own right.

But now it was time to face the serpents and ask myself primordial questions: *What am I ready to shed? And what will I find underneath?*

Carlos parked the car near the stone Temple, which rose up the mountain in tiers of sculpted surfaces. We were the only people there, and he took pictures of me with my staff, then went back to the car to wait. I started to quiet down, as though being in the presence of the serpents cued my body to slow my breathing and still my mind.

Carrying the intertwining serpents on my staff, I walked up the steps of the temple, letting the sacred unseen beings know I was there. I knew from my shamanic study that sacred places all have guardians. And just as we would tread lightly and respectfully on the property of a neighbor or friend, the same etiquette applies when we enter the space of these ancient caretakers.

I reached out and touched the stone of the temple. "I'm here," I said. "I honor you, and I thank you for your wisdom."

I took note of the serpent shape carved into the hard quartz-filled rock over the entrance to the cave. Inside, another snake carving slithered into a ceremonial area where women might once have come to pray for fertility or give birth.

I'd done much work with the feminine side of my nature, acknowledging and exploring the emotions that run through me like the waters that flow through the temple. Now, I stood in a moment of mystery, surrendering my linear thought patterns to a deeper sense of knowing. Why had I been called here today? What was I preparing for?

Looking around, I selected a spot atop one of the tiers of the temple and placed my mesa and staff next to me. I felt called to ceremony, to open the six directions according to shamanic tradition.

Taking the stones from my medicine pouch, I turned to face the south, home of the serpent archetype, and asked to shed my skin that held on to the pain of my past, and to the west, home of the jaguar archetype, the place of letting go all that no longer served my soul's journey.

Then to the north, home of the hummingbird archetype, who reminded me to drink from the nectar of life. And then I turned to the to the east, home of the eagle archetype who reminded me to lift my wings high to reenvision the life I want to live. Then I knelt to Mother Earth, asking for her blessing, and finally to Father Sky, opening my arms wide to receive His blessing.

Then I called in the seventh direction. "To the Holy Spirit who surrounds me and guides me as I walk the Beauty Way." I felt a Oneness like never before after calling in the directions. It was the seventh direction of the Divine. The unified field of Spirit that surrounds all things and all directions. I was breathless. In the stillness of this direction, I welled up with tears, a most holy instant.

I sat down, placing my hands on the stone in reverence and inviting the continued activation of my staff and myself. "May I be filled with grace and wisdom," I said. "May I receive the energy of these powerful serpents." It was a further activation of the serpents on the staff.

As I sat in silence, I experienced flashes of memories about my mother and father, and about my children. I opened myself to the depth of emotion stirring within me, welcoming gratitude and feeling held in sacred energy.

Let go, an inner voice said. *It's time to shed your skin.*

I looked out at the vista in the valley below, taking in the vast stretches of golden quinoa, the thickly planted bushes laden with wild blackberries, the holy waters flowing down from above. The soft fertility of the valley contrasted with the hard rock of the mountains, and all I could see in every direction was the progeny of the two in sheer abundance.

Let go, I heard the inner voice again. *Don't delay your spiritual journey. Be cleansed so you can be born again.*

Our spirits come into our bodies through our crown chakras and leave through that same portal. They summon the power of our physical beings to carry them, intertwining heaven and earth like the serpents on my staff. And so every question—every question that matters—comes back to the alchemy of earth and sky.

The earth gives us sustenance and nourishment. The sky gives us light and energy. As I sat on the stone temple, I was planting seeds within my soul, knowing that I, too, am the offspring of Love and light.

I had experienced the purification of the jungle, and now I was being cleansed by the magic of the serpents, rising from the underworld, and shedding the walls around my heart. To move forward, I needed to lighten my load, unburden myself of old baggage, and honor the places in me that felt most unloved. This, I knew, was the key to getting out of this lifetime alive.

Eventually, I felt my humanness sweep through me and take the place of my reverie. I felt antsy, as though I'd had enough. *It's time to go,* said the inner voice. I gathered my companions—my mesa and staff—and made my way down the temple, thanking the guardians as I went. I took one last look around as the long rays of late afternoon sun bathed the golden quinoa in light, and gave thanks for the promise of an inner abundance to come.

18
Hidden Shrine

When was a kid, I was constantly exploring. Climbing trees, scaling walls, exploring caves. I was invincible, all-powerful. The rest of the world might not have seen the cape flowing behind me as I flew, or the magic sword I carried in a sheath on my hip, but I knew they were there. The imaginary world of play was undeniably real to me, and I pitied the grown-ups whose vision was too clouded by responsibilities to take part.

Fortunately for me, the grown-ups in my childhood home didn't completely shut down my inner rogue. In fact, as much as my mother sometimes dismissed my passions, she and my father both encouraged the adventurer in me. Unlike the helicopter parents who kept their children tethered close to home, I roamed even as a young boy, following the magic of my quest.

It's no surprise, then, that I continued my adventurous ways as an adult, especially when I started my spiritual journey following my divorce in 2004. I felt called to explore the ancient pyramids and cultures I was studying, and with Lizanne as my partner, we flew to some of the world's most exotic and beautiful places to share our inner journeys as well as our outer ones.

In January 2012, just a few months before my first meeting with Men, Lizanne and I traveled to Thailand, ringing in the New Year in a spectacular and exotic land of plenty.

This was the third time we had explored the riches and joys of Thailand, where the friendly people exhibited a grace and ease about life. We were staying in the stunning home of our friend Alan, who had built his place on several lush acres of oceanfront property on the tiny island of Koh Samui, in the Gulf of Thailand.

On New Year's morning, we woke up with a view of the water and white sand beaches. Our villa, like several others, faced an infinity pool. But ours was tucked up into the earth, looking straight out to sea.

"Good morning, love," I said to Lizanne. "Happy New Year."

"Good morning, my amore," she said, giving me a sweet kiss.

The hand of destiny had been guiding our relationship for the past six years. Lizanne first found her way into my heart when I was twenty-four years old. Living in Malibu, California, we met at the crossroads of our lives. I had just returned from traveling in Europe and the South Pacific on and off for two years, and she, like I, was in search of the path forward.

The relationship lasted all of six months before we each embarked on different roads. Lizanne entered the world of fashion and a relationship with a wealthy older man, and I ventured into the business world of real estate, trading my adventurer hat for the sword of the earth conqueror. I took off my beach shorts and put on a suit and tie. My long hair was clipped, like the wings of an eagle who cannot fly.

At that early stage of our lives, each of us got married and conformed to the cultural norms and social mores of the world. Busy with our own lives, we spoke on occasion, and every few years or so we met for lunch. However, we didn't fully recultivate our friendship until the early summer of 2004, at the graduation of our daughters from middle school. Both of us had separated from our spouses six months earlier. I was a broken man with much baggage in tow, and neither of us was interested in a relationship. But a friendship? Yes. We both needed a friend.

Lizanne's gentle demeanor was a healing balm after years of Gigi's wrath. We spent more and more time together, enjoying meals at our favorite spots in Malibu, talking on the phone at the end of a long day. Whenever I saw her or heard her voice, I felt cared for and supported.

With that solid friendship as our foundation, Lizanne and I became loving partners in early 2005. She, too, was an adventurer, and together we explored the world, always eager for the next unexpected discovery. So there we were in Thailand on New Year's Day, 2012, and I was about to make a discovery that would delight Adam the Invincible.

"How are the stitches doing?" I asked Lizanne. On the first day we arrived in Thailand, she had slipped on a rock and sliced her knee open. The cut required twenty-three stitches, and she had to stay out of the water for the entire trip.

"Oh, they're fine," she said. "How was your morning swim?" she asked.

"Amazing," I said, feeling like I was ten years old again. "You won't believe what I found!"

Lizanne smiled, recognizing my explorer self.

"A sacred cave," I said. "Just around the cove." I pointed up the coast about a half mile along the rocky shoreline.

"Really?" she said, sounding excited for me. She relaxed into my arms. "Tell me all about it," she said.

When I set out that morning, I intended to do my morning ocean walk as always in low tide. Even then, I was sometimes up to my waist in water. Because there was no beach access, I wore my water shoes, moving through the warm tidal ocean as fast as I could walk and feeling connected to my surroundings.

Astrologically, I was born under a grand watery trine: Pisces, Cancer, and Scorpio. Because water represents the emotions, I have the capacity for emotional intelligence—even if I haven't always displayed it.

As I walked through the water that morning, I could feel the sea floor beneath my feet and the sun on my face and skin. Air, water, and earth. It was a powerful combination.

I admired the tropical landscape as I walked. Palm trees grew out of the rocky coastline just off shore, and a few well-appointed homes were interspersed with thatched-roof huts.

I made my way past a large rock outcropping just north of Alan's home, still focused on the landscape and the blurred intersection of sea and sky. Then, as I waded through a deeper stretch, I noticed a hole in the rock. I ignored it at first, but it kept drawing my attention. Every time I tried to walk away, I felt pulled back. My inner explorer was not going to leave without investigating.

The opening, I found, measured about four feet by six feet. I stuck my head in it, letting my eyes adjust to the darkness. It smelled like the ocean—salty and damp. And it looked for all the world like an entrance to an underground cavern.

Cool! This held more promise than any fort I'd ever made as a boy.

Feeling my way carefully, I stepped into the hole, which I soon realized was a doorway. I could see an open space down below. The structure felt tenuous, with fallen beams here and there.

Take it slow, I told myself. *If you get hurt, no one will ever find you.*

Thoughts of danger didn't stop me. In fact, they propelled me forward as I navigated with the help of light shining through the cracks. I felt as though I were entering the underworld, the unconscious, the deep primordial waters within all of us. In a few more steps, I arrived at an open space. And what I found next was deeply symbolic of the inner journey—something that made my inner Adam say, "Holy cow!"

There, in the back of the cave, was a shrine. Eight small steps led to an altar on which a gold image of the Buddha sat, dressed in bright orange. He felt vibrant and alive, like the essence within all of us.

Below him was an abundance of riches: offerings of candles and incense, flowered porcelain vases, and small seashells. Despite the vast ocean lapping at the rocks outside, everything was dry and intact.

This discovery was an extraordinary gift, and I felt like had entered into the presence of the holy of the holies. Despite the fact that the Buddha and offerings seemed high and dry, it looked as though no one had been there for a long time. The place was musty and unkempt. When I found a broom leaning against a wall of the cave, I swept the floor as my way of honoring the space.

Then, in awe of my discovery, I sat in prayer, drifting in stillness. What happened next was something even my childhood Adam explorer couldn't have dreamed of—and the beginning of my entire 2012 quest in Peru.

I heard a voice. A familiar voice. It was an ancient one, an invisible being who had visited me in 2007. At that time, he downloaded a five-digit code for me, the numbers 81931. For the next several years, I searched for the meaning of that code, leading to several important findings and a life map that birthed a system I called the Four Roads: red for life in the physical world, yellow for the way we think and feel, blue for our spiritual journey and higher mind, and silver for witnessing our own lives beyond our small ego selves as quantum beings of soul and spirit.

As I listened deeply to the voice, I realized that my solar plexus was warm and vibrating. The voice was communicating to another aspect of my being. I sat still and tuned into the loving voice that came to guide the next turn of my evolutionary spiral.

For nine years, I had worked to become enlightened. I had long hoped to find the Truth of who I am and why I am here on earth. The voice said, "Soon you will take a sacred journey. It will demand that you surrender all that you know and identify with in life. Along the way, be prepared for the sacred marriage of your earthly and Divine Nature. This union of earth and heaven will manifest itself as a sense of certainty, safety, and abundance. You will feel complete and harmonic."

The download continued. "You will experience three seminal events on the Road. They all involve a coupling or union. The first event was your birth and union with the earth. The second event, now unfolding, will be the sacred marriage of earth—the physical, emotional, and mental aspect—with Heaven, the soul, spirit, and god nature. And the third event will occur when you realize completion and harmony.

"Each of these three will unfold according to Divine Will. Thy Kingdom come, thy will be done, on earth so as in heaven. The third and final stage marks a period in life in which you will no longer live exclusively by physical laws but will be wed to Spiritual Law, ultimately transcending all Law. The union of the two will reveal a manifestation of the Life Divine. When complete, these three sacred unions constitute your unification with the Whole of the Cosmos and liberation from a life based solely on the finite reality. The completion of the third and final union will mark the final stage of the Spiritual Being and birth the Divine Being."

I sat for close to an hour in the cave, absorbing the words of the ancient one and feeling called back to my roots as that adventuresome child. I had tasted God's delight throughout my life of exploration, and sitting there in the Buddha Cave, with the sound of the ocean and the light flooding in through the cracks, I said, "Yes. I'm all in. This is what my life is about. I am willing to go to the ends of the earth to birth the Divine Being in me."

Lizanne looked out at the sea as I finished my story. "What a great mystery," she said.

"Yes," I said. "That's it exactly."

Wisdom Teaching 9
Divine Doing

"When you create a balance between the inner and outer environments, you become the Divine Doer who does nothing."
—Men

"The genius Mind is the Divine Doer," Men said.

You need do nothing, he continued, other than be conscious of who is doing the doing in your life. The Divine Doer, who takes action in life, does nothing in the world of the authentic Self. It works with the Divine Genius to create a life of peace and prosperity. The doer who takes action in the world of ego does everything to control life according to its needs. It works independently of the Divine Genius and makes conflict and chaos. Are you doing from the ego mind that separates your life into fragments? Or are you Doing from your genius Mind that creates Oneness in life?

For Divine Doing to become a part of your life, three things need to happen:

1. Reestablish your awareness of the Divine Doer, the genius Mind. Forgiveness of yourself and others for judging yourself as separate creates this awareness.
2. Function as peace and Love. Balancing the inner world of peace and Love with the outer world of conflict and chaos allows the Divine Doer in you to act accordingly.

3. Become the artist of consciousness that actualizes your Destiny. When you are in service of something greater than yourself, you are Doing as a vocation and sharing your unique genius.

Five Insights on Divine Doing

These five critical insights put forth by Men about Doing will help you awaken the authentic Self and genius Mind. As you ponder these insights, consider a relationship that feels most important. Are you experiencing it from the separate ego mind or the Divine Doer, genius Mind?

On the genius path, you are becoming a Divine Doer.

1. **Doing nothing does not mean doing nothing in the outer world.** The Divine Doer paradoxically does everything by doing nothing. You take action in the external world from the genius Mind in your inner world. The Divine Doer instructs the heart and body to act accordingly.
2. **Balancing your physical and spiritual worlds creates the condition for Divine Doing.** The material and nonphysical, spiritual realms are not mutually exclusive. They are one coin with two sides. When you reawaken the authentic Self, they are experienced as Oneness.
3. **Oneness inspires and activates your imagination.** The Divine Doer, being connected to the Divine Genius of the Universe, stimulates portions of your right brain. This area of the brain supports the creative and imaginative aspects of your genius Mind.
4. **Becoming conscious of your authentic Self allows your genius Mind to replace the ego mind.** The ego mind makes your thoughts and actions separate from the authentic Self; the genius Mind unifies your heart and soul's intentions with thoughts and activities of the genius Mind.
5. **Nobody can take away your right to choose the ego mind or the genius Mind.** Free will prevails in the physical world. In

> every moment, you get to choose what aspect of yourself you want to share with the world—your ego or genius.

The sessions with Men had opened my eyes in a new and profound way to the physical and spiritual world. He had shared wisdom and energetic transmissions about Function and Destiny. Why and from where they came from did not matter. My assignment was to receive, experience, and share the wisdom of these treasures. To do this from my authentic Self and genius Mind, I needed to be the Divine Doer.

"This is the next major phase of your evolutionary spiral," Men said. "This is what a joyful life is all about. When you become the Divine Doer, you experience the Divine Life, a Life that is complete and harmonic. You can have all the knowledge and Truth in the universe, but if you cannot put it to good use in the finite world, then it is merely information."

"I get that," I said impatiently. "Tell me about Divine Doing."

I thought about the teachings of *A Course in Miracles,* which say, "You need do nothing." That passage was always a mystery to me until I realized that it speaks to us as the higher Selves that we are.

For instance, instead of doing work to create abundance, the course says we can simply be the abundance we naturally are. Instead of working hard to make a relationship work, we can simply be the Love we want in that relationship and watch it transform. Instead of searching tirelessly for our passion and purpose, we can simply be the light that we came here to be.

The course isn't saying that we're to be idle in this world. Indeed, we're made for doing. But instead of working to control our lives, to do our lives right, we are to allow our natural essence to guide us. The result is effortlessness.

"Doing should be something you and your fellow terrestrial beings are very familiar with," Men said.

"Yes," I said, thinking about how everyone's life seemed to be scheduled down to the second.

"So, let's talk about what you are not doing. How does that sound?" Men asked.

"Sounds good," I said. "I spend way too much time on what I have to do."

"Would you agree that doing is work?" he asked.

"Not always," I said, "but most of the time, yes, doing is work."

"I'm not saying that there is anything wrong with work," he said. "But joyless work promotes stress, leading to disease and death of the body, among other things."

This truth was a sobering thought. How many people did I know who had dropped dead of heart attacks or cancer after long, arduous careers doing work they didn't enjoy?

"You have a choice," he said. "You can work some of the time and enjoy yourself some of the time. You can work all of the time and have no joy. Or you can have joy most of the time and work some of the time."

"Those are the only choices?" I asked.

"You could also have joy all of the time and never work," he said. "But humans need contrasting experience to get the most out of life."

"So, is it truly possible to live in this world of physical form and engage in Divine Doing?" I asked.

"Of course," Men said. "It simply requires five things."

The Genius Process on Divine Doing

This five-step Genius Process on Doing will help you become the Divine Doer who expresses Divine Doing in your outer world. As you begin to practice the Genius Process regularly, remember that the outside picture is a reflection on an inward condition. If you are experiencing conflict and chaos in the outer world, the ego has taken control of how you are doing things. The process will help you see whether your ego or genius Mind is doing the doing.

1. **Ask the question, "What do I need to know about the ego?"** The first action of Divine Doing entails doing nothing.

When you are with a coworker, friend, or loved one, observe the ego's need to separate. Non-doing comes when you do not judge or act upon what you are hearing and feeling.

2. **Listen for the answer, "Whom should I listen to?"** From the state of non-doing, you are guided to Divine Doing. As you do nothing, you are required to simply feel and hear. From this state of mind, spiritual hemostasis sets in your genius Mind. Listen for that which is yet to be spoken. Observe the ego's constant need to talk.
3. **Acknowledge the problem the ego caused in your life by asking, "What do I see that has yet to be seen?"** As you listen, you hear your genius Mind communicating with the authentic Self, the soul, inspiring you to take action. Your imagination begins to reveal your heart and soul's intent.
4. **Be open to the solution by asking, "How do I do things in life without doing them from the ego?"** As you're inspired, you accept the invitation from your genius Mind to step into your role as cocreator. As an artist of consciousness, you can reimagine and subsequently manifest a new life experience. Divine Doing is a choice to live a Divine Life as a Divine Doer.
5. **Activate your genius by asking, "How shall I be?"** Be the Divine Doer by doing nothing. Let go of the first thought, take a breath, feel the peace and Love of the stillness between the breath, listen, and then act or not.

Men made it clear that his teaching on doing was not about doing nothing. His teaching was about me getting out of the way of the Divine Genius and allowing it to work through me and for me.

Soon after I separated from my wife, I wanted to control how and when my children showed up for my allotted time with them. Even though the court ordered a certain amount of visitation, it never worked out that way. By defaulting into the ego's doing mode, I became frustrated and angry. That was followed by sadness. Eventually, I began to meditate on my emotions of anger and sadness. My feelings of rage and loss began to subside. I chose to love the part of myself that felt most unloved and abandoned.

Things changed when my youngest daughter Morgan suggested that we go out and "play."

"So, Morgan, what fun can we have today?" I asked.

"Let's go to the arcade!" she said.

And off we went. For the next few hours, we tried every video game in the place. We laughed and smiled the day away. I was able to let go of the anger and sadness. Instead of acting on my ego feelings of separation, I moved to a place of love and joy. I was doing from a place of my innocence. My imagination was activated. Although I was not aware of it at the time, I was acting from the Divine Doer. It was effortless. That moment was the beginning of a new relationship with my daughters and myself.

Over the years, I've recognized that Divine Doing is a choice in every moment. Now I experience Divine Doing as a way of living. It has become more habitual, even though I sometimes forget. The Genius Process helps me to be vigilant to be the Divine Doer.

When you become a Divine Doer, it upgrades your entire body, mind, and soul. You begin to smile more. Your light and vibration are in tune with your heart. Coherence with others becomes natural. You connect to the whole, and the whole connects with you. You remember you are One.

"Your human vehicle, if you have not noticed, has begun to vibrate at an accelerated pace," Men said. "You are now in full preparation to lift off to a destination unknown."

"What do you mean, 'destination unknown?'"

"Peru is just the place where your journey begins," he said. "As a traveler who loves high adventure, you know that one step always leads to another and another. Where you begin often leads to a completely different outcome."

"I know what you mean," I said. "I feel as if I've been preparing for this quest my whole life."

"You have," he said. "You've been preparing for the return Home for lifetimes."

This notion didn't surprise me. From my studies of *A Course in Miracles*, I knew that Home equates with heaven, the kingdom, or other language used by religion and mythology. The word didn't refer to an actual place, but a state of existence in which we experience the peace of God. On some level of consciousness, I knew the time was coming to integrate my ego and spirit fully.

There are no mistakes. Men was teaching me about becoming the Divine Doer as if my life depended on it. Little did I know that the next steps on my genius path would determine the outcome of the rest of my life.

19
Countdown

June 28, 2012

On day seventy-nine, I awoke from a restless night of sleep. It was the exact opposite of the night before. With only 2,880 seconds (give or take a few) to go until my eighty-first day, I still had no idea what was in store. I reminded myself to trust Spirit. Ever since I was activated along with the staff, I had felt greater peace, following the guidance of something far greater that myself. As Men said from day one, “Don’t question it; trust it.”

I knew the next step on my quest had something to do with the fifty-second anniversary of my conception. And with all the messages I’d received about the end of evolution and getting out of this lifetime alive, I expected a transformation that would symbolically signal death and rebirth. Or maybe it wasn’t so symbolic after all. Men had made it clear that I had to go all in on the return to the Grail Castle. What if I was walking steadily toward my own death?

And then there was the Grail. I suspected that the Grail was equivalent to the Divine Genius, Love, conscious evolution, and the higher Self. I was coming Home to the castle as Percival, completing his quest. But how it would unfold was still a mystery. I tried to focus on completion and harmony rather than life and death.

According to Mayan teachings, the fifty-two-year cycle—as in my fifty-second anniversary since conception—has special significance because it marks the end of four thirteen-year cycles. It also marked the end of what they referred to as my “primary being.”

This is the point where we mere mortals can fully ascend. In that process I had to shed my old skin, just like the serpent. The Mayas and other indigenous cultures called it "becoming a light body," but I thought of it as the journey to genius, to become the Divine Genius of the life my soul yearned to create.

Mayans believed that all individuals, to develop their primary being, move thirteen times through each of the four directions and each of the four roads: red, yellow, blue, and silver. Each time we complete another sacred hoop of life, we move close to the center. And depending on our spiritual maturation, we can return Home to our unique soul center.

With Men's help, I felt as though I was getting closer to my center, but what would it mean to arrive at that place? How would I feel? Would I even know I was there?

Coming to Peru in 2012 was a monumental event in my soul's evolution. I came to celebrate the death of the past and the birth of the future. It was the end of the road through my shadow side and childhood wounds, as represented by the underworld and birth into the upper world of light. I was in the midst of a powerful thrust of the Life Force.

In addition to the Mayan lore, I was being asked to serve the Grail. I could not help but think that I was either going to physically die or I was going to be birthed into immortality. If it was the latter, then I was going to the Grail Castle, the Home of the Holy of Holies to drink the blood of Christ from the goblet. Was I being prepared to become a Knight of the Round Table of God? The sacred architecture was nearly complete. The ink on the Divine blueprint was nearly dry.

I headed into the morning session with Men feeling certain, safe, and confident. More than ever, I felt the absence of my ego fear.

I walked into the park to meet Men, feeling joyous. The wind was blowing at my back, lifting every step into destiny. Just as I was about to make the left turn into the alley, I stopped at the rose garden. The red, yellow, and white roses were in full glory, stunning in their shining beauty and fragrance. I was intoxicated by their scent. I completed the routine and took my seat in front of Men.

"My, you smell wonderful today, Adam," Men said with a smile.

"I feel like everything is coming up roses," I said with a chuckle.

"We are coming to the end of the road," he said. "While our moments are infinite, our time out of time will soon end. You have been a dedicated student, and now you must tell the new myth. Every period of humanity fulfills a purpose, and the coming era requires a new story—one that helps all humans to realize and activate their Divine Genius."

I felt humbled by his words.

"The new spiritual zeitgeist—the Spiritgeist—if you will—has come to earth," he said.

"I'm grateful and honored to have received your wisdom," I said with a small bow of thanks.

"The Involutionary Force now descends upon humanity as never before," he said. "While it always has been present, it has increased in its intensity and flow. It will either crack people open or they will crack up."

"I'm feeling the Force on every level of my being," I said. I knew that what I was feeling for myself was happening on the macro level, for all of humanity.

"We have not been to the Wisdom Well of late," Men said. "Let's drop the bucket into the well. Feel into the Involutionary Force, the impulse incarnating every aspect of your Being from within."

I sat for a few minutes, feeling the Life Force coursing through the body. I began to whisper, *Involutionary Force, Involutionary Force.* I heard words whispered to me. Grace, Divine Essence, Divine Genius. "The seeds of the Force exist within you," the voice said. "They will grant you total freedom to be in form and formlessness simultaneously. To receive the final movement of creation's hand, you must give up the free will of living in physical form."

What did that mean?

"I heard a voice, Men," I said. "It said that to receive the final movement of creation's hand, I would have to give up free will. I don't know what this means."

"Free will when you are in the physical body and free will when you are without form are two different things. When you are in form, your individual self chooses. When you are without form, the movement of creation chooses. Do you understand?"

"I think so," I said.

"In this sense," he continued, "you do not have free will. You are freed from the burden of making a choice. However, in the Divine Genius, the separate self becomes one with the creator and you become cocreators. The force becomes you, and you become the force." I thought, *this is true power.*

With that, Men faded into the sands of the Red Earth.

The Force becomes me when I surrender free will. Wow.

I was quickly pulled out of the space with Men and returned to the hotel room. I felt the need to get into bed and recover. With every conversation with Men, I felt a greater transmission of energy, as though my attunement to the Divine Genius was getting clearer and stronger. This one felt particularly potent.

I covered myself up in the thick wool blankets to feel the warmth of the energy, and I took some deep breaths to relax.

Within seconds, my entire body began to shake uncontrollably. My hands and feet felt like they might fly off with the force of the vibration. I rolled over, trying to calm down, but whatever was happening was beyond my control. It felt as though an electrical current was shooting through my body.

"Men," I said, wondering if he would hear me and explain what was happening. But I heard nothing. No matter what I did, the shaking continued, unabated. I thought about what Men had told me: "Your human vehicle, if you have not noticed, has begun to vibrate at an accelerated pace. You are now in full preparation to lift your ship off to a destination unknown. You are becoming vibrationally intelligent. Soon you will understand the language of light and speak in your native tongue."

Maybe this was what lift-off felt like. A jolt into space. A propulsion into another realm. The words "destination unknown" echoed in my mind, and I felt my dis-ease accelerate.

Then, as suddenly as it started, the shaking stopped. I realized it must have lasted only a minute, even though it seemed like an eternity. For the next few minutes I was not sure what to expect. I wiggled my hands and toes and rolled from side to side just to make sure everything was still working. My body seemed intact, but I knew that nothing would ever be the same.

After the electrical charge left my body, I was ready to sit by the pool and rest. But I knew that was not on the agenda. I would be going to Cusco that day, with my much-anticipated stop at the Philosopher's Stone along the way. I headed off to breakfast to say goodbye to Alberto.

As I walked through the garden on the way to the kitchen, the smell of bacon and a savory mix of morning delights drifted through the air. Still unsure what my body might be going through, I decided to have a piece of toast and fruit. *Keep it light so I can take flight* was my mantra for the day.

"Good morning, brother," I said to Alberto with a half smile.

"You look a little slow today, brother," he said. "How are you feeling?"

"I am a little slow," I said. "It has been a radically transforming forty-eight hours here in the valley."

"I can see that. Do you care to share anything, or can I help you?"

"Thank you," I said. "I just need to integrate it all and rest. I'm heading off to Cusco at eleven, so I want to let you know how deeply I appreciate you and the wisdom you share. Bless you, brother." I could feel our heart connection.

"You're welcome. Please stay in touch," he said. "By the way, what are you doing in Cusco?"

"I'm celebrating my conception day," I said. "It's my fifty-second year on the planet, so I was called to be here. Who knows? I may end up at a wild party."

Alberto smiled. "Enjoy," he said as we shared a heart-to-heart hug.

I headed to my room, packed my bags, and met my driver out at the front of the hotel. I looked out the windows at the immensity of the mountains, the vastness of the sky, and I kept thinking of Lizanne. Tears welled up. I felt so far from home, yet I was Home. I could feel Lizanne's love from thousands of miles away.

The Philosopher's Stone is a monolithic rock like no other in the Sacred Valley. Lizanne and I had seen it when we made our hellacious hike in 2005. The stone was known as an access point for ancient alchemists, a portal into wisdom that transcends humanity. In today's vernacular, we might think of it as an energetic hard drive, holding wisdom for all who know how to tap into its codes.

Although it had been seven years since my previous visit to the stone, I remembered the way. And before long, I realized the driver was taking me on a completely different route than I'd ever gone before. Starting at 8,500 feet on the valley floor, we climbed up to 11,000 feet off the beaten path. The fields of golden quinoa I'd seen the previous day stretched out in all directions, but the road was steeper, windier, and even more remote. I prayed that the driver knew what he was doing.

Finally, above the tree line, the road simply came to an end. Were we lost? I looked off in the distance, trying to get a sense of my bearings. Nothing looked familiar. Then, on the other side of a barren stretch of land, I saw a tour bus. *It must be over there.*

Driving down, over, and back up would have taken an hour or more. So I decided to walk across and find it on my own.

And so I walked, laboring with every breath. I went over one rock hill and down another, struggling up and down without any clear sense of direction. I heard the tinkling sound of bells around the necks of the sheep, goats, and cows who were my only companions. It was desolate. Middle Earth. I had risen from the jungles and the womb of Mother Earth—the lower world of serpents and shedding skin—and was ascending. I was rising into the golden light and the majesty of the mountains.

And I was completely lost.

So I did the only thing I knew to do. I sat down.

A little water was streaming down, spattering over some rocks. Aside from a few small wildflowers, there was no vegetation. Nothing but earth and rocks.

Exhausted, I took my mesa from around my neck and set my staff beside me, feeling comforted by their presence. Then I laid out the rocks from my mesa and asked for shamanic wisdom to guide me.

Tinkling of bells. Soft splashes of water. I listened to the near silence until a message floated in like the wind.

"You are the Philosopher's Stone, Adam. You carry the wisdom."

I shook my head, thinking I must have heard wrong. The Philosopher's Stone was *over there*—somewhere.

"There is nothing outside of you," the message said. "The wholeness and completion are already within you."

I thought about the teachings of *A Course in Miracles*, which describe our human experience as a dream of the ego mind. While we think the dream is real, it's simply disguising our true Self, which carries all the abundance, peace, and clarity of Divine Love, our only Source.

I had climbed the mountain seeking wisdom when I had only to look within. No wonder I was lost. There was nothing on that mountain to find. I felt a rite of passage, another step of preparation, just like my visit to the Temple of the Serpent the day before. Every day, a new adventure, a fresh battle with the dragons on my path, assured me that I could trust my inner knowing.

I put my rocks back in my mesa and picked up my staff, feeling refreshed and confident I could find my way back to the car and my driver.

Now, instead of focusing on finding the stone, my thoughts turned inside, accessing my own portal of Divine wisdom. Tomorrow was the second to the final day before conception day. What would it reveal? What was I to become?

As I traversed the rocky terrain, I asked for help from the ultimate Source.

God, please help me with the transition. I welcome the light and will receive your gift with honor.

20
TRUE WEALTH

If anyone tells you that they belong to a prestigious country club and denies that it feeds their ego, you can bet that they're not telling what's true for them.

We all get attached to a certain lifestyle. For me, my priorities were the health and well-being of my children and myself—and my country club membership.

It meant prestige, image, luxury. Plus, I love the game of golf. But after I sold my ranch at Big Sur, I needed to develop a new relationship with money, to understand a different definition of abundance and true wealth, or wealth with a capital W.

I needed to see through the eyes of the Holy Spirit, knowing that the truly Wealthy are in relationship with creation, and they express that in the abundance of what they're doing in the world.

Being truly Wealthy means becoming the artist of your own consciousness. And that meant shedding everything that wasn't aligned with my higher Self, with Adam 2.0. Fewer belongings. Letting go of the country club membership. Whether literally or figuratively, when you release the items in your closet that no longer fit, your closet isn't empty. In fact, it feels full, because everything in it is truly you.

I began shedding everything I hadn't worn in a year or two. If pieces of clothing didn't fit me well, I either had them remade, as I did garments that I had had custom made in Thailand years before, or I donated them. I was shedding my armor, my skin.

I resized and repurposed, learning along the way that I didn't need to discard everything. I could find new life in it, but only if it could be remade to fit. I was practicing death and resurrection over and over again, recognizing that we can do this with anything in our lives. The end is always a beginning. It's how we evolve. The artist of evolutionary consciousness in me was coming alive.

Repeatedly, I asked the question that *A Course in Miracles* likens to a litmus test: "What is it for?" The power of the question lies in looking beyond the ego need or practicality for a deeper, more soul-resonant significance. If I looked at a pair of expensive shoes that I'd once worn with my prestige suits and asked, "What are they for?" I quickly saw that I'd bought them not for comfort, but to feel important. I didn't buy them for my feet, I bought them for my ego. And my ego wore them well.

But to my higher Self, those shoes had no more significance than a pair of secondhand sneakers. They weren't a symbol of success, just a symbol of an ego that thought it wasn't enough. So the answer to "What are they for?" shone a light on my emerging Self, making it easy to let go.

Over time, I applied that same question to everything—a piece of clothing, a relationship, a country club membership, or an old story. Eventually, I began to notice that there was more space in my life. Things dropped away. Friends, associates, even teachers. I simply witnessed, trusting that my world was realigning with my Divine Genius. That which is not serving will drop away. Everything was becoming "white space." A blank canvas in which to cocreate a new me, a new life—a life that would fit my soul, not the other way around. *Maybe this is what Alberto meant by getting out of this life alive.*

The death of my limited ego beliefs was integral to the Genius Process, knowing that they formed a shield around me, entrapping me in my own fear and need.

Selling my share of the Big Sur ranch was a clear message from the Divine that it was time to go. "Job well done," it was telling me. "Now it's time to clean up other parts of your life."

And so I simplified. Fewer belongings, less travel. I created more space for listening and discernment. The idea of eternal life is to directly manifest—to apply the laws of attraction, then give and receive the gifts you create.

I was at an intersection, in the rigor of choice points.

And then my daughter Ashley made her own choice. And I learned a new lesson about the meaning of wealth.

Despite the acrimony in my relationship with my ex-wife and daughters, my middle daughter Ashley and I had remained relatively close. As she grew up, she developed a sense of maturity that superseded my ex-wife's perspective of the past. Even though her sisters and mother beat up on her emotionally for doing so, she was willing to give me the benefit of the doubt, to see value in our relationships that the others stubbornly would not.

I rejoiced in this. Even though we didn't see each other often, I felt an openness from her.

And then one night, I got a call.

"Dad," she said from the other end of the line, "I need some space."

Immediately my heart clenched with the fear of rejection. Had I done something wrong? Had I overreached? Had my ex-wife convinced her I had horns and a tail?

I tried to modulate my voice so she wouldn't hear my knee-jerk fear. "Is anything wrong?" I asked.

"No," she said plainly. I didn't hear any blame or anger in her voice. "I just think it would be healthy to take a break for a little while. There are some things I want to sort out."

I felt my heart relax a bit. Maybe this wasn't about me after all.

"Well, I can understand that," I said. "You're going through some big transitions in your life."

She had recently finished a yoga training, and she was moving to San Diego to live with her boyfriend, a young man I'd introduced her to. I'd looked forward to seeing her more often since she'd only be five hours away. But her phone call put that desire on hold.

"I'll get back in touch when I'm ready," she said. "Thanks for understanding."

Those were the last words I heard from her for six months.

A part of me felt a bit sad, a little heartbroken around it. But I was in a place of deepening my trust in love. And sometimes, I learned, experiencing a wealth of love in the future means accepting exactly where you are right now.

For six months, I sent Ashley light, love, and prayers. I knew that the challenges we'd had in the family were continuing to trouble her, and her decision to sift and sort through her own emotions was the mark of maturity, of spiritual evolution.

As always happens when someone in our lives chooses their own growth, they create an opportunity for us to grow, too. Instead of fretting over her decision, I chose to ask myself core questions: What am I here to learn? What is the purpose of this? And as *A Course in Miracles* says is the appropriate question for every situation, "*What is it for?*"

Energetically, I could feel that Ashley was on an upward trajectory of her own spiritual journey. I wasn't going to anchor her down with an old story or expectations about our roles. Consciously or not, she was clearing old energy about our relationship. And ironically, while we weren't connected by phone, I could feel a stronger connection with her whenever I took a walk or meditated.

While I didn't know at the time how long the silence would last, I knew that I wanted to create a new meeting place with her. Not one from her old story or mine. But one that the Holy Spirit would design for us, whenever the time was right.

Her letter arrived after six months, our first "real" communication. I trembled a bit as I opened it, realizing how much I had been holding my breath.

As I scanned her words, I saw that her message was simple and heartfelt.

"I still have more to do," she wrote. "I love you, and I need more time."

I took a deep breath, felt my heart expand, and surrendered to her Truth.

And so the six months stretched into nine, and my own lessons continued to take root and grow.

Every time I asked the question “What is it for?” I heard similar answers.

Soul growth. Evolutionary consciousness necessitates a perpetual state of letting go.

Most days, I could relax into that answer. But other days, I asked a different question: “What am I to do?”

The answer always came fast and clear.

Nothing.

Allow, Adam. Simply allow the call for love to be answered by love.

Ashley was claiming her voice as a young woman. She was choosing how she wanted to be in relationship with me, notwithstanding what she’d been taught. She was asserting her own Truth as a spiritual being. And I had nothing to do but respect the wealth of wisdom in her intentional choices.

As the months of silence went on, I observed something profound. In the meeting place designed by the Holy Spirit, she was no longer my daughter, and I was no longer her dad. Our respect for one another had transcended our stories and roles, and we had shed everything but our soul connection.

So one day when I received a text from her, I could feel the completion and harmony in her simple message. “I’d like to see you.”

Tears came to my eyes not just from joy—and, to be honest, relief—but from the feeling that we had accomplished something profound together.

When she came to see me in Santa Barbara, I opened the door with great anticipation. There, standing in front of me, was not my beautiful daughter, but a perfect and Divine soul, complete, mature, and authentic.

She had chosen the wealth of wholeness.

And I had chosen to see her as the Divine Genius she is and has always been.

That, I learned, is what *everything* is for.

Wisdom Teaching 10
Divine Being

"Acknowledgement of the authentic Self can only be found in Being—being in the grace of Divine energy of Love flowing through you as a Divine Being."
—Men

"The acknowledgment you and others seek cannot be found in doing," Men said. "It can only be found in being.

"Human beings are seeking to be known as love in a way that they are not yet able to know themselves," he continued. "This is a great yearning of your time, to be known for the depth of your Love, light, presence, and genius."

"I couldn't agree more," I said.

"Yet humans look for this knowing within the ego mind, where it doesn't exist. This causes immense frustration and the feeling of being invisible. Invisibility engenders feelings of loneliness. When you are in the ego mind, you get in the way of the love you are."

"Yes," I said. "I've felt this myself. So what do we do about it?"

"Nothing," Men said.

Five Insights on Divine Being

These five critical insights put forth by Men about Divine Being will help you awaken to the most sacred aspect of your authentic Self. Doing "nothing" is an inward condition of the genius Mind. This condition experiences the outer environment not as separate but as

One. Your Divine Being, your genius as Love, expresses itself from the inside out. Remember, the heart will lead the way into your Destiny.

The genius path takes us on a journey. The insight of Divine Being and those of the previous nine teachings are now culminating into the place we are One. You have been moving from the outer edge of separation in the ego mind to the inner sanctum of the Divine Being. At this later stage on the path, we begin to sway between form in the body and Love in the authentic Self.

These insights help show us that we are not one or the other; we are formlessness expressing itself in form. The purpose of the body is to be the communication device that amplifies the authentic Self and genius Mind. When we identify with the ego, we are exclusively in form. When we know our authentic Self in the genius Mind, we become the masters of our lives. Here are a few critical insights to contemplate.

1. **Seek not to be seen; seek to be known.** Divine Beingness reveals itself when you identify yourself not as a body but as the energy of Love. With the awareness of this energy of Love, you recognize the same strength in others. Love replaces fear. Oneness replaces separation.
2. **Authentic people meet each other as Divine Beings.** The meeting place for ego minds is in the world of form. This happens exclusively in the body. Divine Beings meet both in the formless world of the genius Mind and in form, where they share their experience(s) through the body. Love of what we share replaces the conflict of our differences.
3. **The intellectual left brain overrides your awareness of the Divine Being.** When the thinking left brain functions exclusively on behalf of the ego mind, it excludes the genius Mind. The difference is this: the genius Mind includes the thinking brain and extends itself as a Divine Doer from a place of Oneness as Love. In this condition of Mind, you are connecting with the Quantum Field, where everything exists.

4. **Divine Beingness feels peaceful.** The genius Mind reflects Peace and Love. The ego mind reflects hate and fear. Fear creates a feeling of lack, whereas Love creates feelings of peace and prosperity.
5. **When you listen and see from the heart, your frequency and vibration attract what you intend.** When you smile at others, you acknowledge the Love that all humans share. Are you listening to and seeing from the heart? Do you feel their energy? When you are connecting in Oneness, you are communicating with others without words. The Quantum Field can then deliver what you have asked to receive.

Men's words about the energy of Love flowing through my Divine Being felt comforting. The relationships that I shared with Lizanne and my children were affirming. When I was with them or even talking on the phone, I began to hear and see them—not just what they were doing, but what they were being.

I began to discern which aspect of themselves was doing the talking and which aspects were being. Were they coming from fear or love? Were they in the head or the heart? To do this, I needed to be more receptive to their feelings. I needed to listen with my heart and not my busy ego mind. I needed to see them not as separate but as one. The greatest challenge posed by the ego mind is its need to judge and project solutions that only create more separation. True Forgiveness is the solution.

One afternoon I had a conversation with Lizanne about her interior design business. She wanted to build more connections in Santa Barbara. At the time, most of her business was in Los Angeles. I could tell she was resisting my ideas about marketing herself in the area. My ego mind defaulted to what she needed to do versus what she was being. She was being fearful in the ego and not in the love of her authentic Self. That all shifted when I changed the conversation to Divine Being.

"So, Lizanne, what do you create for other people?" I asked.

"I help them create beautiful interior spaces."

"And where do your ideas of beauty come from—the client, space, or you?" I asked.

"All of the above," she said.

"Would it be correct to say that the beauty you see and feel is a reflection of yourself?" I asked.

"Yes," she said.

At that point, she began to let go of her fear of marketing herself. She remembered her authentic Self as a person of beauty. This slight shift in our conversation helped her reach out and meet more people in Santa Barbara.

When we have fear about doing something in the world, we can stop and reflect on what we know to be our authentic Self. With this simple choice, fear becomes Love.

I would have thought Being would have preceded Divine Doing. But Men's wisdom teachings were ordered in a way that guided me back to my authentic Self and genius Mind. I am a Divine Doer and Being.

I thought of the lesson in *A Course in Miracles* that says, "I will be still an instant and go home." In that lesson is a line that says, "He [meaning all of us] goes uncertainly out in endless search, seeking in darkness what he cannot find, not recognizing what it is he seeks."

It describes the sadness and frustration of the human search, the constant striving to find what we are seeking. All we need to do to find it, the course says, is to remember our true Home, to be still an instant and listen for an inner voice. No striving, no doing. Just a moment to be. Then we transcend the physical world and remember the Truth of our Divine Being.

"The purpose of being in physical form is to unlearn the ego beliefs and return to the Truth of who you are," Men said. "You are meant to be a living expression of Love."

And how do we do that?

The Genius Process on Divine Being

This five-step Genius Process on Divine Being completes the return Home of your authentic Self and the genius Mind. As you begin to practice the Genius Process, remember that the outside picture is a reflection of an inward condition.

1. **Ask the question, "What do I need to know about the ego?"** Be in the presence of all beings energetically as Love. Creating a sacred space together helps each of you to receive the gift of light and Love. The resulting energy exchange will transcend your exclusive identification with separation and the body.
2. **Listen for the answer, "Whom should I listen to?"** Feel the light within you and around you. Be a witness to Divine Love flowing through you and into the world of form. Know that the only true connecting point from person to person is Love to Love. In Divine Beingness, you can see Oneness rather than separation. Your Beingness lifts all of humanity into Love. When you are still, the voice of Love will speak.
3. **Acknowledge the problem the ego caused in your life by asking, "What do I see that has yet to be seen?"** Release yourself from the grip of the intellectual mind, which asks questions like, "Why is this happening? How can I control this situation? What can I do?" Those questions are the ego mind keeping itself busy and trying to be a hero by focusing on ego doing and being, rather than Divine Doing and Being as Love. As you relinquish this pattern, you move out of fear into Love, from mistrust to trust.
4. **Be open to the solution by asking, "How do I do things in life without doing them from the ego?"** You have a choice: being or Divine Being. Ego being reacts out of fear, whereas Divine Being acts out of Love. Observe yourself in all your relationships. Note when you respond or when you act. Beingness expresses the emotions of Love and Joy.
5. **Activate your genius by asking, "How shall I be?"** Know that you're Divine Being witnessing Love. As you become aware

> of the Love, you are on fire. Your fire lights the world around you. You become free to live your Destiny.

At this point in the genius process, you should be getting clear about the ego and its misuse of the body. You have a choice. Do you choose to remain in the ego mind or let it go and be in the genius Mind? Doing nothing is not an option. Men's teachings put the choices side by side. He invites us to make a choice again. We chose the ego, now we can choose the genius Mind—or not.

"Who and what you are in the outer world of form is a reflection of who and what you are in your inner world," Men said. "If you are functioning in the inner world of separation, then the outer world will be experienced in that context. If you are Functioning in your inner world as your authentic Self and from your genius Mind, then you will experience the outer world as Oneness."

"And what then?" I asked. "Is the journey complete?"

"All great journeys never end," Men said. "When a soul ventures into the wilds of the cosmos, it returns to a Home that it never left. Many souls are making this sojourn, yet the journey can feel so alone."

"I've felt that loneliness," I said. "But at the same time, I've felt that I was never alone."

"Yes," Men said. "The migration from ego being to Divine Being requires the assistance of guides and angels. They are of your choosing and often appear unannounced. They may come in the form of a loved one, friend, associate, counselor, guru, or a mere stranger in passing. They also reveal themselves in nature, symbols, dreamtime, and hidden, often cryptic, messages."

My wife, children, and business partners all served as mirrors of what I needed to learn on the path to genius. Yet the authentic Self was always present. The wounds, traumas, and cultural conditioning acted as roadblocks on the path.

To recap, these wisdom teachings help uphold the bridge to Love and the genius Mind.

Destiny. Men said, "You are actively involved as a cocreator in Destiny, consciously evolving your existence into being. When you activate Destiny, you become a cocreator of the Destiny of humanity." You are not merely a person subject to fate, you can cocreate a destiny of your heart's intent.

Divine Doing. The genius Mind is the Divine Doer. You need do nothing other than be conscious of who is doing the doing in your life. The Divine Doer, who takes action in life, does nothing in the world of the authentic Self.

Divine Being. Men said, "Acknowledgement of the authentic Self can only be found in Being. Be in the grace of Divine energy of Love flowing through you as a Divine Being."

My date with Destiny was fast approaching. I felt guided and connected to this journey. I knew I was being guided because my every move was connecting me to where I needed to go next. This map of sorts took me deeper into my unconscious. I also looked for clues in the jungle and Cusco. I was listening, and Love was speaking.

My ego mind wanted to look into the future, and my genius Mind was intuitively saying, "One step at a time." Where I was to go next remained a mystery. But what I was to be was clear. To gain entry into the Grail Kingdom, to sit at the feast and be One with the Divine, I must first remember that I was a Divine Being of Love.

21
The Assignment

June 29, 2012

"Adam, you are to come to the Temple of the Moon tomorrow night. At the stroke of midnight, you are to lie on the altar of the Divine Grandmother. You will find the altar by entering the Serpent's Cave that lies directly beneath the temple. The serpent's body will guide you down to the earthen altar. Lie on the altar at the stroke of midnight."

Holy shit.

I was startled awake by the voice in the depths of a deep sleep. It was the same voice I had heard in the past, the same voice of the ancient that had given me my eighty-one-day assignment in the Buddha cave in Thailand.

The instruction had come. The Grail Castle was the Temple of the Moon.

In 2005, Lizanne and I had visited the Temple on our first trip to Peru with Alberto. The Serpent Cave and the its opening would be forever imprinted on my mind.

So it was all coming down to this. Lying on the altar at midnight? I could only imagine how dark and cold it would be. I was trusting and listening to my spiritual guides. But every once in a while, my fearful ego still insisted on having a voice. If I thought the jungle was filled with dangerous nocturnal creatures, what would be waiting for me in the hidden corners of an ancient temple?

As I recalled, the temple was located about six kilometers from the center of Cusco. The cave was unique in many respects namely because the serpent's body was carved in stone and served as a handrail to guide you into the cave. The entrance looked like a vagina. Some said it was the cave of death and rebirth.

In 2006, Lizanne and I wanted to return to the temple, but it was closed for excavation. Most of the temple was entombed in earth. From a distance it appeared to just be a large mound of rock. Little was known about the temple, and until recently it was infrequently visited. It wasn't even on the tourist route.

Everything in Peru was mysterious in one way or another, and the Temple of the Moon was no exception.

Having visited the Temple of the Serpent just a few days before, I could see now that it foreshadowed what was to come. Alberto obviously had tuned into the trajectory of my quest and the clues leading me from one step to the next. To come into "right relationship" with the serpent. The direction of the south, the place we shed our skin, to learn how to walk the Beauty Way, to touch and walk softly on Mother Earth.

Tonight I was to return through the vaginal opening, guided by the serpent's body into the womb. Was the serpent's body symbolically an umbilical cord connecting me to the purity of a child?

I was returning to the day of my conception fifty-two years earlier on this exact day on the Mayan calendar, and I could think of no place better than the womb of Grandmother Moon. She symbolically represents the home of emotions, with the innocent magical child within each human being safely housed within.

The moon symbolizes the Divine Feminine and embodies the cycles of time. Each phase symbolizes either the light or darkness of humanity on the individual and collective level. It controls the tides, rains, waters, and seasons. In astrology it is the symbol of the soul. The full moon represents maturity and pregnancy.

It just so happened that moon tonight was just three days from being full.

I decided to spend the day doing reconnaissance of the Temple of the Moon. I had not been there for some time and was not even sure how to find it. After getting a quick bite and packing my backpack and binoculars, I jumped into a cab. The driver knew where the temple was, taking the dirt road from the highway just past the archaeological site of Q'enko. After just twenty minutes, we were within a few hundred yards of the temple.

The temple lies on the side of a hill with two caves inside, one of which is called *Quilla*, or moon. Off the beaten track of the typical city tour of ruins, it is overlooked by many tourists and tends to be quieter and less frequented. Perfectly situated as an observation point, it would have been an ideal vantage point for the ancient Incans to watch for intruders. But it is believed to also have been the resting place of mummies and used for ceremony.

Made of fine stonework, it includes an overhanging cave, a tall doorway, and other structures. It's said to represent the heavens, the earth, and the underworld, symbolized by the condor, the puma, and the snake. A throne or altar carved out of rock sits in the center of the temple, near steps that lead further down. While no one knows for sure where the temple got its name, it may be due to the way the moonlight beams inside at night.

As we approached the Temple of the Moon across the field, we saw workers with wheelbarrows hauling off dirt, and a few others milling around. The site was closed, still under excavation. There was even a guard standing by. *How on earth was I to get into the Temple—much less down into the cave leading to the altar?* My mind began to race.

I tried to quiet myself down. *Don't listen to those thoughts.*

I spent about an hour "casing" the temple and circling around it. I spent most of the time on the west side, trying to figure out if the serpent cave was even open. I took particular note of the guards. They were dressed in dark blue uniforms with trim in a lighter shade of blue. They appeared to be neither well trained nor armed. *Maybe tonight they'll be asleep.*

Over the years, since I had started exploring the four shamanic directions and roads, I'd had many moments when I wanted to quit. I almost gave up my inner journey when I crashed an ATV in the backwoods of Big Sur and was nearly killed. I considered quitting when my ex-wife and her family attacked me emotionally even though I was trying to make peace with her and my daughters. I almost walked away from my journey when I suffered a string of business setbacks and wondered how low my bank account could go.

But every time my ego yelled *uncle,* my conscious evolution refused to retreat. I learned that once you know more about your essence, you can't un-know it. You may still be influenced by the past, but you can never return to who you were before you woke up.

The path I was walking was actually walking me. With every step I took, the path disappeared behind me. I could not say for certain, but I suspected I was being guided. Something greater than my fear and self-defeating ways was pulling me forward into destiny. Call it the Holy Spirit or a Spirit Guide, it was unstoppable. *I guess I was, too.* God just kept whispering in my ear and holding my heart. "Trust," he said over and over, "trust that I am here with you."

These moments were so powerful, they overrode my ego's sense of fear and lifted me beyond the depth of my own being.

I got back in the cab, unsettled yet still certain that I should proceed with the instructions I'd received. To ignore the voice would be like ignoring God. I knew without a doubt that I was exactly where I should be. I remembered the teaching of A *Course in Miracles:* "You need do nothing." My only job was to listen to the guardians and guides who were leading me.

For the past several years, I'd resisted surrendering control of who I am, what I'm supposed to do, where I'm supposed to go and how I'm supposed to do it. My ego insisted that it had the answers and tenaciously held onto the illusion of control. Each time I decided who, what, why, where, and how to do things, I always ended up in the same old place with the same old feelings. I was stuck in the ego design.

On the way back to Cusco, I got sucked into the survival-thinking mind about what might lie ahead. While I needed to follow the instructions I'd received from a higher source, I also needed to make a plan.

I would need a cab to pick me up. I needed to figure out how much time it would take to get to the temple from the hotel, walk through the field in the darkness without being found out, sneak into the cave, and get situated before lying on the altar at midnight. The very idea still made me tremble inside, but I trusted. Everything in the last eighty days had brought me here. I was so scared that I scared the fear right out of myself. Now *that's* the power of the light.

I felt this balance of doing and being as a final test before the eighty-first day. How do we "need do nothing" and still navigate this physical world? I realized it required the skill of a master of consciousness, the artistry of a cocreator, the grace of a magician, and the vision of the Divine Genius. All of the things I'd been gifted in my eighty days with Men.

The old cab chugged its way back down to Cusco from the higher elevation of the Temple of the Moon. Getting back to the temple the next night would not be a challenge, but flowing with my instructions psychologically was something different.

I don't care if you're a master or well-heeled traveler into other dimensions, when you are required to drop into the "It" zone from physical form, it requires a complete alignment with the Life Force.

The energy of my human body would be subject to the energy of the universe, sweeping it up into the higher planes of consciousness. I knew these states are far beyond the typical states of awareness in the body, yet they are available to all.

"*Pare, por favor,*" I said to the cab driver, asking him to stop.

We weren't yet at the hotel, but I couldn't breathe from the exhaust that wafted up through a hole in the floorboard. The narrow streets with their ancient high walls trapped the fumes in tunnels of stone. I got out of the cab.

"*Cuanto dinero, Señor*?" I asked him, pulling my money clip out of my pocket.

"*Veinte soles*," he said.

"*Muchas gracias*," I said as I handed him the fare. I wondered if this cab driver or another would be the one to take me to the Temple of the Moon tomorrow night. Who— besides God—would deliver me to my appointment with the Holy Grail?

22
Inner Child

My dad gave me the name Adam for a reason. Adam, the first man, at home in the garden, but terrified God was going to destroy him. And what did he do? He left paradise. He followed the ego instead of the love of God.

Thoughts are powerful. The mere question of, "Can I think apart from God?" created another thought: "I can." In the individuation of that "I" statement, the ego mind believed it was separate from God and forgot the Genius within.

The "I can do it all by myself" mentality is the path we all take in one way or another until our own quest leads us back Home. As a boy, I was that wild, independent child who refused to listen to anyone else's advice. Even in adulthood, I was determined to succeed or fail on my own terms, which meant I failed over and over again.

It was only through my spiritual study that I learned the difference between the quest of the ego and the quest for Love. We're all trying to find our way back to the Garden of Eden, but the ego mind will never take us there. As *A Course in Miracles* says, we didn't actually leave the garden. The garden is within us.

This return to the heart has been easier in my personal life than in the domain of business. In personal relationships, the mention of the word "love" is acceptable, no matter how terrifying it is to the ego.

Years after my father died, I had a potent dream of holding him and cradling him in my arms while he passed from this life. I was stroking his cheek, whispering that it was okay, and I let him go.

In the dream, my brother was making noise in the next room. "Come in," I said to him. "Come be with your father." But he was too busy. He couldn't spare the time.

When I woke up, I recognized myself as my brother. How many times have I been too self-involved to be present? Too busy to love?

I was able to explore those questions with a therapist named Sandy, who had experienced tremendous trauma in her own early childhood. She was gifted at her work and dedicated to helping others free themselves from the past.

In our first session, Sandy spoke of the magical child within. I knew that the magical Adam was inside me, but I felt disconnected from him, as though not being heard as a child had silenced him.

By using the shamanic practice of lucid dreaming, I was able to observe myself in my own dreams and become aware of symbols and images that held special meaning.

In one dream, I saw my current self walking in nature, where I came upon an outcropping of boulders. As I explored the crevasse, I noticed some movement out of the corner of my eye.

"Hello," I said, "Who's there?"

No response.

I carefully ventured around a rock, and there, looking scared and abandoned, was a boy of seven or eight. He looked at me as if I were an alien.

"It's alright," I said, trying to reassure him. "I've come looking for you." I felt great compassion for him, recognizing him as the boy I'd always been.

He continued to look at me, but was silent.

When I shared the story with Sandy, she asked me a question I didn't expect.

"What do you most enjoy doing?" she said. "Where do you find your fun?"

I had to think a minute. I was so used to focusing on what I didn't enjoy that the answer needed time to break through.

"Golfing," I said. "Hiking, biking, skiing."

"Good," Sandy said. And then she proposed a radical idea. "Whenever you're doing something fun, take your inner child out to play with you. Invite him to go along."

Even as she suggested it, I could feel that magical boy inside paying attention, his fear starting to melt. The idea of being not just acknowledged, but included, made him feel as though he might have some value after all.

True to Sandy's suggestion, I invited the inner Adam to come with me on the golf course and hiking trails. Gradually, slowly, he came out from behind the rocks and began to enjoy himself. Yet something was missing.

Fast forward a few years. I had taken myself on a writing retreat in Chile and had not worked deeply with the magical child within for some time. After writing for much of the day, I would often head out to the beach to enjoy the long stretches of white windswept sand. One day as I was jogging down the beach, flying with the wind and seagulls, I saw a family of four up ahead.

The mom and dad were playing joyfully with their son, who must have been about eleven, and their daughter, who was a little older. I could feel their joy, and I smiled ear to ear as I jogged by.

Next thing I knew, I heard footsteps running behind me. I didn't dare look to see what or who it was, but I glanced down and could see a shadow. I proceeded along, and so did whoever was shadowing me, matching my pace.

After several hundred yards, I decided to pick up my stride and try to outrun the shadow. Before long, the footsteps and shadow went away.

Perplexed by the experience, I looked around to see if it was just my imagination.

It wasn't. There was the little boy, running back to his family. He had been my companion, silent but fully present.

Eventually, I turned around and started jogging back to my starting point. As I ran by the family, I smiled at them and made eye contact with the boy, then gave him a high five.

Before I knew it, he ran out in front of me, and I began to run stride for stride in *his* shadow.

The connection was powerful beyond words. In fact, we exchanged no words, but we were one with each other. Child and adult, sharing the past and the future, brought together in one magical present moment of being.

That night as I reflected on the experience, I realized that I had finally freed the wounded child within to come and out and play. This process of soul retrieval— remembering and welcoming all the parts of our selves that we've forgotten—helped me see that, in one instant, we can experience ourselves as whole beings, perfect and complete, no matter what trauma or wounds we carry from the past.

As I look back over my years of spiritual journeying, I see how often business has been my ego's preferred barrier to being the love that I am. What better smokescreen do we have than "work?" Being hard-working earns respect in this world. We're working for the future, to build good lives for ourselves and our families.

But then the ego takes over the workplace, and there is no love in it anymore.

It's understandable. Being vulnerable, supportive, nurturing, imaginative, and creative in the workplace is not highly valued. At the same time, being intellectual, driven, analytical, and logical is seen as promotion-worthy.

But what if we brought our magical inner children to work? What would be possible then?

I think of companies that are harmonic with the environment in how they source materials and engage with their customers and the earth. Corporations that bring mindfulness and yoga into the workplace. CEOs who allow a free flow of ideas by dismantling the hierarchy so that no walls stand in the way of communication. Trainers and consultants who teach conscious business initiatives to build a better culture.

Maybe we should designate a "bring your inner child to work day." Imagine what quantum leaps might occur if we brought the magic to the workplace and shared it, unrepressed and judgment free.

As I've begun to help others design a new life experience of their making, I've noticed something significant: the more I'm joyfully serving others, the more I'm in my soul. Absent is the judgment, separation, and neediness to be seen or noticed, either at work or at home.

One day as I was reflecting on this, I got a text from my friend and client Steve. I sensed a vulnerability in him, related to the multiple challenges he was experiencing in his life. He had gotten a divorce, his new partner had a serious illness, and he was not happy with his work. While his life seemed to be unraveling around him, he was searching for his soul purpose.

Courageously Steve had decided to design his life going forward from a place of Truth, not by defaulting into his past ego fears. Ultimately, while he was searching for a new job and harmony in his relationship, he was looking for the love inside himself. Without knowing it, he wanted to meet that magical inner child of his own.

Steve was on the short list for a job that would suit his genius and help him move forward. He came to see me at my home the day before his final interview, and the pressure he felt was enormous.

"It's good to see you, brother," I said, inviting him to sit on the couch.

"You, too, Adam," he said. "Thank you for making time on short notice."

"You're most welcome," I said, feeling the depth of his desire for a new direction in his life.

"Are you open to a communication with Spirit?" I asked. He nodded, and I invited him to relax and close his eyes. With that, I invoked the light.

"Dear God," I said, "let us come together with Steve now during this time of great change in his life and work. Please share your light, love, and grace with him so that he may experience his fullest sense of joy. May your purpose be his and support his to share his genius in the world. Amen."

We sat in silence for a moment, then I shared my intention to be there for him.

"If there's anything you want to share," I said, "I'm here to listen."

That invitation opened a door, and Steve spoke for twenty minutes, giving voice to all the fears and anxieties he'd suppressed for so long in the effort to "be a man."

"I've worked so hard," he said, "but it's never enough. I'm never good enough. Everyone expects me to be strong and responsible, but half the time I'm afraid people will find out I don't know what to do next. I feel like a fraud and a failure."

He leaned forward, sat back, shifted in his seat, as though he didn't know what to do with his body. "I want to make my partner healthy and vibrant again—it kills me to see her going through so much pain. But I don't know how to help her, and I'm so afraid I'll lose her. She's been there for me, and I don't want to start over again."

The emotions came flowing out as though a dam had broken open, and after he ran out of words, he wept.

During that time, I sat and witnessed, holding light for him without comment or a need to question. My job was simply to be with him.

After acknowledging the two key pieces that were breaking within Steve—his relationship and his job—I suggested that he take time to fully feel what was happening for him. From my own experience and study, I know that this can be the difference between a breakthrough and a breakdown.

There were moments of silence and stillness. I could hear him taking big breaths on his own. Simple allowing. Just letting him know we were there together in a space that made it safe to be, and where Spirit would join with us. Nothing needed to be done except observe the present.

Afterward, I invited him to share what that feeling was like for him.

"Relieved," he said. "I felt supported. I felt loved."

From there, he imagined ways of being in service to his partner that he hadn't seen before, and he also acknowledged the magnificent job he had done supporting her already.

He also could see how he could be of service in his work. In his mid-fifties, he wanted to take a practical approach to support his children from an earlier marriage, which clarified his sense of purpose and his current priorities.

By the end of our session, he looked like a different person. Lighter. Freer. Softer. He had felt peace and Unconditional Love, and it had given him permission to be himself.

As he left, I knew the transformation wasn't a result of anything I did. To the contrary, I simply allowed the healing power of the Divine to come through and touch both of our hearts and souls.

Like the magical children we are, perfect and complete, we were both returned to the garden to be in the natural grace of Love.

To be the kids on Christmas morning, excited by the wonderment of life.

To be magic.

To be love.

To be.

Wisdom Teaching 11
Divine Evolution

"Evolution is the outward growth of our biological and psychological nature. As a Conscious Evolutionary, you have the capacity to positively or negatively influence the growth of your biological and psychological nature. That superpower in turn can change the world."
—Adam C. Hall

A butterfly that flaps its wings in the rainforest of Brazil creates a hurricane in the Caribbean. Collectively we are the creators of the world we experience. Individually each us has the same power as the butterfly. Each of us influences the world.

Mother Nature evolves according to the laws of the natural world. We, like Her, must do the same. Over the millennia, humankind has taken it upon itself to do as it pleases. The result of this mindset—one that puts itself apart from the natural order of Mother Nature—now threatens our very existence. I'm dedicating the rest of my life to help a billion people change their minds about how we do business and relate to one another and the planet. I need your help.

Scientists say that we are in a period of "punctuated evolution," meaning the rate of evolution occurs at a rapid pace. Throughout history, there have been only five such periods. Each has resulted in a major extinction of species. Sustainability will not be sufficient. We must create a clear intention to adapt to these great earth changes.

Climate change is not only happening in our outer environment but in our inner environment. To survive and adapt we need an evolutionary miracle. The miracle cannot be found in the same ego mindset that created the problem in the first place. We must shift our mindset to the genius Mind. That can only happen when we reawaken to our authentic Selves as Love.

The urgency is an opportunity. The crisis is the birth of the Divine Being. The future of humanity is in our hands. Men's teachings are a step-by-step process showing how you can become the evolutionary miracle and, in the process, find a life of peace, prosperity and Love.

The evolutionary journey requires us to put into practice each of Men's teachings. Now more than ever, with the significant earth changes that are underway, we need to be centered in our hearts as Love. Men's teachings remind us that we must learn to own our power and the responsibility that comes with it—or face with full force the consequences of refusing to do so.

Five Insights of Divine Evolution

> *"For the evolution of humanity to move forward, a titanic rebalancing of mind is required. Climate change and the technological revolution, like the agricultural and industrial revolutions, will mechanize humans. This way of thinking is not good or bad, right or wrong, moral or immoral. It is what it is."*
>
> —*Men*

The following five critical insights put forth by Men about Divine Evolution will help you evolve the authentic Self and genius Mind to the core of your Being. Evolution—like the oceans—ebbs and flows. As you go deeper into all of Men's teachings, continue to look at the life experiences that the ego mind offers. Are you experiencing evolution from the separate ego mind that creates separation and de-evolves? Or are you experiencing Life from your authentic

Self in your genius Mind—the mind that evolves Love and promotes peace and prosperity?

1. **Divine Evolution inspires the separated ego-self to awaken to the presence of Love in the authentic Self.** It acts to intervene with the ego mind's need to divide and conquer, which wants to continuously de-evolve into separation. Just like Love, God, and the authentic Self, the genius Mind is.
2. **When you dissolve the thought that you are separate from Love, you will evolve into the authentic Self and genius Mind.** Stillness promotes peace. Peace creates a condition that allows the genius Mind within to be heard, seen, and known. When the thought that you are separate dissolves, you are freed into Love.
3. **The evolution of humanity depends on your Divine Evolution.** When you remember your Oneness, you share your authentic Self in a divided world. Your evolution will save you from the hate, conflict, and chaos of the ego mind. Hatred, conflict, and chaos will not end, but your participation in it will.
4. **The genius Mind evolves from the eternal Divine Genius, whereas the ego mind evolves from body and dies**. The genius Mind knows that Life is infinite. You are Love that never dies.
5. **As a Divine Being, you are Love and Divine Evolution in action. You are the evolutionary miracle waiting to happen.** When you become aware of how the ego mind creates conflict and chaos in your life, you regain the power to evolve your life instead of life evolving you. As an artist of consciousness and cocreator of your life, nobody and nothing can take this inalienable right away.

The genius path that we walk together according to Men's teachings requires that we do the hard work. You can change which mind you choose—the ego or genius. We do not need to learn genius because we already are genius. We need only unlearn the ego mind.

For much of my life, I had no idea what it meant to be a conscious evolutionary, much less be Love. I woke up with the sun and went hunting for Love, money, and power. The more I felt the pain and suffering of human experience, the more I wanted to escape it. Initially, that was through hard work. Later it was with food, drugs, alcohol, and sex.

When I didn't feel right, I projected my anger and frustration onto others. These outbursts were rare at first, but they became more frequent as I focused on the dis-ease of my mind and fallibility of my body. This mindset functioned in a state fear, conflict, and death.

There are three similarities every human being shares.

1. The separate murderous mindset of the ego.
2. The Oneness, Loving, genius mindset.
3. The ability to choose between the two.

To walk the genius path, we are required to evolve consciously, unlearning the idea that we could be separate from Love. This Truth results in Oneness. All notions of separation fall away.

Men said, "You and others have been selected at this time of great earth changes to lead an expedition to the new frontier of humanity."

I wanted to tell him I didn't sign up for this, but something told me I had.

"Humanity has reached an evolutionary tipping point," he continued. "It is moving in slow motion compared to the speed of the universe. The ego design cannot sustain itself. A new way forward has come to humanity. Today I invite you to consider becoming a radical evolutionary."

"I'm not sure that tipping point sits well, Men. What can we do about it?"

"Nothing," he said. "Climate change and the tech revolution will also bring about many unexpected developments and benefits. By accepting all aspects of the revolution, you will stay in the center. However, from that center, you should and must—along with your fellow brothers and sisters of the earth—shift the collective mindset to the Divine Genius."

"And how do we do that?" I asked.

"Imagine a slingshot," he said. "In one hand, you clasp a small stone, and in the other the frame that holds the band."

"Yes, I can see it," I said.

"As you pull back on the stone, the band stretches. Still following?" Men said.

I nodded.

"Okay, now consider the following," he said. "The energy of evolution is the frame, and the evolution of humans is the stone. The stone has gone stationary, weighted down by the ego mind, and the frame has continued to move forward. At some point, the tension will build to such a degree that humans are launching themselves into the future. This thrust will have a tremendous force, and it will catapult humanity into the highest planes of consciousness. Do you see that?"

"Yes," I said. "So you're saying revolutions happen when the evolutionary energy reaches a breaking point. Then what happens?"

"A birth or paradigm shift emerges."

"So, what's the problem with that?" I said.

"The tension in this evolutionary inflection point has reached such a critical mass that when the stone—or humanity—is thrust forward, there will be consequences the likes of which have not been experienced in a millennium."

"How so?" I asked, trying to stay calm.

"It's the proverbial good and bad," he said. "On the 'bad' front, the sheer velocity of the thrust will burn off those aspects of humanity that are not necessary. Those aspects include war, economic disparity, social injustice, and other cultural influences that are inconsistent with Oneness. These event(s) will likely be the demise of millions of humans."

I took in a breath, trying to process what he was saying. Climate change, fire, flooding, and wars over land and resources are all too familiar. While we cannot control the world around us, we can collaborate with our evolution. The mental climate within could very well determine the fate of humanity. I began feeling a call to tend to my precious genius Mind.

"However," he said, "this will reorient humanity toward a shared destiny."

I felt the enormity of his words. He was laying out the future of humankind. It reminded me of Alberto's words, "There are no safe places Adam, only safe people." As I continued my quest to get out of this life alive, I recognized that my evolution was about the death of my ego mind and its attachment to survival thinking. Men's teachings inspired me to think and act from the genius Mind with a clear intention.

"Adam," he said, "the vast majority of humanity is not prepared for such an event. But you can take steps to mitigate the effects."

"And how do I do that?" I asked.

The Genius Process on Divine Evolution

This five-step Genius Process on Divine Evolution will help you with the effects of the significant changes happening on earth and in your inner Self. As you further practice the Genius Process, remember that the outside picture is a reflection on an inward condition.

Men feels that we ready for radical evolution. He has prepared us to take radical action as Divine Doers. If you're experiencing conflict and chaos in the outer world, your ego has taken control of how you are doing things. It reacts. And the reaction in the face of fear can be dangerous.

In contrast, Love in the genius Mind acts. This process will help create awareness of your ego and genius Mind so you can clearly choose between the two.

1. **Ask the question, "What do I need to know about the ego?"** Lose your mind, meaning set your ego mind aside. Know that you are more than your body, and become the mind that receives messages from the Divine Genius that will support your radical evolution inside and out.
2. **Listen for the answer, "Whom should I listen to?"** Focus on feelings of peace. As other emotions arise, become aware and intentionally return to peace. Radical evolution happens when you are still and in communion with Divine Evolution. This voice is one of reason, wisdom, and soul knowing. This voice does not create conflict and chaos.
3. **Acknowledge the problem the ego caused in your life by asking, "What do I see that has yet to be seen?"** Detach from even your genius Mind. In doing so, you will not lose your ability to function in the world. Instead, you will gain access to radical evolution. You will be given the vision to access the wisdom that has not been accessible to you before.
4. **Be open to the solution by asking, "How do I do things in life without doing them from the ego?"** Ask for spiritual direction in all things. Allow an invisible hand and voice to direct your thoughts, words, and actions. Whom do you choose as your guide—the Divine Genius Mind or the inauthentic self that connects to the ego mind? Your choice will ultimately determine how you find solutions to evolve past the significant earth changes we now face.
5. **Activate your genius by asking, "How shall I be?"** Simply be as you already are, Love. You are activated. You need to do nothing.

The solutions to the world's problems likely will emerge by acting from your genius Mind to see what is yet to be seen. Each of us has an earth mission. It's about how you do what you do, not what you do. Right now, you have a solution to help solve the problems we face. Without you, radical evolution cannot happen.

The Genius Process requires that we stay out of the ego mind. Our genius Mind and hearts can lead us beyond the crisis we face. As I moved into the final part of my quest for the Grail and the return to the kingdom "Home," I felt the Love of others guiding me. However, these feelings were not sufficient. I needed to take action. It was my job to complete the journey at hand and bring back the treasure to share. The fear that drove me at the beginning of this quest became the Love that guided me forward.

"We will talk more tomorrow," Men said. "Perhaps the sun will come out and lighten up this impending evolutionary miracle." With that, he quickly disappeared.

I hoped he was right. I sat for a few moments, feeling the urgency of his message. Maybe my quest to Peru would hold the secret to preparing for the evolutionary slingshot. I was certain that my own evolutionary miracle was at hand.

I found this reassuring, knowing that to be in the Temple of the Moon at midnight, I would need all the guides and angels I could get. Perhaps I would even need a miracle.

And then, as if on cue, I heard one of the cryptic messages Men had told me about.

"When you serve the Grail," it said, "you will Love as One."

23
Temple of the Moon

June 29, 2012

Before I embarked on my final adventure, I immersed myself in a bath. Over the years, I had taken soaks of an hour or more to journey into other dimensions. Attuned to the magical properties of water, I found that a long bath delivered me into the depths of my soul work as I let the warmth of the water surround and carry me while I meditated.

During the past few months, my work with Men had been about riding the winds of great change. But tonight, on the cusp of receiving the Holy Grail, I stepped into the bath with one intention: to align the spiritual essence of water with the spiritual essence of the moon. Just like the staff, activated to receive transmissions from other realms, my body would receive and transmute energy into a feeling, a thought, and a word.

As I lay back in the water, I repeated an affirmation: *I am ready to receive.* Before long, I became nearly immobile as I drifted off into the subtle realm. The bath was working its magic, washing away the anxiety of what I'd been asked to do at midnight. The cab was coming by the hotel at eleven o'clock. Before heading to the Temple of the Moon, I figured it would be best to have a light meal and a cup of coca tea, made from the leaves of the coca plant, which would give me some sustenance and energy for my adventure.

Knowing it could dip near freezing during the night, I put on a pair of jeans, a long-sleeved undershirt, and a sweater. I also planned to bring a Patagonia parka and gloves just in case the conditions warranted it. It was now nearly ten o'clock. The state of ease after my bath quickly wore off. I began to breath heavily from Cusco's ten-thousand-foot altitude, exacerbated by my anxiety.

I hurried to the restaurant in the hotel lobby to order something before they closed for the night.

"*Hola, señor,*" the waiter said with a smile.

"*Hola,*" I said. "I'd like to have a cup of coca tea and shrimp salad please."

"Anything else?" he asked.

"Thank you," I said. "That will be all for now."

Such an ordinary conversation. The waiter had no idea what I was about to do. And, honestly, neither did I.

It felt surreal to be sitting in a restaurant on my way to a life-changing moment. I thought back over all the instructions and wisdom teachings I'd received. I could feel the Divine Genius within me from time to time. But how would I feel two hours from now? Would I be discovered and end up in jail? Would I lose myself in the mystery of the temple? Would I even be alive? If I was to be born into a new paradigm of life, what would happen to me as the old one died?

I felt as though I had one foot in the physical world of everyday life and another that was completely removed. I knew from previous experiences that high adventure meant a high rite of passage, which was always about threading the needle of the finite and infinite. It required the utmost attention, awareness, and consciousness. But I was nervous and losing my appetite fast.

I nibbled on a stale cracker and sipped the coca tea. When I realized the tea was depressing my appetite, I pushed it away and waited for my salad.

"*Muchas gracias, señor,*" I said to my waiter when he arrived with my meal. The salad looked enticing, but I picked at it, wondering if this was my last supper. Was I about to experience the resurrection after death—or the death before resurrection? Something had to die before birth, right?

I am an old soul, but I am yet to be born. A young soul was soon to emerge.

I headed back up to my room to ready my backpack. I double-checked to make sure my flashlight, candles, gloves, and mesa bag were all in place. Fortunately the weather looked clear, but the lack of cloud cover could make it even colder on the mountain. I put on my parka, then strapped on my backpack. So far, so good.

I picked up the guitar case with the staff and immediately realized it was too bulky. Shedding the case, I pulled out the staff and managed to slide most of it into the deepest pocket of the backpack, with part of the double helix serpent and the sun symbol extending out the top. I zipped the pack tight around it to secure it in place. With that, I was ready.

As the hotel room door closed behind me, I stopped for a moment. *Am I coming back?*

I visualized my return from the Temple of the Moon in a few hours, arriving at the hotel and getting back into bed. Clarity of intention was always a good idea when riding the evolutionary edge.

"*Hola, se habla ingles?*" I asked the driver as I crawled into the back an old stinky cab.

"*Un poco*," he said, confirming that he spoke a little English.

"I am going to the Temple of the Moon, please." The driver didn't say anything, but he hesitated, a slight pause. I could tell he was taken aback by my request at this time of night.

Nevertheless, he looked ahead, and we drove down the cobblestone road. The city was empty. Cusco was a place where the people rose with the sun and returned home not long after the sun went down. Only a few tourist bars and restaurants remained open. The temperature had already dropped into the low forties.

The cab wove its way through the city streets and onto the hillside that would take us to the temple. The route was like a snake that coiled in preparation to attack or defend. I looked out the window, quiet and contemplative. Would I become a new person within the temple? Would I come Home to God again? What was really going to happen? And most of all, would I get out of this lifetime—this night, this temple—alive?

The serpent wove its way around my staff, and I would descend into the Serpent's Cave before long. Would I be bitten by the snake's venom or protected by its fierce defenses?

Just as we reached the apex of the hill, I noticed the moon was nowhere to be found. I had hoped it would provide some much-needed light. Instead, it was pitch black out, with only the stars twinkling in the sky.

The cab came to a stop at a parking area about two hundred yards from the temple.

"*Aqui*?" the driver asked.

"*Sí*," I said. "This will do."

It was twenty minutes after eleven. I gathered my belongings and stepped out of the cab into the cold, clear air. I felt certain why I was here. But in the darkness, I was not so certain how to penetrate the perimeter of the Temple.

"*Señor*," I said to the cab driver, "please wait here. I will be back in about one hour. Do not leave until I get back, *por favor*." I wondered what he thought, and if he was nervous about being here. I certainly didn't want him to hightail it back to Cusco. The last thing I need was to get stuck at the temple in the middle of the night.

"*Sí, Señor*," he said. "*Ten cuidado. Es muy peligroso.*"

I appreciated his warning me of danger and hoped he would keep his commitment to stay.

"*Gracias*," I said, taking a deep breath and looking at the shadow of the stone temple against the hillside.

I moved from the parking lot to the edge of a grassy field. The path I had laid out earlier in the day was impossible to see in the darkness. I needed the nocturnal vision of Jaguar Jon. Had it been only a matter of days since I'd met him? How could my whole life come to an end—or a beginning—in such a short time?

I searched for the starting point of the path and, as my eyes grew more accustomed to the inky blackness, finally spotted it at the western edge of the lot. In my backpack were two of the most precious and sacred material things I owned: my mesa and staff. The double helix portion of the staff still protruded from the backpack, with the two serpent heads' ruby and emerald eyes just above the top of my head. I thought of the union of those serpents, intertwining masculine and feminine energy around one central pillar. Somehow I felt stronger with them close by.

Training the flashlight ahead of me, I proceeded with baby steps. At this rate, I wasn't sure I would enter the temple by midnight. I shone the flashlight at the ground directly below my feet, hoping there were no guards to see it.

Suddenly, I could see a light coming from the other side of the temple. *Are they excavating at night?* It was dead silent, except for the pounding of my heart. *These are the moments when you become the jaguar,* I thought, walking as silent as the moon.

As I approached the temple, I saw a flashlight scanning the grounds near the western side. Then a voice cut though the thin, cold night air. It was a guard talking on a radio. I crouched down in the tall pampas grass. The jaguar within me was fully activated, and my senses were on high alert. Even my skin felt the slightest changes in temperature from one step to the next. I could feel the breath of the moon as it rose.

The entrance to the cave loomed about two hundred feet ahead, but it might as well have been miles.

At 11:40 p.m., the fear of the moment suddenly lifted. My heartbeat found a soft, gentle rhythm, in flow with the present moment. Instead of being on high alert, my senses were in a state of high presence. Still, yet fluid, I moved closer to the entrance to the cave of death and rebirth without my flashlight. I was like the jaguar, crouching and stalking the cave entrance.

A floodlight illuminated the temple on the exact opposite side from where I stood, and the guard was nowhere in sight. I was on the dark side of the moon.

I would have expected the entrance to the sacred altar to be on the west, representing the death or surrender of the past, or on the east, symbolizing the birth or emergence of the future. Instead, it was situated on the north side of the temple.

In the shamanic four directions, the north represents the ancient one. It's the access point to the wisdom of the ages. The north is home to the sweetness and joy of living in the world. It reminds us of the hummingbird, to drink from the nectar of life, to live in joy.

It also represents the immortal and eternal life.

I was just steps away from the entrance to the cave. I could see the opening. It was shaped like a *yoni*, or vaginal entrance, and was framed by rocks. The entrance itself was pitch black, a dark hole. But in that darkness, I felt the magnetic Life Force pulling me in.

I quickly looked right, then left. The coast was clear. As I bowed my head, I touched the earth, took a deep breath, and dashed into the cave. Grabbing hold of the serpent railing, I took one step at a time.

My heart was racing now. Inch by inch, I slid my hand across the serpent's cold body. I had forgotten how far I needed to go to get to the altar. As I looked back, the entrance was beginning to disappear. The cave was gently descending from the entrance level and curving slightly to the right.

Before long, I could neither see the entrance or what lay in front. I placed each footstep gingerly, feeling my way along and hoping I wouldn't tumble headlong into the blackness. Then I stood for a moment and took a deep breath, suspended between where I'd been and where I was going next.

24

Conscious Cocreators

It's a sunny afternoon in Santa Barbara, and I'm at the home of the renowned futurist, visionary, and New Thought leader Barbara Marx Hubbard, who Lizanne calls "my other girlfriend." As usual, we're sitting on her deck. She's sipping a pinot grigio, I have a Pellegrino in front of me, and we're actively engaged in mapping the cosmos.

"You're the Holy Host, you know," she says to me. She's said it many times, reminding me of my essence. "Share that when you speak," she says. "*Be* that."

I nod, admiring the wisdom in this radiant silver-haired woman who seems to always be smiling. Deepak Chopra once called her "the voice for conscious evolution," a fitting title for someone who has devoted herself to global change through her many books and teachings.

In her eighties, she is a living example of the Holy Host, and I'm grateful to consider her a close friend. We met when my literary agent invited me to a fundraiser for a documentary about her life, and she invited me to call her so we could get acquainted. In our first conversation, we discussed the challenges we both faced in birthing "the new human."

She eventually invited me to join the Evolutionary Leaders circle and was there supporting me on Morgan's wedding day, when I convened the gathering in Santa Barbara, building community and sharing the light.

Now, countless conversations later, our dialogues are like spirited games of volleyball, lobbing ideas and "what ifs" at one another, effortlessly moving back and forth in our shared roles as teacher and student, master and apprentice.

Today we're talking about her big dream. "What do you want to see for humanity?" I ask her.

"I want to see the interconnectivity of all beings in the whole higher mind of the planet," she says. This is not a random wish. As the author of a seminal work on conscious evolution, she has chronicled that interconnectivity. She knows how it's wired. She knows that one day it will be consciously manifested in us all.

I'm humbled to be in the presence of her genius—and her vulnerability. To see her as a light being and a human one at the same time. We are whole mates, bringing our complete selves to our friendship and creating a holy space for our expression of the Divine.

"We meet in the mind," she says. "The higher mind. The noosphere, the ultimate meeting place in which we serve the greater needs of the planet." Without knowing it, she is sowing the seeds in my mind of a new technology, a system that recognizes people for their genius and guides them toward social interactions and teamwork in which they can share their gifts.

"We will evolve into light beings," she says, taking a sip of her wine. "The *homoluminous.* The universal human. Our DNA is shifting, you know. We're not just skin and bones. When we evolve into the higher spheres of consciousness, our auras will become light bulbs for others to attune to. We will fully express the highest vibration of God's light and love."

I look out over the flowers and shrubs in her gardens and to the horizon beyond. "We are always evolving, aren't we?" I say, more as a reflection than a question.

"Yes," my friend says. "You and I are mappers of that evolution. What was your route, Adam? How did you get where you are now?"

I thought of that question many times. It intertwined with Alberto's question about getting out of this lifetime alive, just like the serpents intertwined on my staff. The more clearly I mapped my own journey, the more I realized it was delivering me to a place I'd never expected.

Solitude.

An inner knowing.

Home.

In all the chaos and angst of my personal and business life, I'd been surrounded by other people and their expectations, which often collided with my own. With each step on my evolutionary journey, I went deeper inside myself. I felt like I was entering a garden with a tranquil pond, and it felt good to sit on the edge of that water by myself, reflecting on its stillness.

I hadn't always been willing to go inside. Whenever I heard others talk of an inner journey, my ego judged them for it, assuming they were crazy to sacrifice their life—no matter how miserable it might be—for the unknown. And besides, were they really prepared to meet the gargoyles and ax murderers that lived within them? As bad as I felt on the outside, I couldn't imagine I'd find anything worth looking for on the inside.

But once *A Course in Miracles* and other teachings gave me the courage to get past the guards at the gate of my own ego, I found myself called further and further within not to a place of drama, but to peace. To that still pond. To a place where I wasn't *by* myself, but *with* myself.

In that place, I learned the power of Source as our abiding companion.

I learned that Truth is the opposite of what the world teaches.

I saw the dichotomies of life. I could be in a cemetery and feel only aliveness. I could witness tragedy and feel only deep love. I could be alone and feel only companionship.

In solitude, there is a knowing that transcends consciousness. A simple knowing of what is true within you. The knowing of Self as God, as love, as joy.

In solitude, I found the fullness I'd been seeking in all my travels, relationships, and business deals. While hiking in the mountains or driving down the freeway, I focused within and found a peace that was always there to meet me. It didn't depend on what I was doing, who I was with, or how much money I had in my bank account. It was the meeting place. The Christ and Buddha mind. The totality of being. My inner genius.

I felt the true power of solitude when I shared it with four hundred people from around the world on one of Barbara's webinars.

She was teaching a one-year online program on birthing the new human. The idea, as we had talked about many times during our conversations in her backyard, was to create a "landing field" for Divine energy within each of us.

While part of our journey is conscious *evolution*, ascending up to the heavens, the other is Divine *Involution*, as Source flows down into and through us. Preparing the landing field means being ready to receive that energy. And where do we do that best? In solitude.

"Would you come on my next webinar and talk about that?" Barbara asked me one chilly day, when we'd moved our outdoor conversation inside by the fireplace.

"Of course," I said, honored to be asked. "Is there something specific you'd like me to share?"

"Talk about your own evolution," she said. "As a species, we've evolved to the point where the Divine nature of being has begun to penetrate the human energy system. How do you experience this in your own life? How can others understand what it means to be a universal human, allowing their Divine Genius to reveal itself in real time?"

On the ninety-minute call, I shared the challenges I'd faced in my life. "They led me to what *A Course in Miracles* calls the Holy Instant," I said. "That's the moment when we remember our oneness with Self, Spirit, and all of humanity. It is an instant in which the Truth is revealed: the only obstacles to completion and harmony are in our own fears. But in our genius Minds, those fears don't really exist. In the Holy Instant, healing happens. You can experience complete forgiveness. Pure potential. Your own inner genius, connected and at one with Source."

By the end of the webinar, after communing with hundreds of people from all over the globe, I felt exhilarated and alive. My landing field had expanded, and I was receiving more Divine love moment by moment.

"Thank you, Barbara," I said to my friend, feeling enriched to be part of her creation. I could feel that something important had happened for everyone on the call. But the moment of deepest knowing happened when Barbara ended the webinar, and I saw all the callers logging out one by one.

Years before, I would have felt lonely, wondering if I'd ever be that connected again.

Now, as much as I'd enjoyed the webinar, I looked forward to the silence that followed. A chance to be with myself and God and experience the involution within.

In our own way, we are all mapping the cosmos and birthing the new human. I was doing it not by being the hero, but by allowing Spirit to flow from the heavens and extend Itself through me. That was my real story.

Evolution and involution, the meeting place of heaven and earth.

Wisdom Teaching 12
Divine Involution

"You are a Divine Being who amplifies the Love of the Divine Genius. Involution is the descent of the Divine into your heart and genius Mind. Through your authentic Self, Love flows into all that you do."
—Adam C. Hall

Divine involution brings us to the end of Men's wisdom teachings. Involution brings us full circle. The thirteenth wisdom teaching completes our return to the place we never left, our spiritual Home. Let me repeat the T. S. Elliot quote from the beginning of this journey to genius: "We shall not cease from exploration, and the end of all our exploring will be to arrive where we started. And know the place for the first time."

Our journey takes us back to the place we set out from to find that everything we were searching for was always here right inside us. The ego did not want us to discover that, so it sent us on a wild goose chase called a spiritual path. On that path, we become eternal seekers and will go to the ends of the earth, swapping out old roadmaps for shiny new ones with more outrageous promises. All we have to show for our searching is discarded and recycled roadmaps, dwindling faith in an empty bank account, and ourselves, still searching for answers in the outside world.

Men inspires us to become conscious of the seeking mindset. These teaching are vital to getting beyond the paradigm of endless seeking. Are you addicted to the ego promise of finding enlightenment and becoming an expert, elite spiritual seeker, teacher, or guru, with the ego prestige that comes with that seeking? Or are you willing to strip yourself bare of all masks and go nowhere but deep into the core of your own false story, to discover beneath it all is that shiny, untrammeled, authentic Divine Source of All Being?

Yes, some people have to go to the ends of the earth and do all this seeking to find the Truth. But we do have a choice. Why wait lifetimes for what you can do now? It is not a question if we get on the genius path; it's only a question of when. We can stop now and let go of all that we are identifying with and start by getting quiet and listening to that still small voice that lives deep within our hearts.

Men inspired me to listen to the inner voice—the one that has the answer to every question you'll ever have. No roadmap, no teaching, and nothing outside of yourself is needed to get you to where you want to go. Why? There is no "there, there." You are already at the exact right place. You need do nothing. When you arrive Home after the long journey of seeking on the genius path, you realize that it's the place you never left.

Your guides may take you somewhere off the beaten track to help you find the Love within. That which you long and yearn for is longing and yearning for you to go deep enough to find it. You get to choose when to take the journey. The planet needs you now. Men came to me to share not only his teachings, but the urgency to activate my genius Mind and share his wisdom with others. He offers this little secret:

"To create a powerful harmony between your evolutionary and involutionary nature, where the functionality of light and soul are in real time, sync with the clock and calendar time. The more you harmonize your evolutionary and involutionary nature, the more you can sync with your genius Mind and the Divine Universal Genius Mind."

My time with Men was coming to an end. I began to realize that I had yet to do the most challenging work. The hardest part of the journey was not about showing up to evolve my consciousness. It was about showing up and fulfilling my mission. The end of this quest was looking like the beginning. I had chosen to take this adventure into an unknown ending, and paradoxically, I sensed that the experience had chosen me to pave the way to a new beginning.

It was becoming clear that I would need to integrate his teachings into my life of relationship and vocation. As you read these words, imagine the journey I took from 2012—when Men shared these teachings—until now. I have spent thousands of hours in deep inner work. Traveled and walked thousands of miles into a destination unknown. Studied, practiced, and shared these teachings to help others, potentially saving them years or lifetimes of searching.

Men's wisdom teachings are a roadmap to the inner world that all human beings share. The teachings take us back to the source of our ego mind. With Men as my guide, I began moving beyond the ego mind and experiencing the genius within. It's not the only map available; there are many. In the end, the only map that counts is the one you create with your unique genius.

The genius map that Men gave me was a straight shot to what lay beyond the ego mind. It's a direct connection to the Source. He helped clear away the obstacles that prevented me from remembering my authentic Self and my link to the Divine Universal Genius, a.k.a. the Quantum Field. Clearing the obstacles links you to your limitless potential.

Men knew that human nature in free will could take you down paths that are dead ends. He knew that the genius path is not for the fate of the heart. It takes courage. Most of all, it takes Love. It takes a guide that comes from beyond the ego mind. We need do nothing and be still but a moment. The guide will come to take you Home.

Five Insights into Divine Involution

"Involution is the power beyond the space-time continuum. It is the power that pulls you with love into Love. Evolution pushes you with fear into

Love. The past pushes from the ego and the future pulls from genius. Involution draws you back to who you have always been as a Divine Being. Evolution aspires to do something. Involution inspires to be authentic."

—Men

The following five critical insights put forth by Men about Divine Involution will help you find the courage you need to complete your journey Home. Insights offer us a chance to look at the existing reality of our lives and evolve that reality into what feels right and true in our hearts.

Men's teachings share that we are the dreamers of the dream we experience. To that end, his map to genius takes us back to the dreamer in the genius Mind. Now we are asked to reclaim the power and Divine Life Force to dream a new dream for the world in which we live.

1. **Authentic power comes from the universe and flows through your genius Mind into the body and the world.** The Divine Involutionary paths of Peace, Prosperity, and Love are not of us. However, they flow through us. Involution flows from a sea of unlimited possibilities. Scientists call this sea the Quantum Field. In this field, everything already exists. To receive this flow, you must be in the frequency and vibration of the Quantum Field.
2. **Ask, and it shall be given.** Your genius Mind has the power of unlimited manifestation.
3. When the genius Mind and heart are in alignment with the Divine Universal Genius Mind, the energy of the Quantum Field can flow into your body and manifest your heart's intent. The secret? You can only give what you have received. Receive the Love that flows with Divine Involution, and what you ask for will be provided.
4. **The heart receives the Love of the Divine Genius. The Divine Involutionary flow connects the heart and genius Mind.** The biological eyes and ears are extensions of the ego

mind. The genius Mind uses your eyes and ears to see and hear from the heart.

5. **The choice for the genius Mind is the choice for Love and Oneness.** Divine Involution creates experiences with a straightforward choice. The opportunity for the ego mind and its identification with the body is a choice for hate and separation. The genius Mind, as Love, does not hate the body, it uses it to share Love. Love nurtures the body to function peacefully and lovingly.
6. **Bonus: There is no Love outside of us.** Divine Involution and Evolution are forces of nature. We cannot have one without the other. Oneness does not separate out love on the outside from Love on the inside. Receiving Love is the same act as giving Love. The Divine Genius Mind gives Love, and the genius Mind and heart in you receive Love. As you receive Love, you can give Love. The more you give, the more you get.

Evolution is a biological force that has evolved our bodies, brains, and entire physical design. Also, evolution spirals us upward into states of expanded consciousness. Involution is the Divine Force that descends into our biological nature as humans in a body. The two meet in the genius Mind. When they meet is unknown. They cannot meet until we awaken our authentic Selves as Love. Men's teachings were a lesson that helped guide me back to Love.

When I was a boy, I learned early lessons about force and power. The explosion of the grapefruit cannon that left third-degree burns on my leg taught me about destructive power, as did my ex-wife's anger and my self-sabotaging use of alcohol and drugs.

But I learned lessons about positive power, too. Power of love for my daughters, forgiveness for my mom, and my soul commitment with Lizanne all served to evolve my consciousness. I was beginning to feel the Divine Force of Involution.

The two kinds of power may seem different, but they're like the electric charges in alternating current. They're part of the same whole, sometimes changing direction. Like the positive and negative terminals of a battery, both are necessary for energy to flow.

That, Men told me, is an apt metaphor for evolution—and the lesser-known or understood involution. The connectivity of positive and negative energy plugs us into our soul experience. But the involutionary current makes us the receptacle of the Divine Will. It is the Holy Spirit flowing through us.

The ego mind equates this Divine energy with death—the end of its identity. But when we see ourselves as receptacles and channels of pure Love, we participate in conscious involution, which holds the key to humanity's destiny.

"The evolutionary nature of your physical life on earth has evolved over thousands of years," Men said. "Evolution exists in the space-time continuum. It propels and pushes you forward."

"Yes," I said. "I see that."

"Involution is the power beyond the space-time continuum. It is the power that pulls you rather than pushes into Love. It draws you back to who you have always been as a Divine Being. Evolution aspires. Involution inspires," he said.

"Then what role does free will play?" I asked.

"You are not asked to surrender your free will," Men said. "Instead, involution brings you into the will of God within you so it may fully express itself in the oneness of who you are. The meeting place with God's will is the altar of grace and God. To go there is no small journey. It's the frontier of consciousness, where it tips into Truth and knowledge. That's the journey."

I thought about how many times I had blindly tried to "fix" my life years before. Not only did I not have the right tools, but I also couldn't see where my problems originated.

As I matured spiritually and deliberately, I understood that my own ego mind was the source of everything I wanted to change. I had evolved in that way. But now Men was describing a step beyond conscious evolution. I was standing at the fulcrum point connecting heaven and earth, with nothing to do but receive.

"How do we take that journey?" I said, looking to Men as always for concrete, practical steps.

The Genius Process on Divine Involution

This five-step Genius Process on Divine Involution takes the final step on the return Home. From here, it's up to God.

1. **Ask the question, "What do I need to know about the ego?"** Surrender to the involutionary impulse of the Divine. Feel this in your body as you relax and trust the higher power of Love flowing through you.
2. **Listen for the answer, "Whom should I listen to?"** Ask for the union of your authentic Self with the Divine Genius. In this instant you'll see and experience Oneness. You will likely feel resistance from your ego, but focus on the emotions of Peace and Love instead.
3. **Acknowledge the problem the ego caused in your life by asking, "What do I see that has yet to be seen?"** See yourself and others without judgment through the eyes of Love, which represents the genius Mind in you.
4. **Be open to the solution by asking, "How do I do things in life without doing them from the ego?"** Be open to receiving and seeing the presence of the Divine in you and the world. For example, look at the magnificence of what humans have created in architecture and art. Know that these are outward representations of the involutionary impulse within.
5. **Activate your genius by asking, "How shall I be?"** Be a receptacle that receives the Divine Involutionary flow of Love from the Divine Genius. Be the Love that you already are.

Men said that Divine Evolution and Involution are not only about what you do with these forces of nature, but about learning the nature of these forces. To fully understand, it's important to see all Thirteen Wisdom Teachings as a progression.

The Foundational Stage of the Body includes True Forgiveness, True Purpose, Death and Divine Life.

The Awakening Stage of the Heart includes Peace, Love, and True Function.

The Activation Stage of the Soul includes Destiny, Divine Doing, and Divine Being.

The Completion Stage of the mind includes Divine Evolution and Divine Involution. These last two mark the completion of the journey to genius. Instead of being apart and separate from the universe, you are whole and One with it. These teachings mark the birth of the new human and the next evolution of humanity. They prepare you for the final step of Oneness that will be taken by the Divine Genius.

Before leaving our session for the day, I was able to see Men in a new way. He was not so serious or in master teacher mode. I could sense that he was pleased with our work and my progress. Knowing that I had much to still experience, Men was preparing to give me his summary of his wisdom teachings.

"This is wholeness," Men said. "From wholeness, you stand in the totality of heaven and earth and make yourself available to the benevolent Divine Force."

"So evolution is like the 'up' escalator," I said, "as we aspire to go higher and achieve more. And involution is like the 'down' escalator, descending from the heavens to meet us where we are."

"That's it exactly," Men said. "It is how grace emerges from the great mystery into your everyday life experience. Evolution evokes an ascent toward something, whereas involution inspires an inner discovery and connection. When these two forces of nature meet in the genius Mind, you can become One with the Divine Genius."

I was about to make the most significant inner discovery of my life, fulfilling my assignment on the altar at midnight. My date with destiny was now. The meeting of my evolutionary and involutionary nature was on the altar in the womb of the Divine Mother. Was I to die or live? The answer to my original question, "Could I get out of this lifetime alive?" was soon to be known.

"Adam," Men said, reading my thoughts once again, "fear not your de-evolution. Simply embrace your involution. The Genius Process can be reasonably gentle if done consciously with wisdom and guidance."

I prayed that God would be with me, and that Men's words were true.

25

Rebirth

June 29, 2012

The cave felt cold and slightly damp. Far enough from the entrance to escape the view of the guard, I turned on my flashlight. In its illumination, it looked unlike an earthen cave. While it descended into the earth, it was constructed entirely with stone. If I had time, I thought, I would listen to those stones. I could only imagine what history they had recorded.

A few steps away was the main chamber. I knew from my previous visit that the altar, formed by a slab of rock measuring about four by five feet, sat in the exact center. I could feel its energy even before I took those final steps into the heart of the temple, then my heart and breath quickened as I felt the magnitude of entering the sacred chamber.

I was in the womb of the Universal Mother. As I stood still and stared at the stone altar, I could feel Her love flowing through me.

I set down my backpack, took out the candles and lit four of them, then placed them around the altar. I set my mesa on the altar and carefully laid the staff next to it. I knelt next to the altar and said out loud the words that flowed through me.

May the light of God shine upon this sacred moment. Thy Kingdom and Queendom come, thy will be done. As in heaven so on earth. Dear Mother, may the light of your heart shine upon my soul.

It was 11:50 p.m. The countdown to midnight had begun. I was now in Divine Time, and only God's hand could determine what would happen from here.

A Course in Miracles says we're living a death experience in our lives every day. Our fears about our physical safety—our bodies, our finances, our relationships, our wellbeing—dominate our thoughts, preventing us from fully living.

Now I had returned to the inner sanctum to find new life, guided by the serpent into the earth. I tried to focus on my conception day, the moment of my beginning. But my ego mind had turned vicious, desperately trying to wield its power. *Don't forget,* it told me over and over, *the Temple of the Moon is also called the Cave of Death.*

At the appointed hour, I rose to stand in front of the altar, placing my hands over my heart. *From my heart to your heart, dear Mother, I live in service to your Divine Grace.* I picked up the mesa with my left hand and held it on my heart. Then I picked up the staff with my right hand and placed in on top of the mesa.

Feeling the embrace and support of their energy, I turned around and sat down on the altar. It was time. The eighty days had led up to this moment. My whole life—and lifetimes before that—had guided me to this place.

Slowly, gently, I lay back until my head came to rest on the stone slab. I felt its cold, hard surface even through my parka and watched the flickering shadows from the candles dance on the walls and ceiling.

How many ancients were there with me? How many souls of the Incas? What had occurred at this altar? What offerings had been made here?

That sacred stone slab held the ancient wisdom of the never-ending creation, the universal Truths of death and rebirth. I lay alone in the stillness and felt a momentary terror of claustrophobia. Would I be buried alone in this cave?

Then I looked into the cylinder in the sky, and I began to feel at ease. I had made a conscious decision to come here for this, my moment of ultimate sacrifice. Not to give up my life, but to give up the illusions I thought defined my existence. My way of life as I knew it.

After a few minutes, I began to still my mind and become fully present. As I opened my eyes, I looked straight up to the ceiling above. The altar was situated below a long cylinder that protruded through the temple. I looked straight to the sky, heaven, the Father above. I was looking directly into infinity.

The cylinder symbolically represented what's known in Hindu tradition as the *lingam*, a phallus worshipped as a symbol of the god Shiva. As I looked above me, I saw this masculine symbol of the Heavenly Father penetrating the vaginal opening of Mother Earth. And my soul center was the exact connecting point of the two.

It was a Divine Union indeed.

I lay still, surrendering to the majesty and grace of universal love. On the slab of stone, I felt as though I dropped and left my body behind. The conception process was underway, and I knew that the fertilization of the Divine in my lone soul was eminent.

It began slowly, almost imperceptibly, as I felt an expansion of every cell in my body. Any earthly boundaries of my body and mind dissolved as the expansion grew and vibrated, pulsing with creation's explosive force. Every cell was opening to receive.

In a flash, light flooded every aspect of my being, as though I was being impregnated with the semen of creation. For several minutes, the light continued, pinning me to the table with a sustained climax of energy and Life Force that felt like repeated bolts of lightning.

My mesa and my activated staff, I realized, were not there to protect me. Instead, they served as magnets for the energy, like lightning rods that drew the bursts straight to my soul.

My heart raced, my breath quickened. I resisted the urge to resist and instead surrendered to the forces at work in my energy field. *So this is what death feels like,* I thought. *So this is what birth feels like.*

I felt tugged forward and back, as though I was descending through the birth canal while it contracted over and over again. As much as I tried to breathe into the process, I felt the sheer terror of leaving my old physical world behind, and my body shook in a tug-of-war between God and my ego.

I was being ripped from the womb, and a part of me screamed silently. *I want to go back. Let me go back.* But I was being pushed from my past into a new reality.

One last push. I had come all the way back to my conception day, and my rebirth was almost complete. Still shaking and cold, I emitted one last gasp, like a squall in the violence of rebirth.

And then I heard it. A soft voice.

The Holy of all Holies, arriving not with a bang, but with a whisper.

"May the Truth be told, let all others know, their voice must be heard and their light must be seen. Serve the Divine. Show and share the new story: Love as One."

I felt the presence of It, the Divine Grace of the Universe, settling into my cellular body. *So this is what it feels like to take your first breath of Life.*

Love as oneness. The complete and total absence of fear. A purity so profound that it could only be revelation and what *A Course in Miracles* calls the Holy Instant.

I was fully spiritualized as a living manifestation of light in the world. After my long journey, I had emerged from this lifetime alive.

I lay on the stone slab inert and numb, unsure whether I still had a body. Slowly I felt my arms and legs again, aware of the hard surface under my back. As I looked skyward, I began to weep from the intense beauty of the experience. But as I came back into my body, I was disoriented, at first forgetting where I was.

When I looked overhead and saw the cylinder of light, I knew I needed to leave quickly. It was the final push of my rebirth. But instead of being reborn into the duality of life, I felt as though my DNA had been altered, understanding the unity of all beings with God.

I had found the Holy Grail: heaven and earth coming together as One. I rose from the altar and gathered the mesa and staff. Then I knelt before the altar and felt the majestic touch of the Great Mother. Her heart had been laid on my soul. The moment had come, and the conception was received.

I packed my mesa and staff in my backpack, blew out the candles, and retraced my steps with the help of my flashlight. When I neared the entrance to the cave, I turned off the torch to stay undetected and slowly found my way out into the night.

As I stepped out onto the grass field, I felt a sense of emergence. The darkness no longer seemed ominous, the cold air no longer uncomfortable.

I looked behind me at the temple and took in a sudden breath of awe.

The entire structure was aglow.

Ahead of me, the moon was rising just above the treetops, illuminating the night sky—and the Grail Castle—with a soft white essence. Symbolically, I had drunk Christ's blood from the goblet—the blood of the Divine Mother giving me new life.

I smiled, silently said, "Thank you," then walked back through the grassy field to the waiting cab. I felt as though I had a whole new set of eyes and ears, a match for my new heart and soul.

26
Letting Go

Just like a wave of energy rises up and falls away, our evolution can sometimes feel like an awakening, but we can also be pulled back temporarily into the old design. By 2012, I knew my mission was planetary stewardship, but I wasn't so sure where or how I would ground myself as an EarthKeeper. I only knew that the answers would come from the only source there is: within.

I became fully engaged in what I now call the EarthKeeper Alliance in real estate, doing environmental work for commercial purposes. I became a benefit corporation. I adopted a quadruple bottom line of people, planet, and profits with purpose. If you don't have purpose, I asked myself, what good is everything else?

My book was coming out, but I didn't know who I was as an author, teacher, and storyteller. I knew I had qualities of leadership and stewardship, but I hadn't fully claimed them yet.

In shamanic traditions, shamans are not simply healers with rattles and feathers. They're storytellers, they're artists, they're leaders. Everyone is a shaman. The progression I adopted was that the priest becomes the healer, the healer becomes the artist, the artist becomes the leader, and the leader becomes the steward.

I was transitioning from my old 1.0 business model—the one in which so many people are living and feeling exhausted—to one in which what I do and who I am are one and the same. That was the choice. And in all my studies and experience with shamanic traditions, I had learned one thing for sure. We always have a choice. Will we make that choice from fear or love?

When I left for Peru in 2012, I carried Lizanne's voice and spirit with me in my heart, and I turned to her over and over again for encouragement and support, just as I had for the past several years. She'd been with me when I felt I'd break under the weight of my financial problems and family challenges.

"Adam," she told me again and again, "as far as I'm concerned, you're the father of the century." After everything I'd been through, she knew how much that meant to me.

Our time together was easy. In the evenings and weekends, we'd head to the beach and play Frisbee or go out for dinner, maybe see some friends. A great cook, she loved to make meals for us at home. When we weren't working, we were connected, spending as much time as we could with one another, even if was a trip to the supermarket or hardware store.

But as we moved into 2012, and as I prepared for the next trip to Peru, I intuitively knew the time was coming for us to wind down our relationship. As easy and comfortable as it felt, it wasn't serving us as it once had. When I asked Spirit, "What is it for?" I heard a clear answer: "Lizanne makes it easier for you to deal with pain and challenges in your life." I appreciated that more than I could convey. However, what was I doing for her? We had established our friendship and romance when our inner trajectories were closely aligned. But our paths had diverged, a natural consequence of growth.

When Men came into my life in April 2012, Lizanne knew me as a metaphysician. She shared my deep interest in mythology and the mystical part of the human experience. While she couldn't relate on a personal level, she allowed me to be in that experience. Yet I couldn't always express to her what I was experiencing. We began needing different things in our own time.

And that, in contrast to the fullness of solitude I felt, created a sense of being alone. At time, I found more fulfillment in my inner journey than in the one Lizanne and I were taking hand in hand.

When I asked Spirit, "Is our soul purpose being fulfilled?" I tried not to hear the response, but I couldn't ignore the Truth. The answer was no.

So when I was in Peru, I thought of Lizanne back home in Santa Barbara—as loving and thoughtful as ever, on her own path of evolution. The death and rebirth of our relationship was coming, and it touched me to my very core.

Relationships, my friend Barbara taught me, evolve through four key progressions: Role Mates, Soul Mates, Whole Mates, and Divine Mates. Lizanne and I began our journey together when we in our early twenties, when it was about exploring a relationship as boyfriend and girlfriend. We played a part in each other's lives and fulfilled a Role Mate need in that moment in time.

Not knowing who we were individually, much less as a couple, the relationship was short lived. Fast-forward twenty years later, and we came back together to take the spiritual journey as Soul Mates. During that time, we evolved and de-evolved individually and as a couple. We realized as Soul Mates that relationships are forever evolving in a perpetual motion. Unconsciously, we were being called to Love.

The period of drifting in and out of each other's lives changed to commitment and steadfastness as we learned how to support one another. She was the one whose love carried me up the mountain in Peru in 2005, past the heart-shaped lake and to the summit, where I could embrace her even in my weakness and be grateful for her strength. She was the one I called when my daughter disappeared in downtown Santa Barbara, reassuring me that all would be well. And she's the one who drove me to the airport for my quest in Peru in 2012, and whose voice spoke to me on that journey whenever I needed comfort and the feeling of Home.

We had grown so close together, the idea of being apart shocked the people around us. As Whole Mates, we were flowering in our lives as one. But it had come time for the flower to recede so it could grow again.

And so, I helped her move to her own place where she could flourish and grow. A month later, my cat was killed on the road, then fire and flood came to our neighborhood. Twenty-three people died, and in my own way, so too did I. And in doing so, we have become Divine Mates. No longer attached to expectations or the roles of romantic love, we are free to simply lift each other up. And in this new place, I want to say the same thing to her that I have felt from the day we met: "I love you. I will always love you."

Both of us were called by Love to receive perfect Unconditional Love of others and ourselves. To do that required that we love ourselves with our whole hearts and souls. To be loved we must receive Love from the One who loves. And that required both of us to heal the aspect of ourselves that feel most unloved. For me, it was the wounded inner Adam who still sometimes hid from the hurts of my mother's sharp tongue and my father's benign distance.

I climbed a mountain a couple of days ago and sat with these memories in absolute solitude, reflecting on them not from my old 1.0 fear, but from the richness and Self love of my genius Mind. I remembered the painful moments of helping Lizanne move out during torrential rains and floods. And as I did, I returned to the inner cathedral of myself, where I know she and I have transcended together. There we are unified, as we have always been. Whole, complete, and one.

Together, we have followed the path of the deepest and highest love. Not surrendering the lives we were living, but stepping into the lives we were meant to live.

WISDOM TEACHING 13
UNIFICATION

"Unification of the Divine Genius Mind with your genius Mind completes the journey Home. Oneness is all there is and all that will ever be."
—Adam C. Hall

Unification of the idea of the separate self with the authentic Self happens when you choose Unconditional Love. Men, as my guide and teacher, was an aspect of my genius Mind. He and I were the same. I chose the mind that unites in Love over the mind that divides in unforgiveness.

Messages from messengers, seen and unseen, deliver their wisdom to you—not to teach something new, but to remind you of what you already know, yet have forgotten. Ultimately, there is nothing to learn. There is only something to unlearn. That something is the ego mind. The unlearning curve can be steep but does not have to be difficult.

Ask yourself, why me, and why now? I invite you to explore these questions. I believe that now is your moment to shine your genius Mind. No longer do you need to live in the future's past. There are no mistakes. You, like the rest of us on the genius path, have come seeking the desired destination. Yet now we know that the journey we share is one of Love. There is no end. The path is infinite. The destination is the means. And the means is the destination. The means to unification is Love. There is nothing else. No more seeking, no learning. You need do nothing.

It is time to emerge from living a life of death, pain, suffering, and struggle—and transcend into merriment, mirth, and joy. Happiness is the nature and the wisdom of unification.

Our only job is to be joyful. The ego dismisses this idea as selfish, but expressing our happiness is how we remind one another of the Light and Love that we are. When we're in our wholeness of Being, we're in the presence of Divine joy and Love of God.

I thought back through the wisdom teachings Men had imparted to me, beginning with forgiveness.

"Forgiveness," he'd told me weeks before, "is a conscious act of non-judgment that restores the memory of God."

Now, because of all the wisdom teachings, I not only remembered God but knew that we are One. As we walk in the world with forgiveness, we walk in joy. And as we walk in joy, we are living reminders and reflections of the Divine light in all. We remember our unification with our Selves, one another, and God.

You're here to share the expression of God's light in the world. This requires your heart and soul. You may still be using your intellectual mind, but ultimately you are in the presence of God and are acting as a vehicle for Love. The unification of physical and spiritual law is truly the point of your human journey. Unification is what Jesus would refer to as coming Home. You already are there.

"Unification is the full emergence beyond fear and separation. It is the connecting point of heaven and earth—that place where there is no above and below or side to side. It is truly infinite, completely entangled in the Light and Love. Unification is harmony and completion."

—Men

The Buddha reminds us of how we can end seeking. "There are only two mistakes one can make along the road to Truth: not going all the way and not starting." God does not seek us, for God never lost us. That which you are seeking has found you. Accept this Love, and you will free yourself at last.

Unifying the light of the Divine Genius that shines through the universe with your genius Mind requires great skill and mastery.

Each day I practice being aware of this light of Love. I sit still in my Home or in nature to hear, see, and feel Love in my heart. I accept that there is no place else to go because the peace of God has descended.

I leave you with these final insights:

1. **Unification necessitates deep practice, honoring, and presence**. In stillness, hold the center point of darkness and light, those ostensibly noncompatible fields of energy. Feel the balance in your body. It will feel effortless because you have shed all judgments and expectations.
2. **If darkness surfaces in your mind, bring it to the light without fear.** Know that this is simply the unconscious nature of your being but has no power to harm you. Breathe in and trust the peace of Spirit and your genius Mind.
3. **Allow the light of God to reflect through you.** There is only a unified genius Mind, or what *A Course in Miracles* calls the "atonement." You've done nothing to atone for. Atonement is Oneness; Oneness is Love.
4. **Be Peace.**
5. **Be Love.**

It felt as though Men's teachings had come full circle and had led to this one apex moment of understanding.

When we heal our wound of separation, we are immortal. We unify into our wholeness and interconnectivity with all things.

We get out of this life alive.

"Yes," Men said. "In the end, this is the simplest teaching of all, because it can be summed up in two words."

"What are those," I asked.

"God is."

Prayer for Unification

Dear God, Great Being of Light and Love,
We stand before you now open to receive your Love
Our hearts yearn to let go into your Grace.

Please guide us down the path of Love.
Show us the way to the Divinity within,
Help us to end the pain and suffering of our lives once and for all,
Take us to the place we never left
Thank you Great Being of Light and Love
for showing us the way Home

Your gentle presence reminds us of what we have forgotten.
We follow the Light and Love you shine upon each step
Together we walk side by side
With faith in our hearts, we know that we are One

Our Journey Home has been long
We are weary and blind by the past we have chosen,
Help us find the strength and sight to see the dawning of a new day,
To choose again to Love as One
Show us the way to Heaven and Earth.
Teach us what we know yet have forgotten.
Thank you, Great Being of Light and Love,
for showing us the way Home

Let us welcome the peace you bring,
May your presence remind us that we are complete.
Let our hearts feel the harmony of being One
May we remember that we are Love
Let us know we are Loved
May your face complete our journey as One.

Dear God, we kneel before your Altar
We have come to receive your blessing
Please unify our hearts and minds,
For we are One
Thank you, Great Being of Light and Love,
for showing us the way Home.

27
Love as One

June 30, 2012

As the driver took me back to my hotel, Cusco was silent. Had I only left for the temple two hours before? How could I have crossed into another world—another life—in such a short time? And how could the rest of the physical world still be sleeping, as though nothing had happened?

I gave the driver a huge tip and found my way to my room. Although exhausted, I took a shower to clean off any dust or lingering energy. As the hot water rained down over my head, I was flooded with tears. Not only had I gotten out of this lifetime alive, I had been elevated to a new and profound understanding of what life truly means.

The Sanskrit word *namaste* translates into “the Divine in me bows to the Divine in you.” The Mayas use the words *In Lak’ech,* meaning “I am another you.”

In both cases, the words acknowledge the Truth of Oneness. Unity. Atonement. Or, as I heard a quiet voice whisper to me while I lay on a stone slab connecting heaven with earth, “Love as One.”

I had studied the concept of oneness for years, through multiple spiritual and shamanic traditions. But studying and knowing are two different things.

A Course in Miracles says that revelation is beyond words because it's a direct experience with God. I had had that experience, and I knew that a life Divine was soon to unfold.

When I woke up the next morning, on the eighty-first day, I felt a fog of malaise. I had no interest in lifting my head off the pillow, much less getting up. I pulled up the blanket around me. Giving myself permission to fall back asleep, I took a few deep breaths and drifted back and forth between a conscious and unconscious state. It was a dawning of a new earth, and that new earth was my life.

I began to replay the events of the previous night over and over. They had occurred in two powerful fields of energy: the limited field of time and space, and the unlimited one of infinity and unification. Even though I was lying in bed in a hotel room in June in Cusco, I was also living in the eternal now. I felt resurrected from the ego design to serve the Divine that resides within the one mind, heart, and soul of humanity.

Once I felt ready to get up, I wondered, was I going to get dressed and walk into the dualistic world? Was I going to function in the same old manner? Or was I going to be *in* the world but not *of* the world? As *A Course in Miracles* says, was I going to remember that I don't just have the keys to the kingdom of God—but I *am* the kingdom?

It was 10:34 a.m., time to get the day started. A part of me wanted to stay in bed, where I could avoid the world and all its insanity. Yet I knew that the very insanity of it all is what makes life so interesting. People, places, and events didn't energize me, but the evolutionary process did. With the light force I'd felt in the temple still pulsing within me like a second heartbeat, I realized that the mundaneness of everyday life can be radically altered, transformed into the pure joy of every moment.

After I showered and dressed, I was ready to take my morning walk to meet Men. What would he share with me today after my meeting with the Holy Grail? Would he be proud of my fulfillment of the quest?

I smiled as I thought of his constant companionship, the wisdom he'd imparted, the humor and surprises that had caught me off guard and delighted me daily. Men had led me step by step to the Temple of the Moon, and I couldn't wait to process this new life with him and see what would happen next.

I sat in meditation and soon arrived in the designated meeting place, just as I had for the past eighty days. But when I looked around, Men was nowhere to be found.

He's up to his tricks, I thought. This wasn't the first time he'd sent me on a scavenger hunt to find him.

I scanned the mesas, hoping to get a clue as to his whereabouts. Nothing.

Hmm, I thought. *He usually shows himself by now.*

Just then, I spotted him off in the distance atop a mesa in the west. He was on a horse with his back toward me, and the sun was just above his head. I waited for him to turn the horse and head in my direction. But instead, he was riding away.

I felt a sense of surprise, then a glance of panic. Where was he going? What about our conversation?

As I looked at him, he turned around. Even though he was far away, I could see his eyes and feel his soul. He raised his left arm high and touched the sun. Then I heard his voice.

"Feel the fire within, Adam," he said. "Follow the light. You are the Divine Genius, and this is the way of beauty and grace, Love as One."

With that, he disappeared into the sun's ball of fire and was gone.

I felt a wave of sadness, the grief of losing a loved one. But immediately, a second wave of emotions came over me.

Gratitude. And strength.

Thank you, Men, I said to him, and to myself. *Bless you. I know you will be with me always.*

As I cracked open the door of my hotel room, a beam of light burst through. I was the newborn chick who just cracked open its shell. Hesitating for a moment, I stepped over the threshold and made my way to the dining room, aware that my body needed nourishment.

The place was alive with tourists of every sort. The spiritual seekers always stood out from the rest. They had a look of curiosity and exuded an energy that they were on the edge of their own existence.

I smiled and sent a silent blessing to them. Spiritual high adventure, as I'd been reminded the night before, is not for the faint of heart. It takes the three Cs: Courage, Cooperation and Collaboration.

You must be courageous enough to step onto the road to enlightenment, peace, love, and liberation.

You must be willing to cooperate with others and the natural world to receive the guidance necessary to fully transform.

And you must be willing to collaborate with others to cocreate.

I had been living an uncourageous life, based on the fears of my ego and its belief in separation. For many years, I thought those fears and symbols of separation were an inevitable condition of being human.

I thought I was cooperative, traveling the world to collect new experiences and ideas. And, similarly, I thought I engaged in collaboration, setting up partnerships at work and at home.

But I never truly gave myself to cooperation or collaboration—not in business or in my relationships. How could I, when a wall of fear always held me at bay and apart from others—and from my true Self?

My journey with Men and his Thirteen Wisdom Teachings, along with my rebirth at the temple, allowed me to demonstrate true courage, to walk right through my fears and see the three Cs from the other side. I saw them not from my ego vantage point of self-protection, attack and defense, but from the perspective of wholeness. Love as One.

Before, the road to completion and harmony seemed long, winding, and difficult. But now, practicing the three Cs in concert with Spirit, I knew I had come Home.

As I sat in the dining room at the hotel and reveled in the energy of others that I had never felt before, I thought about what was next. *Tomorrow I'll head back to the States as a new soul on the new earth.* The rite of passage, coupled with the direct transmission that I received at the Temple of the Moon, was a homecoming of sorts.

On one hand, it was the anniversary of my conception on the earth plane fifty-two years ago. On the other hand, it was the death of Adam 1.0 and the birth of Adam 2.0. And on the third hand, it was a coming Home to the essential Self.

I had been given the rite to pass into the next stage of evolution. I was now the conscious cocreator of my reality, the magician who could dream my world into being. The magnificence and simplicity of that existed side by side.

When a waiter came to my table, I put down my menu, looked directly in his eyes and saw light shining there.

"*Como se llama?*" I asked him his name.

"Juan," he replied.

"*Mucho gusto,*" I said. "It's a pleasure to meet you."

He bowed his head slightly in acknowledgment, and I mirrored that gesture of honor.

We didn't have to speak the same language, wear the same clothes, or come from the same hemisphere.

It was instant connection. Soul to soul. Light to light. Love as One.

I am another you.

I spent the last day in Cusco visiting some of my favorite spots in and around the square. As I looked around, I saw joy everywhere and in everything. Not happiness, but true, pure, unadulterated, complete joy.

We can call ourselves happy within the ego design, but it usually doesn't last long. Someone disappoints or hurts us, we feel guilt and shame, the world doesn't line up to suit or satisfy us. And just like that, happiness is gone because it was an illusion all along.

But joy—joy is everlasting. It is the peace of God, the knowledge of completion and harmony. Light is joy. Everything is joy.

At all times, in all places, the Divine Genius shines the light of joy in the world. Each progression of consciousness brings you closer to the Divine Life of joy. So when you transcend the past, you include those aspects that are part of your soul design into the next evolution of your journey. You die and are reborn over and over again, proving that, yes, you can get out of this lifetime alive.

As I sat at the top of the steps of the cathedral on the square in Cusco, I looked eastward to the hills. High noon, and bells from churches all over the sacred city began to ring. I was struck by the beauty and grandeur of life. My quest had taught me that life is not simply about knowing how it all works. Instead, it's about activating the grand consciousness of the universe—the Divine Genius—within ourselves.

It is available to all of us. In fact, you don't need to go to Peru or to lie on an altar. You are the technology. You are the event. You are the horizon. As the ancient WisdomKeepers would say, we are the ones we have been waiting for.

It's not hard to access the genius Mind within you. And you can start in this very moment. Hacking into your Divine Genius begins with a simple request and question.

"Great Spirit, you have created my genius Mind for a higher purpose. How can I serve?"

Epilogue

In the years since my trip to Peru, I have continued to die and be reborn, understanding now at the deepest level of my soul that death is never a reality.

What remains of the old me will only be known in time, but I see evidence of the new me every day. My relationships with my daughters have continued to improve, I follow my inner guidance about the trajectory of my work, and Lizanne and I continue to be Divine Mates, steadfastly supporting one another as we grow and evolve.

I know that profound healing occurred at midnight at the Temple of the Moon, and my wounded yet magical inner child emerged anew.

How many times during the journey to Peru did I ask myself, Men, and God, "Again? I'm here to die *again*?" And then I would say, "Oh, thank you, God" over and over again. It was alchemy, turning the lead of my existence into the gold of my being.

When I received the message, "Serve the Grail," it inspired more questions than answers. I asked, "How? How can I serve?" And, thankfully, I received the answer. I can serve simply by being the unique genius Mind I was designed to be.

And so can you.

Say yes to this Truth, and a benevolent Divine Force will take over. Then your work is simple: trust it, and follow its light within you.

Without fail, the answers will come. The Grail itself is not a thing, so don't seek it in a person or place. It can only be found at your inner altar. And it will be there whenever you are ready to find it.

The Grail asks little else other than to shine your light and pure heart in the world as a mirror of its luminous light. No amount of darkness from the ego's fears can ever extinguish its flame. You and I are the flame. We are the keepers of the soul, one with Spirit and God's grace.

As evolutionaries and conscious cocreators, we must take satisfaction in knowing that we have fulfilled our part in the evolution of our soul and God's presence in the world. It is not a function of if, only when.

Feelings of peace, love, abundance, and joy are never lost. They get filed away. And when reactivated from their dormant state, life as you know it disappears. Until then we search for intermittent moments of fleeting happiness. Thinking that happiness is an end-all can be an endless search. *All will be fine when I am happy.* Happiness becomes a pursuit of money, belonging, and identity. Happiness attempts to mask the loss, pain, suffering, and guilt. It cures nothing and actually compounds and prolongs the misery. Unless and until you reclaim the joyous child within, life will be an endless chase for happiness. Life at best will seemingly be peaceful and loving, yet underneath a deeper longing will reside.

There is no end. Life is endless and magnificent. Nondiscriminatory. On a soul level and on a physical level, this is our journey, the story that must be told. There is clarity, joy, a never-ending sequence of stepping stones leading to the next moment of Truth and the next.

We are in an early stage of awakening from the dark. But we're on our way. You *can* get out of this lifetime alive. And be assured, your quest will always lead to light as you return Home to the place you never left.

About the Author

Adam C. Hall has spent twenty-seven years as a serial entrepreneur and twenty-five years as a CEO. The founder of three successful real estate companies, he has raised $1.5 billion in capital for development and investment banking.

For more than two decades, he has served as an impact investor, dedicated to the quadruple bottom line of people, planet, profits with purpose. He has lived out this vision in his decades of experience in business and relationship training, along with service to various corporate and philanthropic boards.

A trained shaman and teacher of *A Course in Miracles,* he has been dedicated for the past sixteen years to the conscious evolution of business and culture. The founder of the Genius Process, he is a convening member of Evolutionary Leaders, a speaker and workshop presenter.

His book *The EarthKeeper: Undeveloping the Future* was published by Hay House in 2013.

A father and grandfather, Hall resides in Santa Barbara, California.

Ingram Content Group UK Ltd.
Milton Keynes UK
UKHW011950110723
424957UK00006B/477